# RACE WITH THE DEVIL

# RACE WITH THE
# DEVIL

## GENE VINCENT'S LIFE IN THE FAST LANE

## SUSAN VANHECKE

ST. MARTIN'S PRESS ☒ NEW YORK

www.stmartins.com

DESIGN BY TIM HALL

Library of Congress Cataloging-in-Publication Data

VanHecke, Susan.
    Race with the devil : Gene Vincent's life in the fast lane / Susan VanHecke.
        p.      cm.
    Includes bibliographical references.
    ISBN 0-312-26222-1
    1. Vincent, Gene, 1935–1971.   2. Singers—United States—Biography.
    3. Rock musicians—United States—Biography.   I. Title.

ML420.V377 V36 2000
782.42166'092—dc21                                                00–029676
[B]

First Edition: August 2000

10   9   8   7   6   5   4   3   2   1

For my own G. V.

# ACKNOWLEDGMENTS

Myth, rumor, and conjecture have surrounded Gene Vincent since his very beginning, much of it perpetuated by the man himself. For their patience and generosity in allowing me to poke and prod through over forty years of often quite personal, sometimes quite troubling memories, in search of the facts as they know them, I extend profound thanks to all of the interviewees for this book.

Many thanks to Peter Guralnick for clearing up the Elvis questions.

To Liggett Taylor, David Dennard, Derek Henderson, Chris Welch, Harvey Kubernik, Ken Burke, Peter Jamieson, Andy Gallagher, Ricky Quisol, Sterling Ragland, Michael Ochs, Bob Hope-Hume, and Marc Beard, who went far above and beyond the call of duty in assisting a virtual stranger with photos, music, interviews, press clips, facts, figures, and phone numbers—you have my eternal gratitude.

For keeping the newly discovered music, few-and-far-between words, and larger-than-life memory of Gene Vincent vibrant, relevant, and very much alive, my thanks to Bob Timmers and his Gene Vincent's Official Website, Derek Henderson and his home page and archive, Dragon Street Records, Jerden Records, Derek Glenister and Rockstar Records, and Trevor Cajiao and *Now Dig This*.

To my mom, my best friend, and my dad, my first love, I am forever grateful for your enthusiatic encouragement and steadfast support.

And to my husband, Greg, as much a part of this book as its subject—you make me whole.

# RACE WITH THE DEVIL

**I**

*Well I've led an evil life, so they say,*
*But I'll outrun the Devil on Judgment Day!*
*Move, hot rod! Move, man!*
*Move, hot rod! Move, man!*
*Move, hot rod! Move me on down the line!*

THE GLEAMING TRIUMPH TIGER WAS TOUGH, A REAL BRANDO beast, a "whatcha-rebelling-against-Johnny-whatcha-got?" bad boy. The mighty bike rumbled fiercely between his skinny sailor thighs, hurtling him through the thick, clingy air of southeastern Virginia in July, past the endless acres of glittering green peanut fields, away for a few hours from his native Norfolk and the salty sea and the Navy that had made a young man of this boy.

On the move again, the road spinning out from behind the wild wheels of his chrome-cool motorcycle, he felt strong and contented. Free. Invincible. For the first time in his twenty years Vincent Eugene Craddock saw a future for himself, and it was full and bright.

He was pretty good at this sailor stuff, even if he'd only been doing it for three years. The pay was decent and steady, and he could impress the girls with his medals, a National Defense Service Medal for Korea—though as a boilerman on a tanker he never did see any real action—and his Navy Occupation Service Medal for Europe from a four-month Med cruise last year. Plus, his mama was real proud. So the re-up in March for another six years came only natural. With the reenlistment bonus the big, fast bike was finally his, and now that he was riding courier service, he was on his beloved bike just about every day. Life in 1955 was good.

The narrow highway quavered ahead of him in the mind-cleaving heat, the rows of peanuts steadily ticking off his miles per hour. They whizzed by faster and faster as Gene accelerated. His throat tightened a bit as he glanced at the speedometer, but the hot wind lashing at his sweat-soaked face and the furious forward momentum of 500 ccs felt good. The air, rich with the sweet and fertile scent of living, growing things, seemed electric, the world abuzz with every possibility.

*Gene looked behind him. The road was a gray ribbon, spooled out flat and empty save for a single smoky speck on the horizon. He turned his face back into the wind, savoring the breath-sucking velocity tearing at his cheeks.*

*He eased the accelerator a bit further and watched the needle crest. He was acutely aware of the danger but was thrilled, dizzied—dazzled—by it. His head swirled with the excited imaginings of fearless youth.*

*Gene looked back again. The horizon behind him was empty now, gray road quietly seamed with quickly darkening heaven. He turned back around, unsettled. An uneasy feeling scraped through his belly as inky thunderclouds moved in to foul the sweltering sky in front of him.*

*A few moments passed and Gene looked back again. A sickening chill jolted his body. The speck—first a mere shadow, then gone—was now a looming specter, a terrifying goliath of a car, a churning black chariot swathed in fire and smoke. And it was gaining on him fast.*

*His heart pounding in his ears, Gene twisted the accelerator even further. The bike rocketed forward with a cocksure roar.*

*Yeah, catch me if you can, you son of a bitch! Gene smiled to himself. I dare you.*

*He looked behind him again. The hulking hot rod, a jet black '41 Ford, with crimson flames emblazoned down both sides and spinning silver wheels spewing furious sparks, was closing in, the driver's face obscured by the windshield's dark glass. Gene could just make out the eyes, though. They gleam—glowed, really—red as spilt blood. They terrified him.*

*His heart hammered at his temples as he gave the bike all he could give it, willing his speed machine forward even faster. But* the demon car refused to relinquish its relentless pursuit, its massive chrome bumper now glinting mere inches from Gene's furiously whirling rear tire. He could smell the stinking breath of the car's rasping radiator, could feel its burning brand on his back. It prickled and stung, then moved to his left to prod him beneath the ribs.

Gene was precariously pinned between the flaming car and the pavement's churning edge, an unforgiving green abyss undulating just beyond.

This asshole's trying to run me off the road! Gene realized in astonishment. He tried to make out the face of the lunatic driver through the dark glass. All he could see were the cruel, crimson eyes.

A cold rage seized Gene. It emboldened him.

He ducked his head, now throbbing from the intense heat, down low over the handlebars. The blistering wind screamed over his coiled body. The bike, a bullet, was unstoppable.

The fiery radiator hiss moved back to his rear, biting at his neck. Gene was in agony, but he would not leave the road.

Then it suddenly fell away.

Ha! The bastard couldn't catch him, Gene realized, his body pulsing with pain, fear, and exhilaration. A slow, silent chuckle of relief erupted from his knotted gut.

A triumphant smirk came to his thin lips. He turned to face the glowing red eyes. He glared deep, glared hard into those horrid, hellish eyes shrinking smaller and smaller behind him and began to laugh. Loud. Furious. Victorious.

Swiftly and suddenly the monstrous machine erupted, spewing a heaving mountain of skyward sparks and sputtering, wind-borne cinders. Then, in an instant, it was gone.

Silvery devil-fingers forked across the roiling storm clouds.

Billows of thick, white smoke enveloped Gene as he stepped off the shiny Triumph and laid it on its side at the edge of the road. He walked back to the spot where the hot rod had been, knelt to touch the scorched pavement, laid his suddenly weary body down, *and closed his tired eyes. He dreamt as a cool rain began to fall. Life was good in '55.*

Telling her only son that he'd virtually lost his leg was probably the hardest thing Mary Louise Cooper Craddock ever had to do. Gene looked so small, so broken, in his regulation-cornered bed at the Portsmouth Naval Hospital, where the nurses bustled around importantly and the doctors scribbled on clipboards and shook their heads grimly. He was so heavily sedated that Louise still wasn't sure he fully understood what she'd told him—that he'd been in an accident, that his left leg was severely damaged, and that the doctors recommended amputation. That he would be crippled the rest of his life. The tears came hot and quick once more as she thought of how he'd looked deep, looked hard into her eyes and made her promise, made her swear to the good Lord up in heaven, that she wouldn't let those doctors take his leg.

Louise hovered worriedly over her bruised and battered boy. His eyes were closed, his thin face, at least, peaceful. The rest of him was an angry tangle of bandages, braces, plaster, and tubes. She was lucky to have him, because a young man on a motorcycle— no matter how big the bike, no matter how tough the boy—is no match for a broadside from a Chrysler, no matter how sorry the young lady driving it might be for running the light out west amidst the peanut farms of Franklin. That damn motorbike had been trouble since the day Gene bought it.

Louise didn't need any doctor to tell her she was lucky to have Gene. She felt blessed the moment God delivered the precious, squirming babe into her arms that February of '35 in Norfolk by the sea, at the heel of the mighty Chesapeake and just across the Elizabeth River from Portsmouth and the hospital. A sentimental smile sprang up as she recalled those early days, just her and her handsome Ezekiah, ever the proud papa, and their little baby Gene, moving from apartment to apartment in the Brambleton district of Norfolk, near the busy downtown. They were always just a few blocks from the restless river and its eternal parade of sturdy tugboats, barges hauling coal and timber, ferries shuttling between Norfolk and Portsmouth, and luxury passenger vessels fetching the fancy folks north to Baltimore, Washington, New York, and points beyond. Times were achingly tight—they were always tight, it seemed—but the joy the beautiful babe brought to their lives dulled, if just a little, poverty's cruel and perpetual pinch. Of course, she dearly loved his sisters—Evelyn, who came along three years later, Sarah, thirteen years Gene's junior, and little Donna, a year younger than Sarah—but she kept a warm and tender place in her heart for Gene, her firstborn and only son.

He was such a happy little boy, Louise recalled, cute as a button and always smiling. And forever singing. And when not singing, listening. Like his mama, the "Grand Ole Opry," beamed up from Nashville and broadcast over the NBC radio network, was his favorite. Whenever Hank Williams's keening "Hey Good Lookin' " or that smooth-singing Red Foley's "Rockin' Chair Daddy" would come over the radio, the boy's dark brown eyes would light right up, a grin would open wide and toothy across his narrow face, he'd lay down his toy soldiers and sing along, sweet as a bird plucked from God's blue sky. "You have the strangest palate I have ever seen"—especially high and narrow-roofed—the family doctor would tell him when he was a little older.

Louise remembered how, when he was four or five, he loved so much to go to the movies. They lived next to a theater at the time, and he'd get nickels from his uncles who worked at the shipyard nearby and go to the show. The boy would go in by himself and spend the whole day watching the same movies over and over. Got to be where he'd know every single song and every single line of dialogue by heart. Then he'd come home and act out all the parts with baby Evelyn. Seems he was always performing. When he was six his uncle Roy would take him to the confectionary— well, it was a beer joint, too—out in the country, down in Creeds near the Carolina border, along the mighty Atlantic, where Roy, who was Louise's brother, and his family lived. Little Gene would stand on a chair and sing all the war songs, "White Cliffs of Dover" and "Three Little Sisters" and other different ones, just as pretty as you please. The fellows stationed at the military airfields on the coast would all gather round and listen to the boy, and he'd always come home with a bucketful of money.

Little Gene was living at Roy's house at the time, along with his aunt Hazel and his cousins Leona and Alonso. With Kie off fighting in the second big war and Louise working, too, there just wasn't a way she could look after the kids herself. So Roy and Hazel took Gene for a year, and Evelyn went to her grandmama's. They were good to her boy, Hazel and Roy. Hazel even trimmed one of Kie's uniforms down to make Gene a little sailor suit he'd wear when he was singing at the confectionary. That boy's music even got him on to the radio about that time. Every weekend the kids' granddaddy, Louise's daddy Thomas Cooper, would drive all the way down from Norfolk to Roy and Hazel's. He'd fetch Gene and drive him all the way back up to Norfolk to WCAV so he could sing on the "Joe Brown Talent Show" on Saturdays. Then he'd drive Gene all the way back down to Roy and Hazel's again, out in the country.

Louise remembered how Gene pestered Kie and her for a guitar of his very own, especially after they moved to the lush, sandy-soiled, piney woods of Munden Point, not far from Creeds, and the boy heard the hand-clapping, hallelujah church songs and the curious moaning-low, sad songs of the colored folks who came to the family confectionary for provisions and fellowship. He especially liked hearing them sing "All God's Chil'n Got Shoes" as they went on their way to tend the fields. She remembered those many long afternoons Gene spent on the store's front porch, happily plucking on his guitar for his sisters and cousins and all the Negroes who gathered there to sing their strange, rhythmic songs and gossip and pass the hot, humid hours of southeastern Virginia in the summertime.

Gene wasn't quite so happy when Kie moved the family inland again to Norfolk, founded as Norfolk Towne in 1682, home to

Norfolk Naval Base, the largest military installation in the whole of the world, and also to Cooperative Mills, the big feed manufacturer where Kie worked for years before and then after the war, eventually becoming a supervisor. They lived in Broad Creek Village, which had once been a building project for service people, but after the war anyone who wanted to could live there. Gene's cousin Leona came to stay with them for awhile—she had found a job nearby—and Roy would come up on Friday nights to attend prayer meetings at the house. Gene had his guitar by then, which made him very happy, but he was small for his age and shy, and the bigger kids at school—even when they moved across the river to South Norfolk, near Portsmouth—would hassle him sometimes. But just like John Wayne, that movie star he thought so much of, Gene took no guff off of anybody and he always put those bullies right back in their place. Or tried to, anyway. Yes, sweet Jesus, her boy was a fighter, Louise thought—then and now.

And, oh, how he fought her to join the Navy. The life-and-death frights and sorrows of the two terrible world wars were still fresh in everybody's memory, and Ike's war in Korea—tens of thousands of American boys dead already, MacArthur out before he'd started World War III, and peace talks going nowhere— seemed to be not much different. Kie thought the military would be good for the boy, who didn't seem much cut out for book learning and could never sit still for long. So she finally relented, and Kie signed the papers giving Gene permission to join the United States Navy. How she fretted from the minute her boy left for boot camp, mere days after his seventeenth birthday. But how proud she and Kie were at Gene's graduation from the Naval Training Center at Bainbridge, across the great, blue Chesapeake in Maryland. The boy looked so handsome and official in his clean, white dress-up uniform, those dark curls still uncontainable even under a sailor's hat.

She missed him terribly when he left on the U.S.S. *Chuckawan* late in '52. When the tanker took him to the Mediterranean Sea in '54, she prayed to God every night to watch over her boy so far away on the other side of the world. And the Lord did. When Gene returned home for shore duty, his sea bag and the cheap guitar he'd bought from the Italians slung across his back, he was no longer a boy. He'd put on weight—he was all of one hundred and thirty-one pounds now—and confidence. He seemed excited, cheerful, happy. He was ready to make his own way in the world, she was sure of it.

Now what kind of future would her Gene have?

The smooth-haired, hooded-eyed boy standing onstage in September 1955 was good looking, pretty almost. But it was when he shook all around and swiveled and sneered like a soul done demon possessed that nearly every teenaged girl in the whole of Norfolk Municipal Auditorium at 9th and Granby Streets downtown squealed and swayed and got all sweaty and moist. It was crazy. The thumping songs that boy from Memphis sang sounded like nothing Norfolk, or all of America for that matter, had ever heard, save for his one or two records, which young, adventurous country radio stations like WCMS had been playing only recently. Gene Craddock, in a plaster cast up to his hip and on crutches—dear, sweet Mama had kept her promise—had heard them, songs with the big bull-fiddle slapping out the bottom rhythms, songs like "That's All Right" and an all-fired rendition of Bill Monroe's hill-billy ditty "Blue Moon of Kentucky." Songs that pumped your blood all up and made you want to move, sort of like the other songs on the radio, "Rock Around the Clock" by Bill Haley and his Comets and "Maybellene" from Chuck Berry and that crazy "Tutti Frutti" by wild-eyed Little Richard with his piled-high pom-padour. Rock 'n' roll, they called it. And it moved him.

Those songs sounded, in fact, a whole lot like the music he was fiddling with between hospital stays that fall; the break just above his left ankle was taking its own damn time to heal. Banging and thrumming on the guitar—the one he'd bought for twenty-two American dollars while in port at Naples—in his hospital bed or locked in his bedroom at home—"to keep the neighbors neighborly," he'd say later—the rhythms of the colored folks would come tumbling right on out of him, spilling across the guitar strings and mixing all up with his Hank Williams and Red Foley and even the swinging, new bebop jazz with its wild-running lines that he listened to from time to time. It wasn't at all like the country sounds he and his buddies made when they played together here and there around town. At first it was all a big mess, and people would frown and advise him with stern faces that he should sing songs in an accepted fashion. He'd look them straight back in the eye and say, polite but firm, "No. That's for someone else, not me. Rock 'n' roll is a young person's music and I have a feeling for this style." But he worked on his songs, adding and blending and concocting just so, and it started sounding pretty good, or at least that's what his mama and his sisters and his friends and the other patients at the hospital told him. He thought so too, but he wasn't quite sure what to do with his unholy union of white folks' music and black folks' music.

Now, here, watching this pretty kid from Memphis not much older than himself—just thirty-four days, in fact—seduce boys, girls and, hell, even the angels above with these songs with a deeply colored root—just like his—Gene knew what he had to do.

William Beauregarde Davis was brown-bagging it that day.

He ran the day-to-day operations of WCMS—"Western Country Music Station"—located in the Helena Building at Granby and Plume in downtown Norfolk since the station signed on in June of '54. The Connecticut-born radio man, who also had some TV and acting experience, did his own morning show as well, a couple hours of hillbilly music like Ernest Tubb and Lefty Frizzell and Slim Whitman and Hank Williams that he'd started in the fall of '51 at WLOW, another local station, and brought with him to WCMS. He hosted the "All-Star Record Roundup" as the jolly Sheriff Tex Davis, joined by his trusty sidekick Candy, the make-believe horse. It was nothing like the announcing he did in Waterloo, Iowa, or Dalton, Georgia, or his baseball play-by-play at

WLOW, and it was certainly lifetimes away from his Army war-time experiences. And the very idea of it and the ribbing she'd take from her schoolmates had brought his sweet baby daughter to tears at the dinner table. But the station's switchboard lit up like fireworks on the fourth of July the very moment Sheriff Tex took to the airwaves. Then there were the commercials to cut in the afternoon and the promotions to work on, like bringing that Presley boy to town again, though the Colonel sure wanted a heap more than the two hundred and some dollars Davis paid him the first time he played the Auditorium with Hank Snow in May of '54. Some days there just wasn't time enough for a decent midday meal.

Davis fished out his sandwich and was just getting ready to take a bite when a pale, bony kid in a tee-shirt and dirty pants, his hair greasy and teeth dark and filthy, a huge plaster cast on one leg and a battered guitar slung over his shoulder, appeared in the doorway to his office.

"Mr. Davis, Mr. Davis! My name is Gene Craddock, sir," the kid said, nervous but excited to be meeting the famous Sheriff Tex in person.

"Hi, Gene," the affable Davis said, sandwich still in hand.

"I'd like to sing for you, sir," the kid said. "I can sing."

"Well, Gene, I'm going to have a sandwich right now," Davis told him. "But you come on in and sing for me while I eat."

The boy limped into the office and started to strum a Presley song. As Gene opened his mouth to sing, Davis laid the sandwich down. He would never pick it back up. This odd looking boy with the dirty teeth and the greasy hair and the huge cast could indeed sing, and like no one he'd ever heard before. That voice—smooth as water on a windless day, sweet and high as angels from heaven, but a little bit dangerous, too. And those songs he kept singing—not quite rhythm and blues, not quite hillbilly, kind of a mix of both. Kind of like Presley. It was new. It was stunning. And it was good, Davis thought.

"Where the hell did you come from?" the dumbfounded Davis asked when the boy was finished.

"I told you I can sing, sir," Gene said, smiling.

"You can sing," Davis said, shaking his head. "I don't know what kind of music it is, but you can sing. I have no idea what you're doing."

"Well, sir, *I* don't know what I'm doing," Gene said, polite but firm. "But I like what I'm doing and this is the kind of music I sing and that's the way it is."

Davis liked this kid's voice and thought he had potential in singing whatever he wanted to. He might go over pretty well on the station's new live variety show, "Country Showtime," starting up Friday nights at the movie theater just a few streets up from the station. He invited Gene to try out, and if the crowd liked him, well, maybe he could play every Friday night.

Gene could hardly contain himself.

"Yes, sir, that's what I wanna do, I wanna do that!" he gushed. "Thank you, sir, thank you!"

Bill "Sheriff Tex" Davis was fixing to go on the air when a call came in for him. It was Ken Nelson, whom Davis had met last fall at a radio convention. Davis picked up the receiver.

"My God, where did this kid come from?" demanded Capitol Records' vice president of artists and repertoire, in charge of what songs Capitol would record and which Capitol artists would record them.

"Oh, well—he walked into my office, that's all," Davis said, a knowing grin starting a slow creep across his face.

RCA Victor—one of the giants of the music industry, along with Capitol, Columbia, Decca, Mercury, and MGM—had just signed the boy Presley away from Sam Phillips' tiny Sun label down in Memphis for an unprecedented thirty-five thousand dollars. Now Presley was selling circles 'round other artists with novel rock 'n' roll sides like his echo-laden bump-and-grind called "Heartbreak

Hotel." Davis had figured Capitol Records would want to give RCA some competition, would be looking for a kid who sounded anything at all like Presley. And Davis had found one.

Gene had gone over real well his first week at "Country Showtime." Real well. The youngsters just loved him, the gals in particular, who shrieked and clapped and got all sweaty and moist at his Presley tunes. He won the talent contest at his very first appearance on the show, and he came back every Friday night since, much to the delight of the teenagers in the audience, even when they moved the show across the river to the Gates Theater. He actually started to gig around town, even got a sweet deal on a cherry convertible for playing at the local Chevy dealership. In his shirts with the collars flipped up and his trousers with one leg ripped open to fit that damn cast, he definitely had an unusual way about him onstage, careening about, dropping to one knee, and kicking the mike stand up and around, his white face twisted into a kind of tortured grimace. His act was surely different, a little dangerous, even; there seemed to be a highly combustible violence smoldering just under the surface. He's got something, Davis had thought while watching Gene that first night on "Showtime." I don't know what it is, but he's got something.

Carl Perkins thought the boy had something, too. Davis brought the Sun singer, songwriter, and guitarist, whose "Blue Suede Shoes" was starting to scream up the charts, to the Auditorium on March 21, and Gene Craddock opened the show. Sadly, it turned out to be Carl's last performance for some time; en route to *The Perry Como Show* from Norfolk, Carl and his band got in a terrible car accident. Killed the driver of the pickup truck they plowed into, broke Carl's brother Jay's neck, and put Carl out of commission for months with a broken collarbone. An awful shame.

Prior to the concert, though, Davis cornered Carl backstage and introduced himself. "Carl, I got this boy I'm fixin' to manage, and I want you to come here and watch him," he said. "He's gonna sing a song I'm gonna cut on him. I wanna know what you think of it."

Carl looked on from the wings as Gene tore into that strange, almost sinful-sounding, syllable song of his, "Be-Bop-A-Lula." Perkins watched Gene intently, then offered, "It's kinda like my 'Blue Suede Shoes.' There ain't a lot to it, but it's an effective ol' song."

"That's all I wanted to hear," Davis said, smiling. "That's good enough for me."

Right before Carl went on, Davis brought Gene back to the dressing room. Starstruck and bug-eyed, Gene extended his hand and murmured in a hushed, excited tone, "Man, I hope I can do what you're doin'. I won't ever be like you are, but that's what I wanna do. This here Davis is gonna be my manager, and we're gonna make a record." Carl wished Gene good luck with his song and told him it really had something going for it.

That's why Davis had rounded up the boys to get that odd tune of Gene's down, the song the radio man would later claim to have written with the boy, but which Gene's friends and family would insist was written with one Donald Graves, a buddy of Gene's, who'd sold his rights to ol' Sheriff Tex for a quick twenty-five bucks.

But like Perkins had said, the song wasn't bad. Sounded real fresh, real fun, in fact. Sure, the words didn't exactly make much sense—something about a gal in red blue jeans, the queen of all the teens, this gal's Gene's baby, and he don't mean maybe. It was kind of silly, actually. But fun, all the same. The kids were going to love it. So one afternoon while Gene was hanging around the station—as he did almost every day since first visiting Davis in his office, that beat-up guitar of his dangling over his shoulder—Davis picked up the phone and dialed Cliff Gallup, a fine Chet Atkins–influenced picker with Ricky and the Dixie Serenaders who sat in regularly with the Virginians, the WCMS house band.

"Cliff, you know the boys we use on Friday on the amateur

hour? Can you get the guys together and tell them to come on over? We got a crazy little thing from that new kid who sang last week, Gene Craddock. You remember him?"

"Yeah, I remember him," Gallup said. "He's a pretty good singer."

Tex told him about the strange song. "I think it's pretty good," he said, "so come on by and let's put it on tape before we forget it."

Soon all the musicians arrived. There was the no-nonsense Cliff, twenty-eight, serious and professional, a quietly intense musician who worked in maintenance for the Norfolk County school system by day. Quiet, cleft-chinned Gene, twenty-one. "Wee" Willie Williams, twenty, on acoustic rhythm guitar, who'd come down from Maine in '54 to lead the Virginians. Jack Neal, twenty-six, who worked over at the Ford plant in South Norfolk, borrowed from Garland Abbott's band on big stand-up bass. And there was that wild kid who always went around in a windbreaker with the sleeves rolled up, on drums, Dickie "Be-Bop" Harrell, just fifteen years old but one hell of a stylish hitter.

It didn't take long for them to learn "Be-Bop-A-Lula," "I Sure Miss You," a ballad penned by local songwriter Evelyn Bryan, and "Race With the Devil," another tune Gene had been inspired to write in the hospital after his motorcycle wreck. The players seemed to have a chemistry, Davis noted, and recording—with just a couple of microphones to tape, from which an acetate record could be cut on the station's lathe—went quickly. Cliff, who could make his guitar sing just like one of the fancy opera stars, tossed in his trademark tumbling runs just as he always did when he was playing his country and western dance band gigs over at the Navy base.

"That sounds okay," Davis said, nodding approval.

"Sounds good to me," one of the boys piped up. "But I don't know this kind of music. I don't know what kind of music we're playing."

"Nobody does," Davis said. "But it sounds good, so let's call it a night, boys."

Later, Davis had carefully assembled an airmail package. He addressed it to Ken Nelson, Capitol Records.

Unlike many of his colleagues at Capitol who were content to continue recording their heretofore bankable artists—crooners like Frank Sinatra, Dean Martin, and Nat King Cole—Ken Nelson did not underestimate the significance of rock 'n' roll.

He'd been with Capitol since the company's inception in 1943, survived the company's 1955 purchase by the giant British holding company Electrical and Musical Industries, Limited (EMI) and, at age forty-five, was hardly one to go in for fads or trends. But at some level, Nelson understood that rock 'n' roll represented a cultural turning point that would not only change the face of popular music but also forever alter society, as it coincided with a moment of great social and political change. America, flush from the success of World War II and the Korean War build-up, was enjoying unprecedented prosperity. Jobs were plentiful in the dynamic postwar economy, and a growing middle-class bent on consumption meant secure employment and relative affluence for every member of the family, young and old. For the first time, the younger generation was empowered, if only by its piggy banks. The world would never be the same.

One of the most saleable commodities of the growing youth culture marketplace was popular music. The technology was cheap—transistor radios and record players were now available at prices that easily fit a teen's budget—and so too was the product, the 45-rpm single, which sold for around a dollar and was portable and convenient. With the emergence of Presley and his rocking and rolling peers, U.S. record sales in 1955 had soared to $277 million, a whopping thirty percent increase from their postwar low. Obviously, rock 'n' roll's revolutionary sound—the adventuresome hybrid of "race music," the beat-heavy rhythm and blues and gospel of the black community previously shunned as "the devil's music" by mainstream America, and the melody-driven, Anglo-derived idioms of traditional Appalachian and bluegrass country—was infinitely appealing to the newly independent youth generation.

Nelson knew this. He saw what the kids were going for on his many business travels. He pleaded with the unconvinced Capitol brass, admonishing in meetings, "Look, you guys are out of your minds, we've got to get on the ball with this thing." He anguished over the recently plummeting sales of Capitol's staple artists and the company's foot-dragging attitude toward the hungry, new youth market. So when he'd received the package from the deejay in Norfolk, a demo record of one Gene Craddock singing an odd, new rhythmic number called "Be-Bop-A-Lula," he knew Capitol had to have him. He heard gold in that throat.

"Can you get these people down to Nashville on the next plane?" he now practically commanded the deejay. The smile overtook Davis's face.

Owen Bradley's recording complex was on 16th Street South in Nashville, housed in a small, metal army surplus building fondly dubbed the Quonset Hut. The producer—who'd worked with the Decca label since 1947—and musical director and orchestra leader at WSM, home of the Grand Ole Opry, built the double-studio facility in 1955; with its impeccable equipment and peerless acoustics it would soon become a cornerstone of the country music recording industry. Bradley would later sell the Quonset Hut and relocate to the Bradley Barn, home of the "Nashville Sound," the creamy string-and-chorus-embellished, pop-country mix heard on the sixties sides he produced for the likes of Patsy Cline and Brenda Lee. But before Bradley brought in the orchestra, he, along with his brother Harold, also a musician, worked with some of the freshest names in the strange, new field of rock 'n' roll, including a gangly, bespectacled young Texan named Buddy Holly. The producer was not at all happy with the Holly sessions of just a few months earlier. Bradley didn't understand this newfangled rock 'n' roll. He'd never liked it, and doubted he ever would.

If Bradley wasn't too optimistic about the Gene Craddock sessions, Gene and his band certainly were. They were beside themselves with excitement ever since Davis had made the announcement—not long after they'd made the "Be-Bop-A-Lula" demo—that Capitol wanted to sign Gene to a recording contract.

Sheriff Tex, ever the showman, made a big, splashy production of it, interrupting one of Gene's "Showtime" sets with the news. The capacity crowd went hog-wild with great cheers and applause, as if the home team had come from behind to sweep the season-ender. Gene was absolutely stunned. In his deepest heart of hearts he always imagined a singing career, cutting records and hearing his songs played on radios across the land, performing on television and stage, and making pretty young things everywhere all sweaty and moist with his unusual songs. And here it was, the golden possibility, laid at his feet—even if one of 'em was encased in cement all the way up to the hip.

His warm, brown eyes grew round and shiny as flying saucers, and he fought to hold the hot tears in. His mama couldn't, though, so overcome was she with joyful crying that she was barely able to speak that whole night. And the band was ecstatic, all grins and handshakes and hooting and hollering and back-slapping. "This, I believe, was the happiest night of my life," Dickie, the drummer, would say years later.

Ken Nelson felt a little apprehensive about his latest signing as well. In fact, after he'd hung up with Davis, he wondered if maybe he had just made a big mistake. But after the contracts were officially inked, Gene—nice kid, very young, Nelson thought when they met—and his band, looking like a motorcycle gang in their black coats and hats, arrived at the Quonset Hut the evening of May 4. To their surprise, they found a handful of other musicians—including bassist Bob Moore and drummer Buddy Harman, esteemed Nashville session men, in addition to guitarist Harold Bradley—loitering around the studio.

Puzzled, Dickie, playing hooky from St. Paul's Catholic—not

that he, or the sisters for that matter, minded very much—looked to Cliff and asked, "What's going on here? Are we in the middle of somebody else's session or what?"

"I don't know," Cliff, unpacking his guitar, answered sternly. "Just be quiet, be quiet. Don't mess up everything."

"Gene, what's happening?" Dickie asked.

"I don't know," the singer shrugged, waiting as patiently as he possibly could for the first professional recording session of his life to begin.

Dickie strode determinedly over to Davis and asked what was going on. "I don't know," Davis said. "Let me go in there and talk to Ken. You set your drums up while I find out what's happening."

Dickie assembled the studio kit—bass and snare drums and a cymbal—then pulled out his sticks and the brushes he was fond of using to get a different sort of sound. The other musicians were still hanging around, watching and quietly conferring among themselves, confabulating. Soon Ken Nelson, heavily horn-rimmed and perpetually imperturbable, emerged from the control room and greeted Gene and his band. "Well, we're here to cut some good stuff today. Are you all—"

"Excuse me, Mr. Nelson," Dickie interrupted. "Can I ask a question?"

Cliff cringed.

"Yes, what's that?" Nelson said.

"What's these other fellas doing in here? What are they doing sitting around and staring and all this?"

"Aw, don't worry about them," Nelson soothed. "Just go ahead and let me hear about four or five bars of what you all are going to do." The pros sat back as the rookies ran through—loud, hard, and fast, the way they knew best—bits of the songs they'd been rehearsing nearly nonstop ever since they received their big news. There was "Be-Bop-A-Lula," of course, and "Woman Love," a song Nelson had chosen for them. As the cartwheeling runs of

"Race With the Devil" cascaded cleanly and casually from Cliff's black, pancake-style Gretsch Duo-Jet with its Bigsby tremolo, the studio veterans turned to each other, gasping and muttering in amazement. Gene smiled to himself.

"Okay, fellows, all right," Nelson interjected. The band stopped playing. "That's good. You all can go on home now."

Dickie, dejected, shuffled out from behind his drum kit and headed for the door.

"Where are you going?" Nelson asked.

"I'm goin' home," Dickie said.

"Going home?" Nelson laughed. "No, not you! Those other fellows!"

The session men filed out, and Gene and the band started work on "Race With the Devil," a frenzied tale of a heated hot rod race, which Gene sang in an almost scat style. Run-through after run-through, Cliff handily reeled off head-whizzing solos, truly innovative in their speed and complexity. But the group played so loudly, so aggressively, that engineer Mort Thomasson was having trouble getting the levels balanced correctly; Gene's supple vocals were being overpowered. Owen Bradley, just returned with his brother from taking producer Nelson out for a quick bite, noted that the exuberant Dickie was beating the tar out of the drums and the sound was bleeding into Gene's microphone. These rock 'n' roll guys play it so much louder than the other people, Bradley thought.

He moved Gene to the edge of the tiny hallway between the smaller studio where the musicians were set up, and the vacant larger studio. The band started up again. Those drums were still getting into Gene's mike. Bradley moved the singer and his microphone a little farther into the hallway, and the band gave it another try. Better, but still not there. Bradley moved Gene and the mike back again until finally he was at the farthest end of the hall. Gene could still see what was going on, but he, and his microphone, were totally isolated from the rest of the band. The levels were perfect.

Bradley was pleased. He'd never tried that before. He made a mental note to use that separation idea on some other projects.

Problem solved, and with "Race With the Devil"—complete with a pair of triplet-packed, chromatic-sliding solos from Cliff, whose inimitable technique utilized a pair of metal fingerpicks and a large, thin flatpick—finally in the can, Gene and the band tackled "Be-Bop-A-Lula." It was a slinky, sensual little song, sounding almost dirty as Gene delivered it in a tense, mid-tempo pant, with an anticipatory drum build toward the middle just begging for a climax. So, during one take, Dickie—moved by the moment, just as he'd always been moved by the rapturous, rhythmic gospel songs on the colored radio station back home that he played along with every Sunday—let out a joyful scream, a scream loud enough for the good Lord above to hear. The band broke off abruptly. Gene, quietly amused by the kid's exuberance, fidgeted in the hall.

"What the hell's wrong with you, boy? Are you crazy?" Cliff snapped, an irate frown tugging at his face. "We're making a record here!"

In the control room, Nelson, surprised but unflappable, asked Davis what the scream was for. "I don't know," Davis replied in astonishment. "He's a fifteen-year-old kid. He's liable to do anything!"

"What happened? Something wrong out there?" Nelson asked from the control room.

"No," Dickie said matter-of-factly. "I just screamed. I thought it sounded good. I thought it would add to the record."

"All right, don't worry about it," Nelson said patiently. "We'll get it straight, we're all learning." He turned to Gene, restless in the hallway. "What do you think, Gene? You want to keep it on the record?"

Gene ruminated for a moment. "Yeah, I like it," he drawled.

"All right. We'll keep it on there."

Cliff fumed as the band finished the recording.

Next, Gene and the band launched into "Woman Love," working on it for some time. But Nelson, who initially envisioned the

Jack Rhodes–penned song about some poor fellow sick for some lovin' as Gene's debut single, wasn't pleased with how it was turning out. Some of Gene's words—lasciviously breathy, lustfully tremulous, and lavishly slurred with slapback echo—sounded downright obscene, particularly that bit about "huggin' and a-kissin.' " He wasn't really singing the "F" word, was he?

"I don't know Gene, I don't know about this one," Nelson pondered from the control room. "Bring those words in here and let me look at what you got." Gene obediently took his lyric sheet in to Nelson, who studied it carefully. "Hmm, sure sounds a little different from in here." Assured that Gene's "Woman Love" was indeed clean, though—that "huggin' " wasn't some other word—Nelson seemed satisfied.

They finished up with "I Sure Miss You." Later, the band listened as Nelson played "Woman Love" over and over. "I like that," he enthused. "That's a good song. I think 'Woman Love' is *the* side. Let's release that first."

"Yeah," Gene agreed enthusiastically. "That's a good record. Anything you say—I'm just glad to be on record."

Damn, that Gene could sing, Dickie thought, listening to the tracks. He didn't need a band. Hell, his voice was made for singing.

"Well, I guess that's it," Dickie spoke up.

"We're going to see," Nelson said, warmly shaking hands with each musician. He truly enjoyed working with these boys and had been surprisingly impressed with their talent and cooperation, especially Gene's.

"We might have a hit here. And if we do, we'll come back and cut an album."

Bill Davis picked up the phone. It was Ken Nelson. He sounded excited.

"Guess what! We've got a smash!" he exclaimed.

"What do you mean?" Davis asked. The single had only shipped on the fourth of June and, sure, WCMS was playing the boy's record just about every hour. It seemed to be moving well around town, too. Dickie even got that record shop on High Street to play it over and over through the speakers outside the store; you could hear it all the way to the damn ferry. And the local newspaper had been writing about the boy some. But a smash?

"Gene's got a hit record!" Nelson gushed. It must be true.

"Hey, that's great!" Davis said.

"But it's not 'Woman Love,' " Nelson said.

"It ain't?" Davis asked, a bit bewildered.

"No, it's your side," Nelson answered. " 'Be-Bop-A-Lula.' "

Apparently deejays, concerned about the questionable-sounding lyrics and orgiastic gasps of "Woman Love"—the British Broadcasting Corporation would, in fact, soon ban the song entirely in the United Kingdom—were flipping the single over, spinning the tamer B-side, which Nelson had given to the boy's "Be-Bop-A-Lula." And, as Davis had predicted, kids across the country were crazy about it. It started in Baltimore, where a deejay had put "Lula" into heavy rotation. And wouldn't you know, the song took off instantly, screaming across state lines like hellfire, and on June 16 even entered the Top 100 chart of *Billboard* magazine, the music industry bible, at number seventy-eight.

And Nelson wanted Gene and the band back in Nashville. *Immediately.*

Davis had to hand it to him, Nelson had the magic touch with this one. He chose "Be-Bop-A-Lula" as the B-side. He rechristened the boy Gene Vincent, making his given first name his new showbiz last name, which Capitol further embellished in image-shaping trade ads that excitedly announced the fledgling singer as "The Screaming End." He approved Dickie's plenty marketable suggestion for a group moniker, the Blue Caps, named for the flat, golf-type hats the kid had been wearing for years. And now he wanted to cut a whole album.

The band would hightail it to Nashville as soon as he could arrange it.

Gene needed material and it was up to his management to provide it. In April, he'd signed a two-year contract with WCMS Artist Bureau, the talent agency arm of WCMS, granting the station personal management of his career for fifteen percent of his gross earnings. By mid-June, the station's general manager, Roy La-Mere, and owner, Cy Blumenthal, had formed L&B Talent Management, Inc. and began urging Gene to sign a new and better contract. Now, with an album's worth of new material needing to be cut, the WCMS/L&B staff was frantically rifling its record library for repertoire for their boy. Deejay and program director Joe Hoppel, who'd been perusing the station's old 78-rpm pop records, suggested "Jezebel," a hit for Frankie Laine five years earlier, "Ain't She Sweet," "Wedding Bells (Are Breaking Up That Old Gang of Mine)," "Peg O' My Heart," and Hoagy Carmichael's "Up a Lazy River." They were all tried and true pop standards, most of which also happened to be particular favorites—and suggestions, too—of Ken Nelson's. Gene, still fairly quiet and shy despite his newly rocketing stardom, politely entertained all the recommendations, and he and the band hunkered down in the station studio to learn the songs from the 78s. Nelson also requested they bring in some of their own material, so Gene started sketching out some new tunes, which the band eventually fleshed out en route to Nashville.

Gene was eager to be going back into the studio. The out-of-the-blue success of "Lula" had vindicated him. When his record had first come out, he hobbled into his old Navy barracks, B-17, with an early pressing of the single tucked under his arm, telling his fellow enlisted, "Hey, I cut a record. Wanna hear?" The fellows rallied around him excitedly at first, but the crowd dwindled down to just a couple of sailors by the single's end. The general consensus: the record stunk. He played his debut disc for aunts, uncles, anybody who'd listen—all with the same results. To their country-accustomed ears, the music was awful. But by June 23, the single sold a remarkable two hundred thousand copies. To young people across the country, "Be-Bop-A-Lula" was their new favorite song. And Gene Vincent—the dirt poor, crippled kid from Norfolk, Virginia—was their new favorite artist.

Gene was far more interested in being a star than a husband. But when he'd married Ruth Ann Hand, who listed her age as seventeen on their marriage certificate, on February 11, his twenty-first birthday, he was still recuperating from his motorcycle accident, he was still the property of the United States Navy, and he hadn't even heard of "Country Showtime" yet.

The marriage was trouble from the start. Mama and Daddy did not look favorably on his whirlwind engagement to the cute Portsmouth high school student. And his impromptu proposal was impulsive, to be sure, as he'd only known Ruth Ann for a few months. Even his baby sisters Tina and Donna were dead set against it. They decided that they didn't want some stranger taking their beloved big brother away from them; he had to lock them in their bedroom, accidentally on purpose, of course, every time Ruth Ann would come to the house to discuss the wedding plans with Mama.

But he'd gone ahead with the ceremony anyway, he in his freshly pressed dress blues and dark-haired Ruth Ann pretty as a prom date in her long, white gown. The service was performed by his cousin Alonso, who now went by his first name of James and was a minister of the Church of Christ. It didn't go without a hitch, though, as baby Donna threw a fit and couldn't be swayed from her nonstop crying. They had to lock her in the reception room to keep her from disrupting the service. When it was over, Mama let her out and Gene hugged her and apologized.

Though they were now married, as Gene stumbled onto his new career and his notoriety as a singer began to grow around town, he took to introducing Ruth Ann as his cousin. Man, how she hated that. He quieted her for awhile by saying that his contract with L&B required that he keep their marriage a secret. He explained to her that rock 'n' roll stars were much more marketable to teenage girls if they were unwed. And that it was teenage girls who bought loads and loads of rock 'n' roll records. But it didn't help matters much. Things went pretty much downhill from there.

They started their married life living, at Ruth Ann's insistence, with her parents in Portsmouth. But as he spent more and more time with the band—rehearsing, performing, recording—and his relations with Ruth Ann grew more strained, Gene stayed with friends or with his folks and sisters in the crowded Craddock house in South Norfolk. To Gene, it was a necessity—he had important rock 'n' roll business to take care of. To Ruth Ann, it was abandonment, pure and simple.

Gene and the Blue Caps returned to the Quonset Hut on June 24, knocking out "Jezebel," "Peg O' My Heart," and "Wedding Bells." As he'd thought, Nelson smiled in the control room, the quiet kid ran deep—he had the sensitivity, the feel, for a sentimental standard. His renditions, with their surprisingly tender phrasing, were touching. Aching, almost. Beautiful. After this rock 'n' roll thing had run its course, there was another avenue his boy could take. And "Crazy Legs," the boppin' little number that Jerry Reed, another of his artists, came up with overnight for Gene at Nelson's request, wasn't bad either. A real mover, with Cliff's Chuck Berry–styled riffing.

They set things up a bit differently this time. Gene was placed in the studio with the rest of the band, but hidden away in the corner, not left out in the hallway as before. Each musician used a single microphone, like the one lowered down the f-hole of Jack's bass and the one positioned in front of Cliff's amplifier, a leather-bound Standel on loan from Grady Martin, a top Nashville session player. Dickie, always searching for new and different sounds, pulled pennies from his pocket and put them on his ride cymbal, providing a rattling sustain. Later, he'd get a similar effect by draping a cheap, beaded necklace with a drum key attached over his high-hat cymbal. Another time he'd tape a can of milk to his snare and beat on that. To keep the snare from ringing, he'd improvise by laying a handkerchief or wallet on the drum head. And he was always fooling around with double bass drum kicks. The odd noises drove serious Cliff and rock 'n' roll neophyte Nelson crazy.

The next day they tackled "Waltz of the Wind," "Up a Lazy River," and "Ain't She Sweet," plus the mildly swinging "Gonna Back Up Baby," another of Nelson's suggestions, written by Danny Wolfe, a piano player from Texas. On June 26 they returned to the Quonset Hut and nailed "Who Slapped John," a wild, echo-drenched, scream-punctuated tune of Gene's featuring a unique shout-out interplay between Gene, Dickie, and Willie. They moved on to "Jumps, Giggles and Shouts" next, a mid-tempo rocker involving four different solos, two for Cliff on guitar and one each for Dickie on drums and Jack on the big doghouse bass. The band had some difficulty finding the breaks, though, as each solo was prefaced with the group hollering a personalized invitation to the soloist to "Jump! Jump!" They worked through about a dozen takes before Gene was satisfied with it. Next up was the Nelson-picked "Bluejean Bop," which started out soft and slow— Gene purring in his lower register accompanied only by guitar— and then exploded into a hip-swiveling mover with an inventive twist on the kiddy ditty "Mary Had a Little Lamb" embedded in Cliff's third solo. They ended the day with the stuttering rocker "I Flipped," written by Bobbie Carrol and Bill Hicks.

They moved into their final session with the Gallup-penned "Bop Street," which sported a spoken word intro and exit from Willie and Dickie over Cliff's bluesy bends; "Well, I Knocked, Bim Bam," another Bobbie Carrol contribution; and "You Told a Fib," also composed by Cliff but changed from the more harsh "You Told a Lie" at Ken Nelson's request. They finished up with "Jump Back, Honey, Jump Back," a 1952 Okeh single for boogie-woogie piano player Hadda Brooks that Gene and the Caps transformed into a manic rocker featuring more unison chants from the band and whirling guitar work from Cliff.

Exhausted but satisfied with their results, the boys returned to Norfolk.

It was Gene on the phone. "Dickie, are you ready to go on the road?"

The teenager fell right out of bed, onto the floor.

Since the record came out he'd been living a double life—playing the celebrity when he wasn't messing up at school, cleaning blackboards and emptying trash cans after hours in penance for all his messing up. It was no fun. Yeah, cat, Dickie thought, he was more than ready to go on the road.

Gene swung by and picked him up in the convertible, and they headed to the radio station to meet with Davis. He told them that he'd booked Gene and the band on a three-week tour, starting in South Carolina but mostly consisting of outdoor fair dates in New York—small and intermediate markets, crowds of about two thousand, at places like Hamberg, Whitney Point, Watertown, Syracuse, and Baldwin. The boys were excited. But there was more. They were to play on *The Perry Como Show* on July 28, Davis told them.

National television. They were dumbfounded. The whole country had witnessed what the relatively new technology of TV did for Elvis Presley. By the midsummer of '56 the boy had appeared four times on *Stage Show*, the Saturday night program of Jackie Gleason—who called him "a guitar-playing Marlon Brando"—twice on *The Milton Berle Show*, and once, clad in a black-tie monkey suit and singing to a damn basset hound, on *The Steve Allen Show*. The stunning result was that by April of '56 Elvis could claim six of RCA's twenty-five top-selling records of all time: "Hound Dog" had moved two million copies, "Don't Be Cruel" a cool three million, and both records, along with "Heartbreak Hotel," had straddled the Top Five on the pop, country, and rhythm and blues charts. Plus, Presley had nabbed a three-picture movie deal with producer Hal Wallis for almost half a million dollars. The American pop culture machine, in the lucrative business of making stars, was in full swing; Gene and the band were eager to dive onto the assembly line.

For two weeks before they embarked on their very first concert tour, all day long and every day Gene and the band were in the WCMS studio feverishly rehearsing their show. Dickie happily, gratefully, quit school without a second thought. Jack and Cliff left their jobs. Willie's wife Robbie, a bass player, took over the Virginians for him. Even Davis asked for a leave of absence to chaperone the boys. The lawyers in the office one floor below would phone up to the station, cursing, "For God's sake, do something about that racket!" Gene and the fellows would turn it down for a little while, but eventually they'd get it turned back up again, thumping away in fervent pursuit of the perfect performance.

So that their boys would look their best as ambassadors of Norfolk, WCMS outfitted the band in uniforms—tan pants, rust coats, black shirts, and white ties—from Clayton's menswear store on bustling Granby Street. They looked sharp. The radio station also provided a roomy black Cadillac to travel in, on top of which the equipment was tied and covered with a tarp, and a driver, the rough, tough Red Gwynn, thirty-six, a former shipyard worker and WCMS stagehand at the Norfolk Auditorium. Just before they left for their tour, Gene—overwhelmed with emotion at the start of his journey to national stardom—stopped by WCMS one last time. He said his goodbyes down in the lobby, tears of gratitude running down his face. "I'll never forget what WCMS did for me," he choked.

Gene Vincent and the Blue Caps' first concert tour commenced in Folly Beach, a summer seaside resort town just outside Charleston, South Carolina. Gene was excited—and a little nervous. After all, this would be his first real performance as Gene Vincent, rock 'n' roll star, in front of a non-hometown crowd. It was a coming out, of sorts. But after a pre-show rallying cry of "Let's kill 'em!" to quell any jitters, Gene, dressed in a black shirt with the collar upturned, black trousers, a black sock covering his plastered foot, and a dark tangle of greasy curls spilling over his forehead, hurtled himself headlong into his debut, ricocheting across the stage, torturing his mike stand, and bringing the eager crowd again and again to ecstatic screams and applause. Each musician was wearing his namesake dark blue cap, similar to Eisenhower's favorite golf hat, and in the heat of a charged moment, Dickie, who could so rarely sit still that he regularly drummed standing up, snatched the cap from his head and flung it out into the sweat-soaked audience. The crowd went wild with whoops and applause. Gene loved it and had Tex make sure that from then on they'd always have boxes of hats on hand, first dark blue, eventually light blue, to throw out to the fans.

From South Carolina the band began the long drive to New York. Gene, who had some business matters to attend to in New York City, took a train to Penn Station where, to his immense surprise, he ran into Elvis Presley. Just a couple of months before, the boys in Presley's band—guitarist Scotty Moore, bassist Bill Black, and drummer D. J. Fontana—had given their boss a hard time when they'd first heard "Be-Bop-A-Lula" on the radio; they jumped all over him, positive he recorded it behind their backs. Elvis told them that, no, he hadn't gone into the studio without them, and that the record, which he actually thought was very good, belonged to one Gene Vincent. At the train station one of Presley's boys pointed Gene out to Elvis, and he walked over and introduced himself to the new rising star. "Gene, congratulations on your record," Presley said. "You really got a hit." Taken off-guard and a bit awed to be speaking to the very person who had inspired him to give rock 'n' roll a try, Gene quickly countered, "I wasn't trying to copy you. I wasn't trying to sound like you." Elvis told him, "Oh, I know that, it's just your natural style." The two singers then chatted a bit before each went his own way.

Later that day, in the company of his mother and Roy LaMere, Gene signed a new seven-year contract with L&B, appointing the company his exclusive manager and representative in exchange for twenty-five percent of his gross earnings.

*The Perry Como Show* was a real hoot. Julius LaRosa, the singing TV regular who had a hit with the Sicilian folk song "E Cumpare!" was guest-hosting for the vacationing Como, and pop chanteuse Eydie Gorme was appearing also. Because the set the producers chose resembled the inside of a submarine, the band was put into blue jeans and tee-shirts for their performance. They would have much preferred to wear their new suits—they thought they looked like bums in the scrubby duds—but they weren't about to cause problems on *The Perry Como Show* and cooperated in any way they could. Jack, in fact, was tapped to do a little acting, appearing in a skit with LaRosa later.

As it had for Presley, TV boosted sales of Gene's single considerably. After the band's Como appearance, "Be-Bop-A-Lula"—which Steve Allen had given further exposure with a dramatic recitation of the nonsensical lyrics on his show; whether it was a loving lampoon or sarcastic slam really didn't seem to matter—would vault to number seven on the pop chart, number seven on the retail bestsellers chart, number ten on the chart tracking the most played songs on jukeboxes, and number eleven on the disc jockey most playeds list. "Lula" would spend fifteen weeks in the Top 40 and maintain airplay for a remarkable six months. Capitalizing on the momentum, while they were in New York Gene and the Caps appeared on Alan Freed's radio show, easily the most influential radio program in the nation for young rock 'n' roll artists, performing "Be-Bop-A-Lula" and Presley's "Hound Dog."

The flamboyant Freed did not start out in rock 'n' roll. He had, in fact, been hosting an evening classical music show at WJW in Cleveland, Ohio, when the owner of one of the larger record shops in town invited him to drop by to witness a most unusual phenomenon, white teenagers with apparently disposable income snatching up race music records like there was no tomorrow. Impressed, Freed aired his first rhythm and blues show on WJW in 1952. He called it the "Moon Dog Show," changing it later, after he dropped the stigmatized term *rhythm 'n' blues* from his lingo, to the "Moon Dog House Rock 'n' Roll Party." At the start of every show, with Todd Rhodes' King single "Blues for Moon Dog" playing under him, the free-spirited Freed would howl like a restless hound by way of introduction.

The whiskey-nipping, hooting and howling Freed became the grown-up kids could trust, if only by virtue of the music he played and the colorful persona he pushed. He spoke with a distinctive gravel-throated voice, the result of vocal cord damage from the removal of some polyps in his throat. And his on-air persona— he'd regularly howl and pound out time on a phone book along with the records—was truly unique. Freed was also a tireless promoter and canny businessman, envisioning big profits in live shows that would bring black and white rock 'n' roll musicians—and their fans—together. In March 1952, he assembled a package concert with a panoply of the most popular rhythm and blues acts of the time, including Joe Turner, Clyde McPhatter, the Drifters, the Clovers, the Moonglows, and the Moonlighters. He called it the "Moon Dog Coronation Ball" and held it at the ten-thousand-seat Cleveland Arena. He reportedly sold eighteen thousand tickets, and when the oversold crowd showed up—along with an additional ticketless seven thousand hoping to gain entry—a near-riot ensued. The show was canceled. Freed was accused of overselling the venue, but the charges were eventually dropped. The concert went on a few months later.

By 1954, Freed's show became so well known in and out of Ohio that he was hired by WINS, soon making that station the most popular with the teenagers of New York City. Freed staged many more of his live concert programs in New York with great success, often dancing onstage in a flashy plaid sportcoat and blowing kisses to the audience. Both white and black youngsters would attend Freed's shows, and he would be sharply criticized for "mixing the races" with this regrettable new music. His response: "Anyone who says rock 'n' roll is a passing fad or flash-in-the-pan trend along the music road has rocks in his head, dad!"

Gene and the Blue Caps worked their New York fair dates through early August, fine-tuning their frenetic stage show with every engagement. As the youngest, Dickie's enthusiasm for his work was boundless, and he—along with Gene and Tex—would prod the older members of the band to loosen up, move around and give the audience a real show. Outgoing Willie was easy to talk into some outlandish stage antics, and the other fellows would urge Jack, "Look, man, you got to put this bass in the air and stand on the bass and act crazy and all that. That's what people want." Jack was reluctant at first, but eventually gave in, which pleased Gene greatly and earned the bassist the nickname "Jumpin' Jack." When the audiences would start singing and screaming and dancing in the aisles, Gene would be almost lost in his ecstasy. Cliff, however, was a different story. He was a hell of a nice guy but always strictly business, and he wanted no part of any onstage craziness. All he wanted to move was his fingers. He'd shake his head at his lovably exuberant bandmates and mutter, "You all need help."

After the fair dates Gene and the band moved on to Pennsylvania, eventually joining up with openers the Johnny Burnette Trio—who recorded their "Tear It Up" single for Coral just three days after Gene had waxed "Lula" for Capitol—and Carl Perkins—rested, recuperated, and ready to rock once more, now that Elvis's rocketing rendition of "Blue Suede Shoes" had stolen the thunder from his original—on a six-week package tour. The folks at Gene's booking agency, General Artists Corporation, who'd also nabbed the Como gig for him, must have been aware that New York and Pennsylvania were among six states, along with Ohio, Illinois, Michigan, and California, that by 1958 would account for fifty-one percent of all record sales and booked Gene accordingly.

In Shamokin, Pennsylvania, just outside Pittsburgh, Gene and the Caps played a pair of shows at the Victoria Theater, a cozy movie house. Between performances, Gene moved outside to sign a few autographs and mingle with the fans. An audible "oh" of girlish excitement rose up from the eager throng the moment he stepped from the theater, and the pretty young things of Shamokin, all sweaty and moist, pressed in tightly around him. Smiling, Gene began signing autographs. The crowd pressed in more tightly, moving him along in their primped and perfumed midst. Gene happily continued signing autographs. Soon the impassioned teens had him corralled into a corner. Gene kept right on signing.

Some of the girls decided then that they needed more than just Gene's signature. Stirred deeply by this angelic outlaw who made rebellious rock 'n' roll sound so sweet, one young lady in search of a memento snatched at Gene's tie. The pandemonium was unleashed. Another grabbed at the tie. Hands reached in, buttons were torn from his shirt. Then bits of shirt came off, limp shreds reverently clutched in the tight, waving fists of the screaming, frantic girls. Gene, at first paralyzed in disbelief, tried to fight off his ardent fans. But he was easily overwhelmed by their fervor. Finally the police moved in and rescued the singer from the rock 'n' roll rabid girls and escorted him back to the theater for the last show.

Gene Vincent was no longer a human being. He was a souvenir.

The movie house, without a suitable stage of its own, had erected a portable bandstand atop sawhorses on which musical groups would perform. During the second show, the fans, their rock 'n' roll hunger only whetted by the riotous intermission, rushed the platform. The bandstand toppled over. Gene and the Caps fell to the floor beneath it. And then the lights went out. In the dark, the audience descended on the band like pink, pubescent birds of prey. By the time the lights were restored and the crowd dispersed, the beautiful new jackets from Clayton's were in shreds. Dickie crawled out from the wreckage wearing just an imprint of a jacket front—no sleeves, no buttons, just a couple of lapels. He looked over to Gene, also clad in tatters. He was sitting among the debris, shaking his head and murmuring, "I don't believe it." Bill Davis was furious. "You know how much money it cost for them jackets?" he yelled. Gene and the band looked up at him, looked down at themselves, and broke into hysterical laughter.

From then on, that's how most every show went. A desperate drive to get to the gig, sometimes the second or third of the day in the second or third city of the day. A mad dash to the stage. A mad dash back to the safety of the car, hundreds of screaming girls in panting pursuit. Then back out on the highway. They continued through the Northeast, subsisting on hamburgers with Gene fueled by endless cups of black coffee and an eternal chain of Camel cigarettes, which stained his fingers yellow. It seemed he couldn't carry on a conversation without a lit cigarette in his hand. Gene was still in a cast, albeit a smaller one that ended just under the knee, and he was always uncomfortable. Often his leg would itch so bad that he'd plunge an old coat hanger deep down into the cast, scratching his way to blessed relief. Other times, especially after performances, the plaster would be stained with angry splotches of red, bloody protest from the lingering wound Gene would give no rest.

Traveling back through New York en route to a gig in Contoocock, New Hampshire, Gene and the Caps, Perkins, and the Burnette trio were stranded atop Eagle Mountain for four hours. A dense fog had set in and visibility was poor. Armed with flashlights, assorted band and crew members rescued the show by walking down the mountainside ahead of the cars, safely guiding the way. At one point they decided to stop for a moment, and if Carl's brother Clayton had walked about ten more feet he'd have been off the side of the mountain. The one thousand and some teenagers who greeted them in a pouring rain at Contoocock were a more than welcome sight.

Life on the road was not easy and not for everyone, particularly the married members of Gene's band, Willie, Cliff, and Jack. In September, despite the brisk sales of Gene's debut album, *Bluejean Bop*, which was released a month earlier and would peak at number sixteen on the pop albums chart, Willie played his last gig as a Blue Cap in Fredericksburg, Virginia, before returning to Norfolk, his wife, and his job as leader of the WCMS staff band. Cliff, who had a baby on the way in Norfolk, gave his notice too, agreeing to stay on for one last gig. So without a rhythm guitarist and with the departure of their distinctive lead guitar imminent, the band headed gloomily to Washington, D.C., where they were booked for a two-week stand at the Casino Royale, a large, up-scale supper club that attracted name performers and paid top dollar. Teddy Crutchfield, a WCMS deejay, was summoned to Washington to temporarily replace Willie, but Cliff, he was going to be mighty difficult to replace.

Just down the street, the Tunetoppers, a country band led by Greenville, South Carolina transplant Red Redding, was booked at another nightclub, the Metropole. Red had brought up three other musicians from Greenville to play in his band: Atlanta-born steel guitarist Paul Peek, bassist Bill Mack, and lead guitarist Frank Cosier. Paul and Bill were childhood friends and had been playing music together for about a year, working some gigs with another local musician, the outlandish piano wildman Eskew Reeder, who went by the name of Esquerita. Paul had also played steel guitar in the Greenville hillbilly band Country Earl and the Circle E Ranch Boys. Bill had recently switched from upright bass to electric, and he played his new Fender electric bass in the Tunetoppers.

Paul and Bill, both big fans of "Be-Bop-A-Lula," were excited that Gene and the Caps were also in town and stopped by the Casino Royale one day while the band was rehearsing. They introduced themselves as musicians and invited the band to come see them at the Metropole. Davis and some of the guys, being huge country music fans, did stop by and mentioned to Paul that Gene was looking for a new rhythm guitar player. "I can play some rhythm," the red-headed, prematurely balding Paul fibbed. He was promptly invited to audition. Cliff helped Paul with the chords to "Jezebel," then Gene and the band stepped to the back of the club for a hushed conference. When they returned, Gene handed Paul a hat, proclaiming, "You're a Blue Cap now, man."

Within two days of hiring Paul, Gene and the band were on a plane headed to Hollywood, California. They were going to make a movie.

Like television, film work could make a musician's career. The cross-genre success of singers-turned-actors like Bing Crosby, Doris Day, and Capitol's own Frank Sinatra handily proved the symbiosis between music and film; movies were becoming increasingly important in the marketing of music, and music helped draw audiences to movies. In fact, Capitol itself had been formed from the union of a singer, Johnny Mercer, and a movie executive, Buddy DeSylva of Paramount Pictures, along with Glenn Wallichs, who came from the world of music retailing. The trio's initial investment—said to have been about ten grand—was immediately recouped by the hits "Cow Cow Boogie" by Ella Mae Morse and Mercer's own "Strip Polka." The company went on to gross $195,000 in its first six months, enabling its rapid expansion into rhythm 'n' blues and into the country field with artists like Ferlin Husky, Tex Ritter, and Tennessee Ernie Ford.

Rock 'n' roll provided yet another link between music and film. In February 1955, the movie *Blackboard Jungle*, featuring Bill Haley's "Rock Around the Clock" thumping under the opening credits, was released. Though Decca had issued the single in 1954 to lukewarm reaction—it had sold about seventy-five thousand copies—when tied to the teen rebellion depicted in the movie, the song swiftly lofted to the top of the charts. That movie was followed by *Rock Around the Clock* in early 1956, a slightly fictionalized account of how Haley and his band were discovered and put on television by Alan Freed, who played himself in the film. *Rock Around the Clock* caused teen riots at home and abroad, and, most significantly, grossed five times what it cost to make in less than a year.

To cash in on the rock 'n' roll craze, filmmakers were now working fast and furiously to churn out flicks with vast teen appeal. One of the first big-budget rock 'n' roll movies to be made was the satirical Cinemascope comedy *The Girl Can't Help It*, produced, directed, and co-written by Frank Tashlin. As a Warners' cartoons veteran, Tashlin's specialty was comedy, and he would write or direct films starring funnymen Bob Hope and Harpo Marx, among others, and eventually Jerry Lewis. *The Girl Can't Help It*, in stereophonic sound, starred platinum-tressed Jayne Mansfield and her considerable cleavage—20th Century Fox's answer to Marilyn Monroe—as an aspiring, though talentless, singer, who is groomed by showbiz agent Tom Ewell at the behest of gangster-type Edmund O'Brien, Mansfield's sugar-daddy boyfriend. At a rehearsal facility, Mansfield is given a crash course in rock 'n' roll as she listens in on artists like the Treniers, the Platters, Eddie Cochran, Fats Domino, Little Richard—and Gene Vincent and the Blue Caps.

Being part of glamorous Hollywood—it was the farthest they'd ever been from home—and the hustle and bustle of the Fox movie lot was thrilling for Gene and the Caps. Paul was particularly exhilarated—one night he was playing steel at a club in D.C., two days later he's making a movie three thousand miles away in California. The fellows were excited to see stars like James Cagney and Ernest Borgnine, Ewell, O'Brien, and Mansfield dining in the commissary and out on the streets, though Gene would say later that he preferred "the quiet, plain type of girl. The girl-next-door type. Real sweet, not too much makeup." They hoped to meet Little Richard, one of Gene and the band's very favorite artists, but he finished shooting the day before, the makeup man told them. While they were being groomed and powdered, the makeup department devised a small cap to cover Gene's toes, which dangled out of his cast. The plaster was then painted black. The whole thing looked just like an ordinary shoe when it was done. The boys were impressed.

For restless young men used to the nonstop action of the life of a touring rock 'n' roll band, making a movie—even just filming a cameo—seemed inordinately tedious. All day long, from six in the morning to five in the afternoon, Gene, Dickie, Paul, Jack, and Russell Willaford, another Norfolk guitarist who'd been flown in to take Cliff's spot in the movie, played "Be-Bop-A-Lula" over and over again so that it could be shot from every possible angle.

Though a second single, "Race With the Devil," with "Gonna Back Up Baby" on its flip side, had been released on September 10, neither side had yet charted and "Lula" was the song Tashlin wanted in the film. By midday, the constant repetition ground any spontaneity out of the band's performance, and the director barked, "Damn! Can't you all do something to liven it up a little bit?" So on the next take, when Dickie let loose with one of his robust screams, the musicians all cocked their heads back and the caps went flying. The director was delighted. The band was even more delighted when the shooting day was over.

While they were in Hollywood, the band toured the Capitol Records headquarters at Sunset and Vine, a gleaming circular tower thirteen stories tall, which looked just like a pile of 45s stacked on a skyscraping spindle. The company had been founded to attract the greatest artists of the time, and to that end a state-of-the-art recording facility was constructed on the ground floor of the building. While they were at Capitol, Gene and the Caps also visited the company photo studio, as they would do most every time they were in Los Angeles. Staff photographer Ken Veeder shot countless color frames of the band, the musicians resplendent in black shirts, light blue jackets, and matching caps, with tousle haired Gene, looking gaunt and drawn, dressed in his omnipresent black shirt over a white tee and black pants. Davis and Gene also visited with Ken Nelson—who'd decided on "Bluejean Bop" and "Who Slapped John" as the next single, released on October 8—to discuss the upcoming sessions booked at Owen Bradley's.

Gene and the band arrived in Nashville on October 13, where they met up with Cliff Gallup, who had been persuaded—through a barrage of long-distance phone calls from Nelson, Gene, and Davis—to return just for the sessions. They rehearsed for two days, then entered the studio on the 15th. Seasoned from the road, flush with the exhilaration of their growing stardom, the band was at its spontaneous best. Gene was again placed in the studio with the other musicians, not tucked away in the corner, and the tracks were recorded live, with virtually no direction from Nelson. Gene, always fidgety, was a much more confident singer now, and in his excitement he'd shout and move around, often going off his mike. Nelson had to constantly remind him to stand still.

They kicked off the session with "Teenage Partner," Gene's own rocking paean to adolescent love lost, then rolled out the old Delmore Brothers tune, "Blues Stay Away From Me," and Mel Tillis's comedic "Five Feet Of Lovin'." They concluded the first day with Gene's "Cat Man," a syncopated slice of ominous atmospherics, courtesy of Dickie's locomotive brush work, Cliff's perpetual sliding motifs, and Gene's feral screams.

They launched the next day with the swinging rocker "Double Talkin' Baby," penned by Danny Wolfe, who had also written "Gonna Back Up Baby." Gene's raucous "Hold Me, Hug Me, Rock Me" followed, and they wound down the day with "Unchained Melody," the pop classic, which Gene gave a tremblingly tender read. Gene and the Caps returned on October 17, launching into the Nelson-suggested "B-I-Bickey-Bi-Bo-Bo-Go," a rocking bit of nonsense co-written by Jack Rhodes, who'd penned "Woman Love." Paul Peek's "Pink Thunderbird" was up next, followed by another Wolfe tune, "Pretty, Pretty Baby." They closed out their third day in the studio with Gene's "Cruisin'," adorned with more amazingly high-speed rides from Cliff.

Gene had requested that the Jordanaires, Presley's backing vocal group, be brought in for a few songs, and Ken Nelson happily arranged it. On October 18 the quartet arrived at the Quonset Hut to lend harmonies to Gene's ballad of romantic devotion, "Important Words," by far his favorite of all the tunes he'd written; Cliff's "You Better Believe"; and the Jack Rhodes lament "Five Days, Five Days." The session was complete with "Red Bluejeans and a Pony Tail," another Rhodes-penned number.

After a brief stop home, the group headed north to their first date outside of the United States. They received a hero's welcome in Toronto, Canada, and settled in to a huge, old vaudeville theater called the Criterion for a week's stay on a variety package. For a single admission, patrons got a feature film, several openers—including a performing-dogs act, a magician, and a girl singer named Monique Cadieux—and the featured act, Gene Vincent and the Blue Caps. It was continuous, from noon to midnight, sometimes a grueling four shows a day. Gene became quite friendly with Monique and spent his free moments making out with her in her dressing room. They started a brief affair, but with Gene on the road, it quickly fizzled out.

It was one of the damnedest things Gene and the boys had ever seen. A glittering playground for grown-ups smack dab in the middle of the sunbaked desert.

Erected from a dusty Union Pacific railroad stop, Las Vegas had managed to bypass the Depression, largely because of its legalized gambling industry and the jobs-producing Hoover Dam construction just a few miles away. Nearby Nellis Air Force Base became a key military installation during World War II, bringing countless personnel to live—and play—in Vegas. And did they play. The postwar building boom saw casino hotels spring up like great neon weeds from the shifting, shimmering sands, lining the two-lane highway leading into the desert city from Los Angeles. The Last Frontier, Thunderbird and Club Bingo. The Desert Inn. The Sahara. And Bugsy Seigel's Flamingo, the lavish "carpet joint" modeled after the resort hotels of Miami, which attracted the rich and the famous, deep-pocketed patrons and top-name entertainment.

Many of the Flamingo's showbiz luminaries jumped ship, however, when Jack Entratter from Manhattan's glitzy Copacabana was installed as vice president of the newly opened Sands Hotel. When the place opened its doors in December 1952, Dean Martin, Jerry Lewis, and others headed straight to its stage without a second thought, such was their respect for Entratter and his boss Frank Costello, head of the New York mob. Entratter also managed to lure Sinatra, Lena Horne, Tony Bennett, and other A-list talents who'd played at the Copa out to his brand new hotel on Highway 91.

Gene and the Caps were booked into the smaller gambling lounge of the Sands for a few weeks. They shared the lounge bill with the Mary Kaye Trio and the Four Lads; each act played a twenty-minute set every hour from midnight until sunrise. As one of the first rockabilly bands to play Vegas, Gene and the Blue Caps were something of a novelty. As one of the wildest bands to play Vegas—not many acts in town featured a screaming, hiccuping, mike-hurling singer, an upright-tossing bassman, and a stage-diving drummer—they were something to see and drew jam-packed crowds from their first night.

On the third night, about one or two o'clock, Davis felt a tap on his shoulder. It was Entratter. And he didn't look happy.

"Tex, look around," he said.

"Where?" Davis asked, confused at such an odd request.

"Around the room."

Davis scanned the lounge. "What do you see?" Entratter asked.

"The people," Davis answered.

"A lot of people," Entratter corrected. "And what are they doing?"

"They're watching Gene," Davis said.

"And I'm losing a million dollars a minute."

Davis winced.

Gene was just too loud, too showy, Entratter told him. Couldn't he get the boy to tone it down, he asked, though it was a command more than a query—"Just do some ordinary singing, some Frank Sinatra stuff? Or maybe just the band?"

Davis knew that asking Gene to tone it down would be like asking him not to breathe. It would be futile. But he assured Entratter that he'd give it a try.

Back in the hotel room after the set, Davis told Gene about Entratter's request. Gene was upset.

"No, no," an irate Gene said. "I'm gonna perform."

"You can't," Davis implored.

"Well, I don't care what they say," Gene said angrily. "I'm gonna perform."

"Gene, you can't," Davis snapped, quickly becoming exasperated at the boy's stubbornness. Certainly it was only common sense that if the fellow signing your paycheck wants you to pipe down, then you'd better pipe down. And most especially if that fellow happens to be Jack Entratter. "Gene, the guy said you can't do it. There's millions of dollars involved."

"Yeah," Gene shot back, "but it's my life. And I want to do what I want to do."

Fed up, Davis surrendered. "Okay, Gene. You do what you want to do."

They went back down to the lounge. When it was time for Gene to go on, he limped onto the stage, sang one song, looked at Davis out in the crowd, stuck his middle finger straight up, and walked off, leaving the band to finish out the set.

The boys were having a ball in Vegas. The place simply oozed decadence. Stars and millionaires were everywhere. Lena Horne, who was also playing at the Sands, caught their act. So did powerful gossip columnist Hedda Hopper. Some rich old man sitting in the front row bought the entire band dinner after one show. Elvis had been in town for a few days, vacationing before the premiere of his first film, *Love Me Tender*. Frank Sinatra and Dean Martin, Eddie Fisher and Debbie Reynolds, and Peter Lawford and Sammy Davis all played the big room at the Sands. Dickie'd even run into Jerry Lewis at the slot machines. One night Liberace, who just opened at the Riviera, came in with his brother. Dickie ran outside to gape at his flashy Cadillac convertible with the keyboard seats. The flamboyant piano man, a favorite of Gene's, went backstage to meet him.

"Let me tell you something, son," Liberace advised Gene, turning deadly serious after they were introduced. "If you do what these people tell you to do, you'll work the rest of your life right here in this place. If you're not going to do what they tell you, you'd just as well pack your bags and go back to Virginia."

"Well, uh, thank you very much," Gene murmured, mulling the showman's words over in his mind.

Gene wasn't having as much fun in Vegas as the band. He just didn't like the place. Sure, the money was great, over three grand a week. And now there were four or five other places that had invited him to perform, plus the Sands wanted more dates. But it wasn't like playing the concerts. He liked to hear those kids screaming. Their applause was his paycheck. He told Davis that Vegas just wasn't his bag, that he wanted to get back into the concert business.

The Blue Caps could tell Gene wasn't happy in Las Vegas. They could see that the virtually nonstop months on the road had taken a painful toll on Gene's leg, which increasingly agonized him. Gene occasionally took a drink or two before a show if he was nervous; Paul noticed that Gene was now starting to drink a bit more than usual. One night, when Gene went into one of his familiar poses—right leg bent down low, that bum left leg kicked out straight and stiff behind him—he slipped on the footlights. Nobody in the audience seemed to notice, but blood was seeping from his cast after the show. Gene had had enough.

"Bill"—Gene always called him Bill—"I wanna go home," the singer informed Davis back in the hotel room.

Davis was dumbfounded. "What do you mean?"

"I wanna go home."

"You can't go home. You have a commitment that you made with these people when you signed the contract for $3,250 a week. That's a lot of money. And you've committed for a whole month, so this is the way it's gotta be."

"Not for me," he said. "I'm leaving in the morning. I've already got my flight planned."

"Gene, you can't do that."

"I'm gonna do it." There was no changing Gene's mind.

The two argued some more, until Davis, infuriated by the boy's impetuousness, his downright orneriness, finally barked, "Gene, you go home. You just go on home. And the boys can go home with you. This is it for me."

Gene finished out the night and returned to Norfolk the next morning. Davis was with him.

"Mama," Davis told Gene's mother, "this is the last you're gonna see of Tex Davis. Gene, you're back safe and sound. You're on your own."

**II**

*Well, me and the Devil, sittin' at a stoplight,*
*He started rollin', I was out of sight!*
*Move, hot rod! Move, man!*
*Move, hot rod! Move, man!*
*Move, hot rod! Move me on down the line!*

THE NEW YEAR DAWNED DARKLY FOR GENE.

He returned to the Portsmouth Naval Hospital around Christmas time for yet another operation on his leg. The doctors, alarmed at how badly the wound had deteriorated—Gene had refractured it in Vegas—sternly advised Gene that he must quit singing—and now—or he'd almost certainly pay dearly later. Actually, it didn't much matter. He was forbidden to play anyway by court order.

In mid-February attorneys for L&B secured an $11,000 attachment on Gene's earnings, then filed suit for back commissions from July 3 to December 1, 1956. They also filed for the injunction that restrained Gene from performing for or securing the services of any other agent. The suit claimed Gene grossed about $32,000 in that five-month period—entitling L&B to $8,175, or twenty-five percent as stated in the contract Gene had signed in July—but that he'd only paid L&B $562.50. They wanted the remaining $7,612.50.

Gene's lawyers countersued, asking the U.S. District Court in Norfolk to void his contract and restrain the agency from prosecuting the $11,000 attachment. His lawyers were also seeking compensatory and punitive damages, claiming he rescinded the contract around August 24, 1956, on grounds that it was void and one-sided. The suit also claimed that Gene cut short L&B's representation partly on grounds of alleged fraud, misrepresentation, and undue influence. He was, after all, just a kid with absolutely no experience in business or contractual matters. Gene's lawyers also filed a motion to dismiss L&B's suit on the grounds that L&B, a corporation formed in Delaware, had no authority to do business in Virginia, and that the firm was never franchised and licensed as a manager or booking agent in accordance with requirements of the American Federation of Musicians. It was all a big headache. And it was all about money, as usual.

The release of another single, "Crazy Legs," with Gene's favorite, "Important Words," on the flip, on January 7 was a bright spot, especially after "Race With the Devil" had peaked at a dismal number ninety-six and "Bluejean Bop" at an almost as dismal forty-nine on the October charts, and "Lula" had fallen off entirely in November after a dazzling twenty-week ride. And the opening of the group's film debut, *The Girl Can't Help It*, around the holidays was exciting. The boys—Paul chomping gum and pumping his guitar like some kind of humping hoodlum, and Gene, grease-soaked strings of hair in his face, trembling, breathless, and clench-fisted with lustful tension—looked and sounded like no other act in the film. It was a brilliant performance, even if only a minute of an entire day's worth of footage wound up being used. But even more encouraging was the whole new group Gene formed during his enforced vacation.

He had plenty of time to think about how he could make the music more exciting, make the performance even more entertaining. The first thing, he thought, was to avoid old, married guys like Cliff, Willie, and the departed Jack at all costs. And Russell Willaford, whom he'd picked up for the movie, turned out to be kind of hesitant onstage. Gene was looking for something different. He wanted a show band, with guys who weren't afraid to get a little wild. A band that would rock the place down. So he approached a young kid he knew, Tommy Facenda.

Tommy, who went by his nickname Bubba, was a lifelong buddy of Dickie's. They'd attended St. Paul's Catholic together, but Gene became quite friendly with him as well. He and Dickie would go watch Bubba play basketball for the school when they could, and Bubba would go out on the road with his pals from time to time. Facenda was a good-looking Italian boy, and Gene knew that he could sing because he spent a lot of time over at Bubba's home—Gene loved his parents—and they'd often goof around with doo-wop songs, sit around and watch TV, or spend the night at each other's houses.

"I want a band that entertains," Gene told Bubba one evening while they were staying up late, sitting under a streetlight, just singing and talking. "I want young guys that want to do things on stage. Get crazy. Move around. Look, why don't you go with me and sing background?"

"Well, what are we talking about?" Bubba asked, a little stunned at Gene's request. "Are we talking about four people? Are we talking about a bass and—"

"No," Gene said. "We're just talking two. I would just like to have maybe you and another guy, lead and a tenor."

Bubba was flattered. He'd fiddled around with music all his life, even blew a little horn in school, but he never, ever thought of singing professionally. He was on his way to college—he was thinking about Notre Dame—or maybe he would embark on a military career. It was going to be one of the two. But this thing with Gene, making music, it was something Bubba'd always loved. Hell, the only thing he'd ever really done in his seventeen years was make music and play ball. And he liked what Gene was doing, this show band thing, because "you get onstage, man, you wanna move, you wanna do your thing," he'd explain years later. And Gene was going to give him that opportunity. Plus, Gene was a big star, had a hit record, and was in a movie. Bubba had always wanted to give acting a shot. And Gene must've been making some real good dough, too, Bubba thought.

Bubba appreciated the offer but told Gene he needed some time to think it over. But it wasn't long before Bubba was helping Gene audition countless locals for the other backing vocalist spot. Bubba and Paul worked together to show the auditionees what Gene was looking for—some singing, some dancing, some hand-clapping. But no one seemed to please the boss. Gene was getting more and more frustrated with every prospective singer who hadn't a clue what the star wanted. One day Gene just said, "Well, Paul, you do it." He figured it would be a lot easier to pick up a rhythm guitarist somewhere than find the perfect showboating background vocalist. So Paul traded in his six-string for a pair of dancing shoes.

Paul found Gene some damn fine players back home, too, all friends of his, to round out the band. He took Gene down to Greenville to catch a Country Earl and the Circle E Ranch Boys gig. They returned the following day with the rest of the new lineup. There was Bill Mack, who'd been playing with Paul in D.C., and his Fender electric bass. Gene was thrilled to have an electric bass in the band, it was so loud and different and took up much less space on stage and in travel than the bulky doghouse bass. And then there was Johnny Meeks, who played a big ol' three-neck guitar. He'd bought it from a buddy in Greenville who fashioned it from old Fender parts. It had a six-string guitar neck, a twelve-string guitar neck, and a mandolin neck up top for the high notes. The gimmick just knocked Gene out. He even bought it off Johnny a little later. But Bubba had no idea what Gene was talking about when he and Paul returned from Carolina—"I just hired a guitar player with three necks," Gene had said. Damn, Bubba thought, Gene always did have a little P. T. Barnum in him. And now he's done hired some sort of freak!

Once Bubba and Johnny were introduced, though, and Bubba heard how Johnny could play, he had all the respect in the world for him. A lot of other fellows would have come in and tried to imitate Cliff. Not Johnny. Even though he was a little hesitant to join because he didn't think he was a fine enough guitar player, he went ahead and played his own sound. Gene really liked that. And Johnny was good. Sure, Cliff was a genius, was great with his triplets in a Les Paul and Chet Atkins kind of way, but Johnny was pure, rough, and rock. The whole sound changed. And that was exactly what Gene wanted.

The out-of-towners all moved into the Craddock house on Leckie Street in Portsmouth, sleeping on the sofa, the floor—wherever—when they weren't rehearsing or horsing around. Gene's mama was patient with the hubbub, but they drove Gene's daddy absolutely buggy with all their racket. He'd shuffle around the house, frowning and muttering, "This stuff is driving me *crazy*." He thought they were all nuts, what with the rehearsals at all hours of the day and night in the living room, Paul and Bubba working out dance and hand-clapping routines, and the new fellows learning all the songs. But Kie respected the boys' ambition and his son's quest—which included riding the boys pretty hard—for the perfect rock 'n' roll band.

The rest of the family couldn't help but get involved, too. Little Donna—Gene's baby sister whom he'd rechristened "Pipes" because she was constantly singing around the house—would often sneak out of bed to watch her big brother and his crazy rock 'n' roll band rehearse. She'd sit at the top of the stairs at night with her sister Sara, whom everybody called Tina, their tiny legs dangling between the balustrades, and listen and watch for hours. Gene's mama would complain to the boys, "The girls won't go to sleep!" and they'd all chase the kids back to bed. And, oh, the pillow fights. They ruined many of Louise's pillows with their frequent battles, the girls plotting and scheming elaborate strategies to defeat the boys for the glorious booty of pizza, ice cream, or candy bars.

With his new band taking definite shape, Gene was restless and itching to get back on the road. One morning he called up Dickie, who was staying at his mama's house.

"What's happening, man?"

"Nothing," Dickie said.

"Let's go somewhere. I'll come by and get you."

Gene picked Dickie up in his flashy two-tone T-Bird, and they rode around Portsmouth as they often did—Gene wasn't much for sitting still—cruising back and forth on High Street downtown.

Out of the blue, Gene said, "Let's drive to Nashville, man."

"Nashville? For what?" Dickie couldn't believe it—that was a full day's haul.

"Let's just ride to Nashville," Gene answered.

So they drove to Nashville, riding low and sporty the whole way in the pretty—but, for a husky guy like Dickie, pretty damned uncomfortable—Thunderbird. By the time they got there, Dickie felt like he wouldn't be walking for a week. They stayed in Nashville just three hours before Gene turned around and drove back home. Every time they hit a bump, the little car would bottom out on the cement. Dickie was miserable.

"Son, we can't do this no more," he lamented to Gene, his rear end in mortal anguish.

"No, man," Gene beamed. "This is great!"

Gene's second album, *Gene Vincent and the Blue Caps*, was released March 4, and Gene knew he should be on the road to promote it. So, defying the court order that prohibited him from performing, he and the new, improved Caps joined a package tour of Ohio called the "Rockabilly Spectacular." Along with Gene it featured Sanford Clark, who had a Top 10 hit the year before with "The Fool"; Gene's buddy Carl Perkins; Sun rockabilly Roy Orbison; fellow Capitol artist Sonny James, whose "Young Love" would top the charts that year; George Hamilton IV, singer of the 1956 Top 10 teen ballad "A Rose and a Baby Ruth"; singer, songwriter, and guitarist Eddie Cochran; and others.

The crowds at the auditoriums were full and responsive, but the old coots running the house sound systems didn't quite know what to make of the rocking and rolling hoodlums. During one show, when Gene hit the deck with the microphone stand and thrashed about wildly with it to the music, the elderly, white-haired sound man who'd probably been working the venue for some thirty years sprinted onto the stage and tried to wrestle his precious microphone away from Gene. They grappled for a while. But the more the old man fought for the mike, the more Gene just rolled around with it, keeping his elderly persecutor at bay.

The musicians were wild, especially Gene and Carl and his brothers. The booze would be flowing and they'd all get to drinking. One night in Cincinnati, after playing at a fairground directly across from a racetrack, Carl took the car he'd been traveling in out for a spin. He took off around the track mighty fast, but about the time he reached the other side, he saw another set of lights pull out onto the pavement. It was Gene. The two tore off around the track after each other, chasing one another for quite a while, then finally quit when every time they passed the bandstand they saw Sheriff Davis waving his arms frantically. They didn't want to give the poor guy a heart attack.

Then it was on to Philadelphia for the week-long "Rock 'n' Roll Jubilee of Stars" at the Mastbaum Theater with a cast of fifty artists, including Al Hibbler, the blind jazzman whose "Unchained Melody" and "After the Lights Go Down Low" had become pop hits, and Nappy Brown, the blues and novelty-song singer. Cochran was booked for the "Jubilee" as well and since his group was without wheels, he rode with Gene.

On the surface, the two couldn't have been more different, charismatic Cochran's all-American, milk-fed good looks a stark contrast to Gene's underfed, anguished fragility. Cochran was born in Minnesota to Oklahoman parents in 1938. When the family migrated to California in the early '50s, Eddie, already a formidable guitarist, was introduced to honky-tonk singer and songwriter Hank Cochran (no relation) with whom he started performing as the Cochran Brothers. They recorded three singles for the Ekko label in Memphis before parting company, Eddie then teaming up with musician-producer Jerry Capehart for a single on Crest. On the strength of his appearance in *The Girl Can't Help It*, in which he performed his "Twenty Flight Rock," Eddie was picked up by Liberty, which released that song and, in early 1957, Eddie's echoing cover of J. D. Loudermilk's "Sittin' in the Balcony," which became a million-selling Top 20 pop hit. Gene and Eddie did share, however, a sweeping passion for rock 'n' roll and an instinctive ability to interpret a song, and both worked tirelessly to achieve the fully realized sound each heard inside his head, particularly in the studio. They became fast friends during those weeks together.

The new Blue Caps show was going over like gangbusters. Johnny would break out the heavy three-necked guitar and Bubba and Paul would move all around the stage. They'd worked out all sorts of dance and hand-clapping routines at the Craddock house back on Leckie Street, which they would perform standing on either side of Gene. All three would share the same microphone, mostly out of necessity because the venues would rarely furnish two microphones. But Bubba was glad that it had turned out that way, actually; now he got to hear Gene's sweet voice in his ear every evening. And it sounded just like his records, like he had a little echo chamber right at the back of his throat. But the mike sharing was not without its perils. One night, when Gene screamed out his customary "Rock!" at the bridge of a song, he picked up the mike stand with such gusto that he accidentally whacked Bubba in the mouth with the heavy metal microphone. Bubba fell to the ground. When he stood back up his mouth was a geyser of blood. The crowd went crazy. Dazed, Bubba reached for his handkerchief to wipe off his face. Gene stopped him. "They love it!" he yelled, smiling ear to ear. Oh, crap, Bubba thought, now I'm gonna have to get my mouth busted every night?

Most times after Gene sang a ballad, he'd lay his Gretsch guitar down on the stage. In those few moments of darkness, Dickie would light a cherry bomb and drop it on the ground. It was a great effect: the thing would explode and the band would tear into a rocking number. But one night, on a bill with Sonny James, Paul was standing in front of the guitar. No big deal, Dickie figured, he'd just roll the bomb, it would hit Paul's foot, veer away from the band, and go off. But Paul moved his foot as Dickie dropped the lit explosive. It rolled under Gene's guitar. With a deafening bang the instrument vaulted forty feet in the air, then came down with a terrific thud, a huge hole blown out of its lower portion. Stunned, Gene picked the instrument up and looked over at Dickie as smoke wafted out of the hole. Lord, I better pack up right now, Dickie thought, it's all over. The audience started screaming. Gene was elated. "It's wonderful!" he gushed. "It's the best damn thing that's ever happened! We'll do it more often!" Dickie was relieved, of course, but he still felt bad about ruining Gene's guitar, so he took it to Sonny James' guitarist, who was something of a specialist. "Hey, can you do anything with that?" he asked. "Yeah," the guitar player said, "put it in the trash can." Dickie loathed telling Gene the bad news. But his singing friend simply said, "Don't worry about it. It looks good. It works good." And he continued to use it.

The battle with L&B was not the only litigation following Gene in early 1957; at the end of April he was ordered to pay his estranged wife Ruth Ann one hundred dollars per month for support. The L&B flap was settled a month later, with Gene shelling out thirteen thousand dollars. The figure included monies advanced for expenses, plus a consideration for his immediate release from the contract. At least that mess was over. Now Gene could concentrate on his music once again. Working to promote "Five Days, Five Days," which had been released March 25 with "B-I-Bickey-Bi-Bo-Bo-Go" as its B-side, the group gigged their way back to Portsmouth, then down to Greenville, where Gene let bassist Bill Mack go. He was immediately replaced with Bobby Lee Jones, yet another of Country Earl's Circle E Ranch Boys, who, like Bill, played a Fender electric bass. Johnny recommended him, and it didn't take much persuading to get Bobby to join; he'd actually become a paid-up member of the Gene Vincent Fan Club earlier that year.

Finally free to find other representation, Gene was eager to hire a professional manager, a real hard-ass, someone who knew his way around a deal. Ken Nelson suggested Ed McLemore's Artists

Service Bureau in Dallas. McLemore managed Gene's label-mate Sonny James, as well as fellow rockabillies Buddy Knox and Jimmy Bowen of the Rhythm Orchids, Johnny Carroll, who'd waxed his first Decca recordings at Owen Bradley's studio just a few days before Gene arrived for his first session, and many area musicians and songwriters. McLemore also ran the "Big D Jamboree," a largely country and western show similar to the "Grand Ole Opry," "Ozark Jubilee," and "Louisiana Hayride." The "Jamboree" was broadcast from Dallas' Sportatorium—where McLemore also booked popular wrestling matches—every Saturday night on radio station KRLD and nationally over the CBS radio network. Gene was duly impressed and signed on.

McLemore quickly set Gene up with a tour manager—balding, middle-aged Lawrence Thacker, a stoic businessman-type whom the band would come to aggravate to no end, gleefully and on purpose—to supervise things on the road, and supplied the band with a nine-person Chrysler station wagon, "the only car which could stand the strain of road travel to gigs," Gene would recall later. "We used to hit it like hell and it used to stand up to anything. We sometimes hit ninety miles an hour with that half-ton trailer on the back and it would stand up to it. Gigs were a minimum of two hundred to three hundred miles apart in those days, and we used to have what we called 'long jumps,' which were for a thousand-mile gig. They were usually overnight trips and we'd get noisy and tight in the Chrysler."

McLemore, a classy dresser himself with an affinity for cashmere, also outfitted the fellows in all-new stage gear: green jackets for Paul and Bubba, red jackets for the other musicians, and a variety of shirts in satin and crushed velvet for Gene, who wore a different shirt for every show. Gene always traveled real light, sending Dickie, whom he long ago appointed his clothes keeper, out for new shirts at almost every stop when they were on the road. He'd toss the kid some money and say, "Here, go get me something." Dickie'd run down to the local menswear store, pick up some crazy shirts, sometimes pants; Gene never did wear stuff long. Back in the early days, Gene would always cut the side of the pants so that his cast would fit. Now that he was wearing a metal brace, he could wear his trousers like the rest of the band. Gene never carried a big suitcase, though, and half the time there wasn't a damn thing in it, Dickie couldn't help but notice, just cigarettes and a bunch of junk.

Tom Fleeger was a Texas oilman turned self-styled music magnate. He'd picked up the publishing rights on a catchy little ditty written in five minutes by one Bernice Bedwell, "Lotta Lovin'," and he thought it would make a perfect comeback hit for that breathy kid from Virginia, that Gene Vincent. He'd heard and liked "Be-Bop-A-Lula," a fine song, but the fellow hadn't sold be-bop-a-lula of any of his other records, Fleeger thought. So he tracked Gene down in Portsmouth, Virginia, played him a tape of the tune over the telephone, and left him his phone number so that Gene could call when he arrived in Dallas.

Gene, who thought he heard a hit, too, did call when he got into town for his "Jamboree" appearance. Fleeger immediately carted him and the Blue Caps over to his mother Jan's apartment for an impromptu demo session, which he captured on his recently purchased reel-to-reel tape recorder. Johnny brought along just his acoustic guitar, no amplifier, and Dickie brought just his sticks, no drums. Improvising with an overturned trash can to keep the beat, Fleeger had Gene and the boys rehearse and record "Lotta Lovin' " and "In My Dreams," another Bedwell title, and Mary Tarver's "Nervous," which would later become a regional hit for Dallas singer Gene Summers. That boy was pretty clever, Fleeger thought. He seemed to know exactly how he wanted things to sound, halting the band's second go-around of "Lotta Lovin' " with a gentle but resolute, "Somebody's off there, man." "That's good!" Mrs. Fleeger exclaimed when they finally polished up "In My Dreams." Gene gave "Nervous" a couple of tries, but the words just didn't seem to fit right in the damn song, so he gave up. During a break, while the boys were just hanging around,

Gene idly whistled a pretty tune, "On My Mind," which Fleeger also caught on tape. Within a few days Gene and the band were at Dallas' Sellers Studios to cut proper demos of the Bedwell tunes.

Gene and the Caps played the "Big D Jamboree" on May 11, and shortly afterward Fleeger, Bedwell, and Gene met with Ed McLemore at the Artists Service Bureau offices. McLemore, too, sensed a hit when he heard Gene's demo of "Lotta Lovin'." And he wanted those rights.

"Tom," he said, leaning back in his big chair, puffing on a long cigar, "I like this song, but I'm interested in the publishing."

"Well, what's there left for me?" Fleeger asked.

"Well, you just make a deal with your girl songwriter," he said.

Fleeger was offended. "Mr. McLemore, I don't deal that way. That's impossible. I want to get the song out. I'll be willing to split the publishing with you."

McLemore didn't hesitate. "No," he said. "I want all the publishing. Or Gene doesn't do this song."

Gene looked down at his feet. The tension in the office was positively suffocating. He was paying McLemore to be an asshole, but did Ed have to do it at the expense of a surefire hit? Once again, it was all about money.

Now Fleeger was outraged. "Mr. McLemore, there's no way," he said through clenched teeth.

"Well, if there's no way that you can give me all the publishing," McLemore said calmly, taking a long puff on his cigar, "then Gene Vincent isn't going to sing this song."

Fleeger looked at Gene. He felt bad for the boy. "Well, sorry we couldn't make a deal, Mr. McLemore," Fleeger said to the boy's manager. He turned and walked out of the office.

Fleeger was waiting in the dark shadows under the staircase when Gene came out of the office.

"Gene, I'm sure sorry about all this," Fleeger said.

"I am, too, man," Gene said. "I just don't know what to do about it. This was a hit!"

Fleeger could tell the boy was sick about the situation. "Well, where are you going from here?" he asked Gene.

"I'm getting ready to drive to California tomorrow. I'm going out to Capitol Records for a recording session."

"Gene, do one thing for me, will you," Fleeger said. "You know 'In My Dreams' real good and you know 'Lotta Lovin' ' real good. Play it for your A&R man when you're out there for your recording session. If he likes it, maybe we can get the thing out anyway."

Gene brightened a bit. "I'll do it," he said, cracking a smile. "I'll play it for Ken Nelson."

They took the long way to California, cutting up to Missouri for an appearance on the "Ozark Jubilee" on May 22, then playing a string of country shows, including the "Top Record Stars of 1957" package, also featuring Sonny James; Johnny Cash, the Sun singer with the spare, simple country sound of hits "Cry, Cry, Cry," "Folsom Prison Blues," and "I Walk the Line"; Capitol's female rockabilly belter Wanda Jackson; "Big D Jamboree" host and singer Johnny Hicks; and Sun's piano-pumping Jerry Lee Lewis.

Gene and Jerry Lee got on famously. Gene loved Jerry's music and even incorporated his "Whole Lotta Shakin' " into the band's repertoire. Jerry Lee liked ol' Gene's downright cockiness. They'd race each other to the next gig, each in his own car, and, once there, would carry on like a couple of potty-mouthed schoolboys, holding contests to see who could make up the filthiest word and passing flagrantly profane song lyrics back and forth. The band got a kick out of ol' Jerry, too; he'd show them little tricks on the piano or just socialize. One day Bubba and Jerry Lee were sitting in the dressing room and Jerry, said to him, "You know the day's coming ol' Jerry Lee ain't gonna be the opener." Bubba guessed he was probably right. Gene and the Caps then played their way to Topeka for a May 25 show with Sonny James and Patsy Cline, the tough country songbird with the voice as big as all outdoors, before gigging on to Kansas City for a stint with Sonny James,

Bobby Lord, and Ferlin Husky on May 30. Then they worked their way west, arriving in Hollywood for the first of two days of recording on June 19.

The studios in the bowels of the Capitol Tower were enormous, large enough to accommodate Nelson Riddle's entire orchestra, and with their vaulted ceilings and polished floors, as swanky as Ol' Blue Eyes himself, the fellows thought. A lot was riding on this session. It was eight months since Gene had last seen the inside of a recording studio, and though "Lula" had exceeded all expectations, his last five singles failed to crack the Top 10. He needed a hit; both he and Ken Nelson were committed to creating one. Since none of the new Caps had any recording experience—including Johnny on the vitally important lead guitar—Nelson invited some insurance to sit in, a young, crewcutted session picker named Buck Owens.

The group began their work with a pair of tunes Nelson had picked up, "I Got It," a mid-tempo rocker by Hollywood singer, songwriter, and guitarist Dick Glasser, and the sweet ballad "Wear My Ring," which had been sent to Nelson by two young writers named Bobby Darin and Don Kirshner. Darin would soon have a solo singing career of his own, waxing the rock 'n' roll novelty hit "Splish Splash" before turning pop with "Dream Lover" and his swinging "Mack the Knife." Kirshner would go on to become a successful publisher and the eventual music supervisor of the prefab TV band the Monkees. Nelson relaxed as soon as he heard what the new fellows could do. Johnny was actually a fine player—Nelson moved Owens to rhythm guitar—and the boys singing backup—particularly Paul, who gave "Wear My Ring" a lovely, high intro—added a new melodicism to the total sound. But it was "Lotta Lovin'," peppered with Paul and Tommy's rhythmic hand-claps and percussive harmonies, that showcased the full textural vitality, the astounding cohesion, of the new Blue Caps. Nelson, too, agreed that this one was a hit. They finished out the day with the raucous "Rollin' Danny."

Buck Owens was impressed with Gene. The singer seemed to be real creative, wanted to hear what the drums were doing and the bass and the guitar lines. But he seemed to respect the musicians' input, too, sometimes just turning to Johnny or Buck and saying, "Play me something." He was obviously very passionate about his music. And insistent, too, sometimes telling Mr. Nelson, "I feel that if we put it like that, it'll work." Some of the time Mr. Nelson would say, "Won't work, Gene," and Buck would think to himself, "Now who's making the hit record here?" And that voice. He absolutely had magic. No doubt about it, Buck thought, Gene was an exceptional young man.

Since Nelson liked to cut in the daytime, the boys were finished by four or five o'clock each day. With nowhere to be but back at the studio the next morning at ten, they goofed off around town. They loitered at the corner of Hollywood and Vine, watching the pretty girls and hot rods go by. They caught a flick at the Pantages, or they swung by the Palomino for a drink or two. Buck enjoyed palling around with the guys. Gene seemed to be a fun-loving fellow, very sociable, and got along well with his band. Buck could tell they were pretty darn close and liked one another a lot.

The next morning they started with "Time Will Bring You Everything," a calypso-flavored ballad written by Gene and Paul, moved on to Gene's romantic "True To You" and Bedwell's "In My Dreams," and finished up with the spirited "Dance to the Bop." Ken Nelson sat inside the control room as Gene sang, doodling with his pencil and his paper, rarely interrupting. Once in a while, if he thought one of the players was out of tune, he'd say, "You there, the guitar player"—he didn't remember names very well—"Are you in tune? Is that in tune?" Johnny or Buck would say, "Which string, Mr. Nelson?" And Nelson would say, "This one—" and sing the note in question. He trusted Gene's instincts and, for the most part, left the sound up to him.

For Johnny, the whole thing was a thrill. It was the first time he'd ever been inside of a recording studio. Hell, it was the first time he'd ever been outside of the state. One day he was just some local yokel from Laurens, South Carolina, and then, all of a sudden, there he was in the Capitol Records tower in glamorous Hollywood, California. It was beyond his wildest dreams. And for the rest of his life, he never forgot the thrill that came over him when he heard the tape playback of "Lotta Lovin' " coming through those big studio speakers. In the session, he hadn't been sure of exactly what he was going to play on that tune, and when Gene said to him, "Kick it off, Johnny," he picked out the first thing that came to his head. But listening to the finished song, he could hardly believe it—it sounded so great. He never heard anything like that his whole life. And to think that it was him, Johnny Meeks, playing that music—well, it was something he'd remember forever.

To be closer to his manager, Gene purchased a roomy, ranch-style house, complete with swimming pool and a maid, on Dyke's Way in north Dallas and soon moved his mama and daddy and two of his sisters in with him. With his divorce from Ruth Ann finalized on June 24, there was nothing to keep him in Virginia. Louise had heard about the dangerous twisters that came rumbling across Texas from time to time, so when she arrived in Dallas she insisted that Gene build a tornado shelter out in the roomy backyard. Gene thought it was downright silly. But he loved his mama and wanted her to be comfortable, so he put one in for her, laughing the whole time. The kids seemed to take to Dallas, too. Gene took them clothes shopping not long after they arrived, since the school year was soon to begin. The girls had a ball—anything they picked out, Gene bought it for them. And when they were all too pooped to shop anymore, Gene simply walked into one store and said, "I'll take two of everything in their size." Louise was none too happy when they got back home and she saw how much Gene spent on the girls. She even had the maid return a good portion of it the next day. But when Gene found out, he marched right back down to that store and bought everything all over again. Gene and his mama went back and forth about it for a while, until the store finally called and asked them never to shop there again.

The local musicians were thrilled to have a real star in their midst, and Gene became quite friendly with many of them. When he was in town, he'd pick up singers Johnny Carroll and Joe Poovey, plus Howard Reed, who played guitar for both of them, and they'd all pile into Gene's red convertible and cruise the Oak Cliff section of Dallas. They'd drive around Adams High School, ogling all the pretty young things. Then Gene would pull over at the Orange Inn and within minutes there'd be two or three hundred kids around the car. He'd be signing autographs just as fast as he could.

Gene wasn't at the house for long, though. By mid-July, he and the band were back out on the road, touring across the States and up into Canada. They were quite a sight, with their mountain of gear piled high atop the station wagon, which was covered—headlight to taillight—with lipstick autographs. Every time they'd pass through a town, all the squealing girls would want to write on the car. They'd scrawl "I love you, Gene" across the windshield or draw hearts and other mushy stuff on the doors. It was a real pain in the ass, because when the fellows would go to get their equipment off the top, they'd end up with greasy, red smears all over their clothes. The band hoped and prayed for rain every day.

They ate—usually burgers—at whatever roadside diner or all-night truck stop they could find. They all looked forward to passing through Nashville, where you could buy a burger for just thirteen cents at the Tick Tock diner. All the fellows would buy ten or fifteen of them, put them in a big sack, and carry them to the car. When they finally got to their hotel, they'd take the shade off the lamp and heat the burgers up over the hot lightbulb. Often when they arrived in the next city—typically at three or four o'clock in the morning—Dickie and Tommy would call or swing by the local radio station before they went to bed just to let everybody know that the band was in town and ready to play. Gene didn't like to go out to the stations much; he preferred to stay back at the hotel and rest up. He was usually exhausted. It took him a good while to wind down after a show, and more often than not, he'd end up staying awake all night. His leg was always hurting, and it slowed him down. He liked to sleep when he could; he needed to get his energy back for the show the following day.

Johnny marveled at Dickie and Bubba's boundless energy. The two just seemed to be naturally hyperactive. In fact, Johnny never saw Dickie take a drink, smoke a cigarette, or ever take any kind of pill. Bubba seemed pretty clean, too. Now Paul, he was another story. He got a little wild. Gene would drink—he always had a pint or something around somewhere—though Johnny never saw him drunk or out of control. Even Thacker would take a drink, though he was mature enough to know when to quit. He was like one of the band, but being older, he knew when to knock it off and take care of business.

The boys were always finding new and inventive ways to amuse and occupy themselves on the road. Once, in Philadelphia, they were playing cards, as they regularly did, and Paul was down. It seemed that every time they played cards, Paul always lost. So he told them, "This is it, I'm gonna end it all! It's finished! Leave me alone!" and stormed out of the room. Next thing they knew, they heard Paul shouting off one of the balconies above them. "Boys! Boys!" he yelled. "Don't bother me! Don't mess with me! I'm ending it all!" As they looked toward their open window they were horrified to see Paul, all wrapped up in a bedsheet, hurtle to the ground. They ran out, fearing the worst, to find the bed linen chock full of rocks. Paul and Bobby, gleeful partners in crime, laughed their heads off.

Another time in Philadelphia Paul passed out on the couch. The boys then moved it over to the window and opened the window up so the snow could blow in. Twenty minutes later, Paul looked like a snowman. "I'm so cold," he murmured through chattering teeth, never fully waking. "How's about giving me a blanket?" When he started turning blue, Johnny raked the snow off of him, then let it pile right back on top of him again. It tickled the others to no end. Then there was the time they nailed Gene's shoe, which was attached to his brace, to the floor while he was sleeping. When he woke up, he tied on his shoe and almost broke his neck. Another time, at a tour stop on the way to Los Angeles, they were cutting cards for money. Paul was drowning his sorrows; he'd just received a "Dear John" letter from his latest girlfriend. When, as usual, Bubba cleaned him out at cards, he broke down. "I lost my woman and I got this letter and I lost my money," he moaned boozily. "What else can happen?" He grabbed the liquor bottle, finished it off, and hurled it over his shoulder. It crashed through the television screen, sending silvery splinters of glass everywhere. Bubba couldn't stop laughing for an hour. And they were always pulling practical jokes on each other, squirting shaving cream over the first fellow to fall asleep, or filling the beds with it on the sly, giving a weary musician just looking for some shut-eye a not-so-pleasant surprise.

It seemed there was always another riot just around the corner, too, like the one in Chicago at the "Howard Miller Show" in front of tens of thousands of kids at the local stadium. Mr. Nelson was there; he came to present Gene his gold record for "Be-Bop-A-Lula." The band played, and as Dickie and Gene's uncle Will, who'd been chauffeuring the band at the time, were out loading the equipment into the station wagon during a drenching downpour, the thousands of kids being held back by a line of policemen linked arm-in-arm broke free. Dickie and Will jumped into the car, locked the doors, and prayed for the best as the sea of kids quickly swept around the car, rocking it back and forth. Bubba, who hadn't quite made it to the station wagon when the melee broke out, jumped up onto the vehicles parked nearby, hopping from car to car in the rain. When it was all over, Bubba's clothes were ripped off—the girls took every damn stitch and he was left holding up half his underwear and hollering for his mama—he lost his school ring, Gene lost his keys, the instruments were gone, and Mr. Nelson's glasses were knocked clean off his face. "Never again," Nelson told the cussing Gene in astonishment. "I'm going back to California. It's safe there."

And there were always a few mishaps during the show. One night Dickie hopped off the stage with his snare drum, marched through the crowd, and straight out the front door. The door slammed shut—and locked—behind him. It took a good ten minutes before he found his way back to the stage. Another night, as he was making his way back from a foray out into the roiling crowd, some zealous fans pulled his pants right off as he was climbing back onstage. He didn't really mind baring his ass for the shrieking mob; all he cared about was getting his wallet full of cash back.

The fellows enjoyed the fringe benefits of being on the road. By the end of every night they had a pocket full of money, they knew they were going to get paid again the next night, and hundreds of cute, little baby dolls, all sweaty and moist, were drooling at their feet. The world was one giant rock 'n' roll playground. Bubba and Johnny were always running around with the girls, and Gene would always have with him someone with whom he'd fallen in love—again. For all of his onstage freneticism, Gene often revealed a softer side, like during his performance at the armory in Mankato, Minnesota, that summer. Watching Bubba and Paul's hand-clapping routine from the back of the stage between song verses, Gene noticed a girl standing at the bottom of the steps to the stage. She was holding a small kitten. He made his way to her, held and stroked the tiny animal, carefully returned the kitten to her, then returned to the stage in time to resume his screaming vocals. But like his tender encounter with the kitten, Gene's concert tour romances were brief; Gene and his new love would travel together for a little while, then it was over about as quick as it started. The fellows' romantic dalliances didn't always come without a price, however. One night in Canada, as Bubba came off the stage, he noticed people pointing angrily in his direction and yelling, "That's him!" He sure hoped there was somebody behind him.

There wasn't. Bubba was promptly arrested for suspicion of statutory rape. He was dumbfounded; all he knew was that he didn't rape any statue. But he knew what rape was—and he knew he was in one big mess. It turned out that a girl he had a little fun with told the authorities that Bubba had promised to take her to the States with the band if she'd go to bed with him. She was just sixteen and apparently wanted to escape her very troubled home life. Bubba was madder than a hornet. He wasn't but seventeen himself and couldn't understand why she hadn't been arrested, too, once he learned the meaning of the word *statutory*. It took a good long while to iron the whole thing out, but in the end, Bubba beat the rap. Later, en route to a fair date in Billings, Montana, he'd never been so happy to cross the border.

It was called "The Big Show." Little Richard; Gene Vincent and the Blue Caps, whose latest single, "Lotta Lovin'," and "Wear My Ring," entered the U.S. Top 100 not even a month after its July 22 release and soon vaulted to the number thirteen position; Eddie Cochran; and Alis Lesley, known as "the female Elvis Presley," who'd performed some with Gene and the Caps in California. It was a groundbreaking tour, the first American rock 'n' roll show ever to come to Australia. And every single date was sold out.

The crowds were phenomenal—much wilder than the fans back home—and the musicians were having a lot of fun. Johnny, who like the others had been thrilled to see Hollywood, was simply astounded to be there. He wasn't even sure where Australia was. Bubba would delight in egging on the passionately screaming Aussie girls, motioning them to come up to the stage, and winking and kissing at them. Gene didn't much care for Bubba's show-stealing antics; he actually fired Bubba a few times, always making a dramatic show of reaching deep into his pocket, pulling out a wad of money and angrily throwing it on the ground at Bubba's feet. But Gene always hired Bubba right back within a couple of hours.

Gene was in high spirits in Australia. He loved it there. One time he phoned up his mama and asked her if she had room in her house to keep his new kangaroo. He was just joking, of course. He thought very highly of the Australians he met. There was something very special about them, a sincere honesty that touched his heart. And naturally he was thrilled to see his good friend Eddie again, and to be working with Little Richard, whose "Long Tall Sally," "Tutti Frutti," and "Rip It Up" had been part of Gene's new show band's repertoire since the very beginning. To their regret, the Caps had not crossed too many paths with Richard in the past, because, for one thing, he was black and they were white, and they just didn't get booked into the same clubs. And even if they did happen to both be in the same city one night, Gene would always end up playing on one side of town and Richard would always play on the other side. Now they finally had the opportunity to work together and get to know each other.

Of course, there was always a little friendly competition going on. Each night Richard would say, "Well, Gene, how long you gonna sing tonight?" Gene'd answer, "Oh, I ain't gonna do too much, I don't feel so good." Gene would go out and do a short show, maybe twenty minutes; Richard would go out and do an hour and a half. The next night it would be the same thing. Richard would say, "What are you going to do tonight?" Gene would answer, "Oh, I don't know." Gene would go out and play a full hour; Richard would go out and do two hours. It cracked the Blue Caps up.

Despite their good-natured professional rivalry, Richard came to consider Gene a good friend, albeit it one who could be a bit annoying at times, especially when he was drinking. Often while they were traveling along the highway from gig to gig, a drunken Gene would try to put Richard out of the car. Richard liked the guy, but thought he was completely insane when under the influence of alcohol.

One night in Sydney, the bands were all playing on a futuristic revolving stage. The place was triple-packed. As he loved to do, Dickie came out from behind his tiny kit banging on his snare drum. The crowd roared. When the husky boy jumped up onto the gleaming baby grand piano, one of its legs collapsed, sending the piano skyward and catapulting Dickie out over the stage and into the band pit. The crowd went wild. Gene loved it.

The fifth date of the two-week tour, October 4, was at an outdoor arena. Forty thousand screaming teens came to witness the rock 'n' roll mayhem. That night Russia launched the world's first artificial satellite, *Sputnik*. The Americans were stunned; the Communists had beaten them into orbit. Little Richard was distraught. He raised his eyes to the sky and it looked as though that big ball of fire had come directly over the stadium, just two or three hundred feet above the vast, pink sea of undulating limbs. He came face to face with the ugly strain of his own damnation. It shook his mind. It was a sign. He got up from the piano. "This is it," he swore, "I am through. I am leaving show business to go back to God." As they were in the bus leaving on the vehicle-carrying ferry to the next city, Richard informed his band of his decision. They didn't believe him. To everyone's utter amazement, Richard started throwing his glittering diamond jewelry into the water behind the boat. Then he started giving away his other showbiz trappings; Gene got some of his flashy suits and Paul received an expensive pair of glittering purple shoes. Richard soon jetted away from half a million dollars' worth of canceled bookings in Australia, remanding himself to religious seclusion upon returning to America.

Dickie was done. Rock 'n' roll was great fun, but he was in love with Bubba's sister Verna and he wanted to go home—for good. Besides, he didn't care for Ed McLemore, Lawrence Thacker, and that bunch all that much. There was just something about them. Every time he turned around, they were trying to slide this guy in and that guy in. Gene was quite upset at the startling news. After all, Dickie was the only Blue Cap left who'd been with him since the start. But he wished his friend well and then hit the road again, heading west for gigs in California and the Pacific Northwest, borrowing drummer Dude Kahn from Sonny James. He also hired seventeen-year-old Max Lipscomb (who later pursued a solo career as Scotty McKay) from Dallas, supplied by McLemore's agency. Max began his life as a Blue Cap as a backing singer, but was soon moved to rhythm guitar, and then piano.

But Gene needed Dickie. There was no two ways about it. He wasn't about to go on *The Ed Sullivan Show*, in front of millions of people, without him. Dickie thought Gene sounded kind of scared when he called to ask him back, but Sullivan was a big deal. As Elvis proved, if you were on *Ed Sullivan*, you had it made. Dickie traveled to New York for the show, which also featured former Capitol-turned-RCA songstress Kate Smith and the ubiquitous Julius LaRosa. Gene was a little uptight—as he always was when there was a high-profile gig to do—but the Caps performed well and he seemed pleased when it was over.

After a lecture on how to behave on live television, they were organized into a sort of pyramid shape, with Bubba, Gene, and Paul in the front row, Johnny, Max, and Bobby behind them, and Dickie high up on a riser behind them. Though Gene, clad in a light, monogrammed smock over matching trousers, was supplied with a hands-free microphone to hang from his neck rather than his customary mike stand, the performance was still exceptionally dynamic. Bubba and Paul, sporting their crisp velvet-collared jackets and black trousers, ebulliently snapped and clapped their way through "Dance to the Bop," dancing loose-legged and knock-kneed on either side of Gene during Johnny's solo and joining the singer on his knees for a chorus. Up top Dickie threw in loud, exuberant shouts, and his hulking body could be seen recoiling from the two-fisted walloping he was giving his snare. On television sets across the country, the band shared a split-screen with a pair of jiving couples, though the added action certainly wasn't necessary. Like their Como appearance, the Sullivan spot would give the single a firm boost; it entered the charts within three weeks of the TV broadcast.

To Gene's relief, Dickie agreed to stay on to record another album's worth of material, fifteen songs in a brisk four days back at the Capitol Tower in Hollywood. Buck Owens was not necessary—or even available, as his own country-western career on Capitol was taking off—this time around, with Max Lipscomb handling both rhythm guitar and keyboard duties. And they were now armed with the very latest in the Fender guitar line, a modified version of the Telecaster called the Stratocaster. Just prior to the sessions, some of the Caps drove up to the Fender factory, just north of Los Angeles, where Mr. Leo Fender himself demonstrated the new instruments for the boys. Actually, Johnny had been playing a Stratocaster when Gene hired him, but Gene preferred Gretsch guitars and had bought a sunburst Gretsch for him. Now, with the endorsement deal Ed McLemore's agency arranged, Johnny and the Caps gleefully picked up three shiny, white Strats, a matching solid-body electric bass, and one of the company's new 50-watt speaker/amplifier cabinets.

They went into the studio on December 6, starting off with the Hank Williams classic "Your Cheatin' Heart," then working out "Baby Blue," a satisfyingly earthy blues song Gene wrote on the road with bassist Bobby that vaguely resembled Presley's "Heartbreak Hotel." "Walkin' Home From School," a sweet ballad co-penned by Sylvester Bradford and Al Lewis, Don Kirshner's partner in the publishing company Vanderbilt Music, came next, followed by "It's No Lie" by Otis Blackwell, who supplied Elvis and Jerry Lee Lewis with several hits.

Nelson always found the Capitol sessions quite challenging. The studios were cavernous and the band made a lot of noise; the sound was extremely difficult to pin down, instantly dispersing like water through his fingertips. It was maddening. He'd assemble the band in a corner to get them closer to their music, but the sound would bounce and spread and distort, and it was difficult to get a good balance in the mix. So he'd have to compromise, boosting guitar or keyboard levels during solos and turning down the rest of the band behind them, which particularly muffled the locomotive feel of the drums and bass. But he was recording in mono, mixing to tape as the group played, and there was little else he could do.

The group returned on December 9, finessing the bluesy rocker "Should I Ever Love Again," the novelty ditty "Flea Brain," "Brand New Beat," written by Joe and Audrey Allison, who also composed for fellow Capitol acts Jerry Reed and Tommy Sands, and a revved-up rendition of the old folk song "Frankie and Johnnie." The next day they tackled Pee Wee King's hillbilly swingin' "You Belong to Me," Jesse Mae Robinson's "Keep It a Secret," and "Yes, I Love You Baby," a rocking collaboration by Gene, Paul, Max, and Bubba on which Johnny picked with a penny to achieve a hard, scratchy guitar sound. They'd come up short of material, so they'd huddled in a corner of the studio, scribbled the song down in fifteen minutes, and knocked it out in no time. Their day was brightened with the heartening news that "Dance to the Bop," issued on November 18, entered the charts at number forty-three. It would peak at twenty-three.

They finished up on December 15 with the pop standard "By the Light of the Silvery Moon," another Bradford and Lewis tune called "Right Now," Rodgers and Hammerstein's "You'll Never Walk Alone" from the musical *Carousel*, and "I Got a Baby," a raucous rocker that Gene felt sure would be a monster hit. The next day, Gene flew to Philadelphia for a performance on the influential television show *American Bandstand*.

The program, an informal teenage dance party originally aired only in Philadelphia, had recently been picked up for national broadcast by ABC. It was now seen across the country every weekday after school, from three to five in the afternoon, and was helmed and hosted by the boyishly handsome, always conservatively necktied Dick Clark. Between song spins, the fresh-faced, poodle-skirted, and sport-jacketed adolescents—*Bandstand* enforced a strict dress code—engaged in record-rating contests and delighted to lip-synched performances from their favorite artists. *Bandstand*'s pervasiveness and immense popularity made it an extraordinarily powerful promotional tool; more often than not, musicians who appeared on the show jetted to the loftiest spots on the record charts.

More important, *Bandstand* began to tame the wild beast. Clark, closer to thirty than thirteen both in age and mindset, was well liked by American parents because he was able to remove that third, objectionable *r* out of "rock, roll, and riot." "Rock 'n' roll provokes participation," he reasoned the following year. "Confine kids to theater seats and of course they break out. Give them a chance to dance and they work off steam and have a good time." And often they were dancing to the music of artists in whose success Clark had a financial interest. Clark was part-owner of the small independent record companies Cameo-Parkway, Swan, and Chancellor, which were label homes to the likes of Chubby Checker, Bobby Rydell, Freddie Cannon, Frankie Avalon, and Fabian, all of whom would wring hit records from their homogenized take on rock 'n' roll—helped in large part by their frequent *Bandstand* appearances. Everything that Gene Vincent, "The Screaming End," was, *American Bandstand* definitely was not.

"Well, backstage at the Georgia Auditorium is the man that got here early," young Canadian Red Robinson announced in his best disc-jockey voice late in 1957, "one of the very few acts that ever gets into Vancouver early, Gene Vincent. How are you?"

Now this kind of promotional appearance, where the deejays come to you—Gene could handle this.

"Just fine, sir," Gene said softly and politely. "How are you?"

"Very good," Red answered. "You're looking quite good. How was the ride up? Kind of a drag?"

"Oh, it was," Gene said. "It was raining the whole way, you know."

"The question we always ask: Did you have any trouble at the border?"

Gene laughed. "Sure did. I stayed there about two hours."

"Two hours!"

"Yes, sir."

"Well, I had a bet on with a fellow in Vancouver that you would be there just that long because most of the groups are. Hey, your record 'Dance to the Bop' and the other side 'I Got It' on Capitol is doing real fine in the Northwest here."

"Well, thank you, sir," Gene said.

"When did you record that?"

"Same time as 'Lotta Lovin',"" Gene said, then laid on the country-boy charm. "Do you mind if I call you Red?" he drawled.

"Yeah, it would be better," Red said, warming up to the informality. "Look, I don't wanna call you sir, either."

"Well, Red," Gene continued, "we cut that the same time we did 'Lotta Lovin'.""

"Hey, where'd you get your big break? Could you tell us the short story of how Gene Vincent and the Blue Caps got out to the West Coast and got success?"

"Well, sir, I sent a record out there first," Gene said. "And Capitol was holding a big contest and they had two hundred and fifty entrants." Well, at least that was what the publicity department had said. "And I was one of the last ones to send mine in. And out of the two hundred and fifty entrants there were two hundred and forty-three that were singing Elvis Presley songs, and the song I sang was named 'Be-Bop-A-Lula.' And that's the one—"

"Of course, the original that made it for you. What did it do, a million and a half, something like that?"

"Uh, well, it's close to two million now."

"That's crazy. 'Be-Bop-A-Lula.' That was great. Every time we play it, we get phone calls, even today. Sometimes on our Saturday session, which is five hours long, we play, well, half an hour of Gene Vincent and when we play that we get a lot of phone calls."

"Sure do appreciate all you've done for me, Red," Gene drawled beguilingly, "and I'd like to thank the public, too."

"What have you got in the way of records coming out, Gene? That's always a good question for a jockey to ask a big star."

"I made a record, and the start note went—" Gene imitated the opening guitar riff to "Baby Blue."

"The start note was like that," he continued. "And then I was gonna put that out this time, but a fella named Elvis Presley come out with 'Jailhouse Rock,' with—" He imitated the opening guitar riff to "Jailhouse Rock," which sounded almost identical.

"So we held that one and put out 'Dance to the Bop,' " Gene explained. "And the next one will be a song called 'Rollin' Danny.' "

"What do you think about rock 'n' roll?" Red asked. "You're one of the rock 'n' roll greats, do you think rock 'n' roll is slipping down? This is a question I have to ask myself all the time because I've been associated with it since it began, too. What do you think?"

"Well, if anybody thinks it's slipping down, you look at *Billboard*'s Top 30—"

"Or *Cashbox*," Red interjected. Gene laughed in approval.

"I say *Cashbox* 'cause we follow that just as close," Red explained. "We have our own, of course, too."

"*Cashbox* is real, real good—" Gene began.

"It's good," Red said. "Nice big picture of you in it, in this week. Did you catch it?"

"Yeah. No," Gene said. "I caught *Billboard*, it was in *Billboard*, too."

"Nice big spread they gave you there," Red said.

"Yeah," Gene laughed.

"Where do you do your recording? Down in the Capitol Tower, in the bottom part there?"

"Yes, Red. Uh-huh. You know, all their studios is underground."

"How 'bout giving us a lineup of the boys in the band."

"Uh, well, sir, Johnny Meeks plays the lead guitar. Bobby Jones plays the bass. Dude Kahn plays the drums. Red, Pred, I say—" Gene smiled at his own twisted tongue. "Paul Peek on the rhythm. We call him Red."

"Gotcha," Robinson laughed.

"And Max Lipscomb on the piano."

"That's terrific. And of course Gene Vincent, you play guitar. What kind of guitar have you got?"

"Gretsch."

"A Gretsch guitar. That's a good commercial for one of our sponsors, I'll slip it in right about now."

Gene laughed.

"No, not actually," Red said. "Um, what I was going to ask you next is, is Gene Vincent your real name? That's a thing I always throw at show business people."

Gene smiled. "My name is Gene Vincent," he fibbed softly.

"Your real name is Gene Vincent," Red affirmed. "Where do you hail from? What part of the United States?"

"Virginia. I was born in Virginia and come from Dallas, Texas."

"The girls ask me," Red said, "the girls of the Northwest asked me to ask you how old you are."

"I'm twenty," he fibbed again.

"Are you married?"

"No," he answered with an embarrassed chuckle.

"You're not married?"

"No," Gene repeated, still chuckling.

"What are the plans?"

"Um, well you know how this road is—"

Robinson laughed.

"You never—" Gene tried to explain. "You never hardly meet anybody long enough to know 'em that well."

He thought of pretty Darlene Hicks, the young lady the promoter Pat Mason introduced him to at his show the month before in Klamath Falls, Oregon. He dedicated "Wear My Ring" to her at the next evening's gig in Eugene. And she showed up at most of his shows during his two weeks in Oregon. They got to know each other pretty well, and he was sad to leave her when he had to drop down to California for a few nights at the Garden of Allah in Niles and the ILWU Union Hall in Broderick and for the sessions at Capitol.

"You never stay in one spot long enough," Red said.

"I swear," Gene agreed.

"Well, I don't know, I always ask this question, too," Red said, "but you've been on the road for how long now, Gene?"

"Since July the tenth."

"Since July tenth," Robinson echoed. "It kind of gets—it wears on you. I mean, not the audience—I don't mean that—but I mean being on the road all the time."

"Yeah, well, the traveling, mostly, is what wears on you, boy," Gene explained. "It gets horrible sometimes."

"Do you ever get home?"

"Yeah, once in a while," Gene laughed, "once in a while. I've been off about eight days since July the tenth."

"Where does your mom and dad live?"

"Well, they live in Dallas, Texas."

"They live in Dallas," Robinson reiterated.

"Yes, sir."

"That's a big state there, man."

"Sure is," Gene agreed.

"Gee, I was talking to Buddy Holly of the Crickets right here where we are standing right now about two weeks ago. No, three weeks ago now. He's from a place called Lubbock. Where's that?"

"That's down south of Dallas."

"South of Dallas, huh?"

"Yes, sir."

"What have you got coming out around Christmas time, Gene?"

"Well, sir, we won't have any Christmas albums coming out. We're kind of afraid to do hymns now 'cause, you know, Elvis done some hymns."

"Yes."

"So we're scared to do that."

"By the way," Red said, "there's an old rumor off the press that you met Elvis Presley in the Knickerbocker Hotel back in 1956 and he said to you—I'll quote the press and then you can tell me if it's true or not—he said to you, 'Gene, my mom heard your record and she thought it was me.' Did he say that?"

"That's true, yes, sir," Gene said with a laugh.

"What happened there anyway?"

"Well, that was my first record, 'Be-Bop-A-Lula.' And Elvis is done one of the greatest guys I ever known. To me, he has. And he's just helped me along."

"Did you meet him somewhere Gene, before you ever—"

"Oh, yes," Gene said.

". . . got into the big show business like you are now?"

"I've known him ever since almost he first come out," Gene said.

"How did you bump into him? On road shows yourself?"

"Well, they brought him into Norfolk," Gene said. "I remember they paid him fifty-three dollars." Well, it sounded good anyway.

"I'd like to see the check for fifty-three bucks for Elvis Presley, it would be a great deal, eh?" Red asked.

Gene laughed. "And then he came in with Hank Snow."

"Uh-huh."

"And that was the first time I ever met him," Gene said. That sounded pretty good, too.

"Well, Hank was a local promoter for Elvis in the beginning, wasn't he?"

"Yeah, I believe so, yeah."

"Well, who would you say gave you the big start? Or did you manage this whole thing yourself?" Red asked.

"Well, Capitol Records managed it for me," Gene said.

"They did?"

"Well, as you know, I spent a lot of time in the hospital with my leg here—"

"Hey, what happened to your leg?" Red asked. "Do you mind if we bring that up, Gene?"

"Well, I broke it riding courier service for the Navy," Gene answered. "I was in the Navy, and I was riding courier and I got run over."

"Is that right? Gee, how long ago was it that you were in the Navy?"

"Uh, it was two years ago since I broke my leg," Gene said. "I stayed in quite a bit after that. I've been out about—uh—just a little after 'Be-Bop-A-Lula.' I've been out about thirteen months."

"Well, what numbers are you gonna do for us tonight?" Red asked.

"Well, the first two numbers will probably be more or less ordinary rock 'n' roll," Gene said. "And then, as you probably know, maybe they don't, but as you probably know, rock 'n' roll was derived from the old blues records, you know."

"Yes," Red said.

"So I'll do a blues song for 'em, then I'll carry through with the show."

"Sure," Red said, then asked, "What would you say to an up-and-coming youngster who was interested in going into the music business? What would you say to do? You know, give them credit where credit's due, and some of them, some of them feel at times it's not worth it and they'll never get there. What would you advise them on the road up, Gene? I mean, you did it yourself."

"Well, sir, I'll tell you," Gene said, his voice taking on a more serious tone. "I've heard people sit around and say, 'Boy I wish I had a break' and this, that, and the other. You can make your own breaks. 'Cause there's no record company today that if you take them a dub record that they won't listen to it. And if it's good, they'll record it."

"Because, after all they're in the business to make money, too," Red added. "Isn't that right?"

"That's true, that's true," Gene agreed. "More so today, you know, as it was back when I first started."

"Yeah, the younger group, namely our group. How old are you again, twenty?"

"Yes, sir," Gene fibbed once more.

"That makes us both the same age," Red said. "How about a shake on that?"

Gene laughed as he shook Red's hand.

"Anyway, the younger people now," Red continued, "they've sort of taken over the record industry."

"That's true," Gene said. "That's true."

"And I think, like you say, rock 'n' roll is here to stay for a while, don't you?" Red asked.

"I think it's here," Gene answered. "I think it's gonna stay here for an awful long time myself."

"But say tomorrow—you know how the hit parade charts change—say tomorrow things all of a sudden changed over to ballads. You can do ballads, can't you?"

"Uh, yes, sir," Gene said. "In my new album that came out, you probably—"

"Yep, we've got it," Red said. "Both of them."

" 'Unchained Melody,' " Gene said. "Well, the guitar work on that is beautiful. If you get the right instruments, you can do ballads."

"Well, who would you consider—now that we're talking about guitars—the greatest guitar player in the pop field today?"

"Well, there's been a lot of arguments," Gene considered, "but between Chet Atkins and Sugarfoot Garland."

"What do you think?" Red asked.

"I tell you," Gene said, "I think—I think Chet Atkins."

"So do I," Red concurred. "I like Chet. I like Sugarfoot, too, but I think Chet Atkins is an artist in the true sense, and his music is so original. It really is."

"That's true," Gene said. "Well, it's funny for a guitar to play his own rhythm. And he does."

"It's real odd," Red said. "People can't believe it when I announce on the air that this is Chet Atkins and the way he's playing this guitar, it is not done elsewhere."

"That's true at that," Gene agreed.

"They can't believe that there's one man doing all this. What have you got for the future?" Red asked as a horn section began warming up somewhere behind them. "What have you got hopes for the future? I mean, say it all caved in tomorrow. Not that it's going to. But say it did cave in tomorrow, what would you do, Gene?"

"Well, Red," Gene drawled, "I'm one of the lucky ones that's got something to fall back on in the industry. I've done pretty well and I've saved my money and I've got some things I can fall back on."

"Some things to fall back on," Robinson echoed again. "Definitely. Have you any occupation that you'd go into if you got out of show business?"

"Radio. I own a quarter-some interest in some radio." Okay, that sounded pretty good, too.

"Where?" Red asked. "Do you? Where do you own half a radio station or a quarter?"

"Well, uh—" Gene fumbled, "I own some in Peoria, Illinois. And I own a half of one—not half a one, but a third of a one in Lubbock."

"Lubbock, Texas," Robinson echoed yet again. "I was talking to Jimmy Bowen—apparently he has some shares, too. You ever met Jimmy Bowen on the road?"

"Jimmy Bowen's manager is the same as ours," Gene said.

"Oh, no, is that right?"

"That's how we all got in together, see."

"That's terrific, because I was talking to him and he said, 'You know, I'm only nineteen and I've got an ulcer already.' "

Gene laughed. Sometimes he felt like that, too.

"I look at him," Red said, "and I can understand the whole thing."

"Yeah," Gene agreed.

"Well, Gene, thanks for taking time out here backstage before the show at the Georgia Auditorium to talk to us about your career and everything else. And is there anything you'd like to say to the thirty-four thousand members of the 'Teen Canteen' show?"

"Yes, sir," Gene drawled lovably. "I'd like to tell 'em what a fine disc jockey I think they've got. You're a real nice guy."

"Thanks," Robinson said, blushing. "Thanks, Gene. I'm turning red. I better go."

The holidays were exceptionally happy for Gene. At his invitation, Darlene and Debbie, her young daughter from her first marriage, joined him and his family at the big house in Dallas. He lavished them all with thoughtful gifts, surprising his baby sisters Tina and Piper—Gene's nickname for her had evolved—with a shiny, new bicycle with a bell on Christmas Eve. He told the girls they'd have to share it, but then Christmas morning he wheeled in another bike from the garage. "I told Santa to leave only one," he said, "but he left two!"

And the new year was off to a great start as well. "Lotta Lovin' " and "Dance to the Bop" were still lingering on the charts. On January 20, Capitol issued "I Got a Baby," backed with "Walkin' Home From School." Gene had high hopes for the single's success, and rightly so now that his most formidable competition was to be virtually sidelined; Elvis Presley had orders to report for induction into the Army in March.

But it wasn't all peachy. After an appearance on the "Big D Jamboree" with locals Johnny Carroll and Joe Poovey, the band hit the road once more. Crisscrossing the Midwest, Paul and Tommy quit, each burned out from playing in every single state in America, coast to coast, plus Canada, and each with hopes of kick-starting his own solo singing career. Paul returned to his hometown of Atlanta and signed with the new NRC label, which Bill Lowery, whose publishing company owned the rights to "Be-Bop-A-Lula," had just launched. Tommy returned to Norfolk, hooked up with Legrand Records owner and producer Frank Guida, who negotiated a deal with Atlantic, then headed to New

York City to begin recording "High School USA," a novelty song with twenty-eight geographically-specific versions, each mentioning the high schools in that region. To expand his newly diminished band—Max Lipscomb had bowed out, too, at the end of the year to return to school—once again Gene looked to Greenville, picking up piano player Clifton Simmons, who'd played with Paul, Johnny, and Bobby in the Circle E Ranch Boys. With his receding hairline and spectacles, Simmons looked more like an accountant than a wild rock 'n' roller, but his distinctive keyboard technique, relying on emphatic one-note successions rather than the grand ivory swipes of, say, Jerry Lee Lewis, set him apart.

They worked their way through the South, stopping in Austin for a show with Sonny James and rockabilly singer Bob Luman, promoting his first record on Imperial, plus a gaggle of local acts, including Joyce Webb, the Debs, the Slades, and Ray Campi, most of whom were recording for the independent Domino label. After the lesser-known artists performed on the outdoor stage on the south side of the Colorado River, Luman went on, followed by James. Then it was Gene's turn. Ray Campi never saw anything quite like it—so much movement, the mike-tossing from side to side, the ferocious screams emitted at all the right places. It was spectacular. Ray was dying to meet this terrifically unusual singer, so he and his buddies went up to the stage after Gene was finished and the musicians were packing up. Gene was very friendly to the young players, and even showed them the brace on his leg. "Sometimes it hurts when I jump around," he told them, "but I wasn't about to let them cut this thing off." And from the way he reeled around the stage, Ray would never have suspected Gene was in any pain.

Then it was on to the "Louisiana Hayride" in Shreveport, where Gene did some country numbers—a little Johnny Cash, a little Hank Williams—and then headed right back out on the highway. It was almost becoming a blur. Racing from state to state, joining up with Ferlin Husky, the Champs, and Bill Justis for a package tour, and playing endless dates with Sonny James, Jerry Lee Lewis, Buddy Knox, and Jimmy Bowen. It seemed the highest points and most dire moments were the only memorable benchmarks. And there were plenty of dire moments. In Nebraska, Gene suddenly demanded that a rhythm guitarist be added to the lineup. Artists Service Bureau quickly dispensed Dallas guitar player and songwriter Grady Owen to Omaha. And in Milwaukee, there was yet another riot when Gene leaned out a little too far over the front of the stage and thousands of screaming kids snatched him and passed him around above their heads. When he was returned to the stage he was shirtless, shoeless, and had scratches all over his face. Then it was out to Philly for another *Bandstand* spot without the Blue Caps, a rendezvous with the band back in Green Bay, and yet another leg of the tour all the way back down to Dallas.

Gene was nervous. Ed McLemore had landed him another movie. This time the band would be featured prominently, and Gene would even get to do some acting. His current lineup, assembled haphazardly as musicians had come and gone—Dickie was the latest to quit, again, replaced by Dude Kahn, again—was not as strong as he'd like for such an important gig. Plus, there was another round of recording scheduled at Capitol at the end of March. He needed a real show band once more, with players he could trust. Like the group on the latest album, *Gene Vincent Rocks and the Blue Caps Roll*, which Capitol issued March 8, culled from the June and December '57 sessions.

Gene talked to Paul, who thought the movie would be good promotion for his new single "Skinny Jenny," coupled with "Rockaround," the very first NRC release. Joe South's "Games People Play" was the second. "Rockaround" was given to Paul by Esquerita in gratitude for Paul's bringing the piano player to Gene's attention, who'd promptly gotten Esquerita a deal with Capitol, too. With Paul back on board, Gene gave Bubba a call in New York. Gene explained his predicament, then asked Bubba to come to Los Angeles and do just the movie, plus one show en route to California.

Bubba was hesitant.

"Gene, I don't know," he said. "I'm getting ready to do a session on my own and everything—"

"Look," Gene interrupted. "I didn't want to have to tell you this. I know how you are about acting. I've got you an acting part. You and me are the only ones who got an acting part in the movie. I know how you like to play character roles. Well, you get to beat an old man to death with a bicycle chain."

Man, Bubba thought, what a role. He just couldn't pass it up.

"All right," he relented. "Just the movie."

That night Bubba went out to 182nd Street in the Bronx and bought himself a bicycle chain. He stayed up all night practicing, elaborately choreographing just how he was going to work that chain in his film debut, how he was going to beat that old man to death in the most dramatic, most sensational way the world had ever seen. The role was going to win him an Oscar, for sure.

Sixteen-year-old Juvey Gomez could hardly believe he was in Hollywood.

It all started back in March, when some balding, middle-aged fellow named Thacker—said he worked for Ed McLemore's Artists Service Bureau in Dallas—asked him if he'd like to join Gene Vincent's Blue Caps. Juvey and his school-aged band the Vikings, along with Johnny Carroll, had opened up for Vincent at the Will Rogers Coliseum in Fort Worth. Apparently Vincent caught the act and really took a shine to Juvey's swinging style, which was rooted in jazz and the Latin rhythms he'd learned as a child folk dancer. He had, in fact, only been playing drums a few months. Juvey's mom didn't know exactly who these Blue Caps were, but she was a shrewd lady with a sharp business mind and negotiated a great deal for him. It would be hard on him, since he was, after all, still in school; he'd have to bring his homework along with him on the road so that he could pass his exams in a few months.

They'd practiced at Gene's house in Dallas for a few days, then headed west to California, stopping on the way for a show at the National Guard Armory in Globe, Arizona. In the middle of "Be-Bop-A-Lula," a massive brawl broke out among the locals in the audience. There seemed to be a couple of Indian tribes going at it, or maybe Mexicans and Indians; the band wasn't quite sure what set it all off. But the authorities came and had to fire tear gas into the joint to get things quieted back down. Juvey had taken cover underneath his drum set. Outside, speaking in Spanish, he asked one of the kids from inside what started the fight. Gene's fans were angry that he had not bothered to show up for his radio interview that afternoon, the kid told him. It was quite an initiation for Juvey.

Juvey thought the world of Gene. He felt kind of out of place with the older guys at first, but Gene took him right under his wing. Little Juvey was particularly clothes-conscious and was quite concerned about how he could, quite literally, fill the departed husky Harrell's shoes—and jackets. How can I wear this Dickie Harrell coat? he agonized. It's purple! It's huge! "I am not going to wear this," he fretted to Gene, making a big stink. "Look, I can't play, the sleeves are down here!" Gene just looked at him and cracked up. He gave Juvey a reassuring hug and said, "Wear whatever you want." So before they left Dallas he started buying his own stage clothes, vests, moccasins, things like that. And though he'd done it a couple of times at first, Juvey refused to stand up to drum. "I'm not Dickie Harrell, man," he said. And when Thacker wanted to give him grief about it, Gene said, "Let him do what he wants to do." Gene didn't seem to like Thacker too much, Juvey noticed, and the feeling seemed mutual. Juvey didn't care much for Thacker's attitude toward him either, and he later got Thacker back by loading his coffee-to-go with syrup of blackdraw, a powerful laxative. Juvey also noticed that Gene was constantly in pain and drank a lot to relieve it.

And so here he was in Hollywood, underneath the Capitol tower, cutting a rock 'n' roll album with Gene Vincent and Eddie Cochran. Since Cochran lived in Los Angeles and was such great friends with all the guys that he was practically a Blue Cap himself, he sat in on four of the five days of recording. On the first day, March 25, after Gene and the band finished with "Dance in the Street," Eddie joined in on "Git It," with its layered doo-wop vocal backing. He said, "You know, a bass voice would fit perfect there." "But we don't have one, Eddie—whatcha gonna do, run out and get a guy off the street to sing?" Bubba cracked. "No, I'll sing it," he said. "Just don't tell Jerry Capehart or Liberty Records." So Eddie crawled into the cave of sound baffles they constructed in the middle of the studio, adding the big, fat bottom to Bubba and Paul's "well-oh-well-oh-wop-wip-wip-wips."

The next day Eddie also helped out with vocals on a new version of Gene's "Teenage Partner," which Eddie arranged for him, "Peace of Mind," and Grady Owen's "Lovely Loretta," after Gene worked through "I Love You," also penned by Grady. On March 27 they knocked out the Holly-ish Bobbie Carrol number "Little Lover," and "Rocky Road Blues," Gene's revved-up version of Bill Monroe's bluegrass number, plus "Somebody Help Me" by Texas songwriter Bob Kelly, and a second version of "Five Feet of Lovin'," which he originally waxed, along with "Teenage Partner," in October 1956. "Five Feet" and "Somebody Help Me" again featured Eddie helping out on backing vocals.

Eddie couldn't make it on March 28—he was waxing a song of his own called "Summertime Blues" at the nearby Goldstar studios—when Gene and the Caps worked out "Look What You Gone and Done to Me," a song bass man Bobby wrote six years earlier; Hank Williams's "Hey Good Lookin' "; a wildly innovative, bluesy read of "Summertime," the Gershwin classic from the musical *Porgy and Bess*, which Gene ornamented with gorgeous vamps and bends; and another Hank Williams classic, "I Can't Help It." But Eddie was back with his buddies again on the 29th, helping out on "The Wayward Wind," a hit for Gogie Grant in 1956, and "Now Is the Hour," another pop classic.

The sessions were loose and relaxed, and the easy feeling transferred nicely to tape. Nelson had Juvey's kick drum miked and a small mike on the snare, but everything else was right off the top of the drum heads with mikes suspended from the ceiling. Gene was placed in the middle of the room, away from all the noise. Nelson brought in a lot of writers' demos on acetates that he played for his singer, saying, "Gene, this is a new artist," or "This is a guy that's written a song. Wanna hear it?" Gene would listen to them and respond with a "wow" or a "nah" or something like that. Sometimes Gene would say, "I want to do this, what do you guys think about it?" And when he'd say, "Okay, let's go with this one, let's do it," they'd all work out their parts after listening to the demo a few times. Juvey, who, like Dickie, liked to play with both sticks and brushes, would always manage to throw some jazz licks in.

Juvey thoroughly enjoyed the week in the studio. They went in at ten each morning, took a break around noon, then went back until five to finish recording. They were working in Sinatra's room, Studio B, and the impressive music stand with the big gold quarter note on it never let them forget it. One day during the lunch break Juvey heard some fantastic jazz music coming from Studio A. God, that sounds familiar, he thought. He peered in. He could hardly believe what he saw. It was pianist George Shearing, guitarist Toots Thielemans, and percussionist Armando Peraza, three giants of the jazz world, and they were rehearsing their new album. Juvey was fascinated by the intricate and involved music and the intensity of the rehearsal. The jazzmen invited him to hang out and listen; for the rest of the week he spent all of his lunch breaks in Studio A.

In his spare time in Los Angeles, Juvey, ever fashion-forward, did a lot of shopping for clothes. Eddie would sometimes join him. They got to know each other pretty well in the studio and Juvey really liked Eddie. "Where'd you get those shoes?" Eddie asked Juvey one day, admiring the kid's crazy moccasins. So Juvey took him shopping.

Eddie's manager, Jerry Capehart, was the associate musical supervisor on *Hot Rod Gang*, the American International picture Gene and the Blue Caps began shooting as soon as the album sessions were complete. Capehart also managed and produced John Ashley, who played the lead in the film, which was written and produced by Lou Rusoff and was being directed by Lew Landers, a veteran of the silent-film era. In the movie, Ashley played a teenage hot-rod car driver dating the lovely Yvonne Lime, in real life a gal pal of Elvis's. Ashley's character attempts a singing career to earn money to build a better car. Eddie's stage and recording band, the Kelly Four, backed Ashley in an early singing sequence. Jody Fair's character, the love interest who ultimately lands Ashley in the end, just happens to know Gene Vincent. Gene helps Ashley out by putting one of the hot-rodder's songs on the flip of his own single and performing at a benefit concert.

In the film, Gene and the Caps—billed Gene Vincent and Group—first appear in a rehearsal for their show that evening. They perform "Dance in the Street," the whip-thin Gene, in a sequined black shirt with the collar flipped up and light trousers, kicking his leg over the mike stand and gazing at the floor or searching the rafters as he sings—as usual, looking everywhere but directly at the audience. He and the band then step to the beat, snap their fingers, and clap their hands while a tape playback of "Dance to the Bop" accompanies a trio of dancing couples in rehearsal. The Blue Caps then back Ashley, who warbles "Annie Laurie" in his most earnest Elvis impersonation. Later, "Lovely Loretta" is heard in the background of one scene, and Gene and the band roll out "Baby Blue" at the benefit show. It is quintessential Caps, Gene in a monogrammed black shirt with a rhinestone-tipped collar looking downward or heavenward, Gene kneeling during Johnny's guitar solo, and Bubba convulsing uncontrollably on the floor under Johnny and then doing his "freeze"—his signature full-body shiver with upstretched arms—as he, Paul, and Gene gather around the single microphone.

Shooting went smoothly, the boys singing and playing along to tapes of their songs. But because Juvey was too young, according to California law, to work more than half a day, he had a stand-in who took his place when he wasn't available. Juvey was irked;

the stand-in ended up with more screen time than he did. The boys enjoyed the filming, but didn't appreciate the strict direction too much. They wanted to show what they could really do, but they were limited by the script and the small performance space. The band could tell that Gene didn't much like performing on film, either, just as he hadn't much cared for making *The Girl Can't Help It*. He loved the screaming kids and missed them when they weren't around.

Gene was given some dialogue, though, which he pulled off quite competently, his easy drawl and slight stutter giving a degree of naturalness to slang-larded lines like "You know, we've got the shaggy mane and the shivering spine and the rubbery legs. Why not dress him up in a cool set of shrubbery and some real classy threads, you know, like one of those Greenwich Village cats who's on cloud nine?" And his bony-faced, snaggle-toothed visage, a sharp contrast to Ashley's matinee-idol good looks, gave Gene a ragged authenticity.

Bubba liked filming all the band scenes, but he was eager to get to his acting debut, too, that scene with the bicycle chain. One shooting day, he was told he wouldn't be needed until the evening so he and Eddie decided to go to the movies. They caught the latest Elvis flick.

"Well, I hope you enjoyed that movie," Gene said smartly to Bubba when he returned.

"Yeah, it was pretty good," Bubba said. "Why?"

"Because you weren't here to do your scene," Gene said.

"What?" Bubba exploded, his movie-star dreams evaporating like summer rain on a sunbaked sidewalk.

"Yeah," Gene said, shaking his head.

Bubba was furious. "I was told that we wasn't going to shoot until this evening!"

Gene tried to suppress his laughter. "And they were gonna shoot that part with you and the bicycle chain," he said, unable to hide his smirk any longer. "Now it's on the cutting-room floor."

Bubba knew he'd been had.

While they were in Hollywood, Gene would hold court in his hotel room every evening after work. It was just too inconvenient for him to go out. He was now an oddity, a spectacle, a celebrity who attracted hordes of gawkers and groupies wherever he went. And his leg was a major impediment. He just couldn't get around like the other fellows in the band. They could effortlessly jump out of the car, run in and get a hamburger somewhere, hop back into the car, and head back to the hotel. He couldn't. He'd have to ease slowly in and out of the car, take stairs one labored step at a time, and have someone hold the elevator until he was fully aboard. The boys—who'd now come to love each other as brothers—could sense it bothered him. Here he was the star, the breadwinner, and he was a prisoner of his hotel room. But there wasn't much they could do about it.

So while the Blue Caps were down in the hotel lobby or next door at the beer joint or making it with some underage chick, Gene was holed up in his room. They'd moved to the Knickerbocker after the staff at their first hotel, fed up with the noise, the vandalism, and the endless stream of girls coming in and out of the rooms, had asked them to leave. Gene would accept visits from pals like Johnny Cash, Bob Luman, and Eddie Cochran, of course. Also Lefty Frizzell, John Ashley, and the young actor and singer Ricky Nelson, the baby-faced star of TV's popular *Ozzie and Harriet* who had a double-sided million-seller in 1956 with "I'm Walkin'" and "A Teenager's Romance." Ricky would go to the hotel every afternoon after taping his show to be near Gene Vincent, whom he seemed to regard with sheer reverence. His brother David would come after him at eleven o'clock each night, parking his motorcycle downstairs and then calling up to Gene's room to ask for Ricky. "Get your butt down here," he'd scold sternly, "because we've got to be up at 5 A.M. and be on the set at six in the morning." Ricky wouldn't be doing anything more than smoking a cigarette, just real quiet, and he and Juvey would sit and talk.

Since they were both teenagers, Ricky and Juvey often hung out together around the hotel while the older fellows carried on. One evening at about seven o'clock, there was a lot of drinking going on in Gene's room. The kids were bored. "Hey, you wanna take a spin?" Ricky asked Juvey. They went down to the parking lot, along with Jimmy Burton, Ricky's guitar player, and jumped into the kid's 1957 Plymouth Fury that he'd souped up. The car was a beauty. They drove around the Sunset strip, goggling at all the pretty girls and showing off their sweet ride. When they stopped at one intersection, a bevy of young lookers recognized Ricky and started screaming and hollering. When the light turned green, Ricky popped the car into first, waved his middle finger in the air, and tore off down the street, wheels squealing all the way. Juvey thought it was a gas.

Juvey returned to Dallas for exams immediately after the shooting was done, and by May, Gene's band was very different. Despite the hopeful release of "Baby Blue" on April 14, with "True to You" on the flip, Johnny called it quits. He'd had his fill. He was tired and he just wanted to go home. Gene was sad to see him go, but Johnny couldn't be talked out of it. Bobby had gone back to Greenville; he was married and decided he needed to be at home with his wife. Paul and Bubba departed, as agreed, after the movie to pick up their solo singing careers. Howard Reed, guitarist for Johnny Carroll and Joe Poovey back in Dallas, was recruited to take Johnny's place, Grady moved over to bass, and Max Lipscomb and Dude Kahn joined up once more. Gene's personal life was a little different, too. On the first of May, after she'd taken him up to Oregon to meet her parents, Darlene married Gene.

After ten months of playing gigs around Greenville, Bill Mack received a call from Gene asking if he would consider playing bass in the Blue Caps again. Gene had decided he wanted a show band once more, and wanted bassist Grady and Max to become his new backing vocalists for the six-week tour of Canada that was booked for him. Bill, who'd kept up with the band's activities through his pal Paul Peek, told Gene he was happy to join. So the Artists

Service Bureau wired him some money and Bill caught the next Delta flight out to Winnipeg. When he got there, he was held by airport security for two hours. He seemed suspicious to them; they just couldn't believe he'd be traveling all the way across Canada with only a small suitcase. After the authorities sorted things out with a phone call to the Sportatorium, Bill was finally released and he made his way to the little town of Regina, where the next show was to take place. It was so early, and Bill was so exhausted, that when he finally got to the gig he crawled up on a table and went to sleep. Later the group came in and woke him up.

The band was very different from the last time Bill was a Blue Cap, plus Dude had dropped out on the way to Canada. Elvis Presley's drummer, D. J. Fontana, was quickly recruited for the forty-date tour. He received a phone call from Thacker, who was in Fargo, North Dakota, asking if he'd play drums with Gene Vincent. "Sure, when do you want me?" D. J. asked. "Next week?" Tomorrow, Thacker told him. So D. J. packed up his drums, hopped on a plane, and—after an hour's rehearsal—was playing behind Gene in Moorehead, Minnesota, the very next evening.

The Mounties, the Royal Canadian Mounted Police, haunted the group at almost every turn. After their engagement in Winnipeg, a couple of the boys brought girls with them to the next gig. They'd just settled into their motel when Cliff, D. J., Bill, and Grady were startled to see the door to their room suddenly burst open and a Mountie come galloping in, accompanied by a thoroughly distraught mother in search of her daughter. The Mountie popped the dumbfounded Cliff in the mouth, knocking the glasses right off his nose and the pipe out of his mouth. D. J. was so surprised he spilled his drink down the front of him. Grady took cover in the shower.

In Canada, Eddie—who was on the show too, along with Bill Justis, the Champs, and several other acts—turned Bill on to "bennies," pep pills. Truck drivers took them a lot, and many of the traveling musicians took them, too. The bands would often have to rush onto the stage straight off a several hundred mile haul from their last gig and they'd need a little pick-me-up to perform at their best. Gene had already been taking the little pills, Benzedrine and Dexedrine, for some time. He loved them. He used to get them from Johnny, who took them from time to time when he was still in the band. Johnny got them from a doctor back in South Carolina who gave him all he wanted. The doctor knew exactly why he needed them, so Johnny dropped by whenever he was home for a visit and left with a prescription for twenty-five or so. He'd take four or five of the pills for himself, then sell the rest to Gene. Johnny figured that as long as he could still sell the pills to Gene, he wasn't hooked.

At one point the Canadian tour took them almost into the Yukon to perform in Dawson Creek, British Columbia. The recently cleared roads, the Alaska and Hart highways, were treacherous, rocky and winding. Gene and the boys were in a two-car caravan and the dust and stones kicked up by the first car would ricochet off the windshield of the second, leaving cracks in the glass. After the show, they had to leave the same treacherous way they came in. Another time, Max was at the wheel of Gene's car when he saw some kids throwing rocks at wild horses near the side of the road. He tried to scare the troublemakers into dropping their rocks by racing up to them, but he lost control of the car and it crashed off a cliff. The fellows were fine, but the car was a complete loss. They had to buy a new one to finish out the dates. Gene was not pleased. When the tour was finally complete and they crossed the border into the States, the boys, their nerves frayed and patience worn thin, gave the Mounties the bird and kissed the blessed American soil.

D. J. did a few more dates with the band in the Midwest before quitting. He'd had fun with the guys. At every diner Gene and the Caps would go into, he'd make a beeline for the jukebox, punch up all the Elvis Presley songs, sit across from Gene, and tease, "Man, listen to those drums!" He thought the world of Gene, and could understand why he drank so much with that leg giving him constant pain. Sometimes that nub would be oozing so much pus

Gene's pants would be soaked. But Gene would still sit on it, lay on it, throw that leg around like there was nothing wrong with it—he was a hell of a showman, D. J. thought. And though the money was good, better than most actually, he was tired of the touring life and wanted to go home. The band worked their way down to Dallas, playing the "Big D" a few times and the Yellow Belly Dragstrip, a local club. The band members who didn't have homes in Dallas stayed at Gene's house or at the nearby Alamo Plaza motel, where they'd crawl up to the roof and jump into the swimming pool at night for kicks. One evening, Bill was over at Gene's house. The two had a few drinks and got to talking about cars. Thinking of Johnny Meeks's Cadillac,s Bill mentioned to Gene that he thought a Cadillac was a much better car than a Lincoln. Gene actually owned a Cadillac, but had defiantly purchased a Lincoln as well when he realized that every other star in the world seemed to drive a Cadillac. But a certain mood moved over the singer at Bill's casual remark, a fearsome rage, cold and red. He pulled out his gun, put it to Bill's head, and ordered him out of his house. Badly shaken, Bill walked the three miles back to the Alamo Plaza.

It only took a few weeks before Johnny Meeks was on the phone to Gene, begging to come back. Gene was all for it, though the Artists Service Bureau hemmed and hawed about it; they had plenty of talent right there in Dallas. But Gene wanted Johnny, no one else. And Gene won. So Johnny was quickly flown out to Seattle, taking his slot back from Howard. Soon Juvey Gomez, who'd returned briefly for some West Coast dates, departed once more, taking a gig with the more sedate Buddy Knox and the Rhythm Orchids. The teenager had tired of the band's shenanigans, though not before he and Cliff got back at the fellows for turning all their hotel room furniture upside down in Arizona by coating the instigators' room with raw eggs and white shoe polish. Plus, he could see the writing on the wall; radio stations didn't want anything to do with Gene anymore because he never made interviews. He was really kind of messing himself up, Juvey thought. Drummer Butch White was sent immediately from Dallas to take the kid's place. While the band was in Washington, they met Darlene's mother and went to see their pal Ricky Nelson, who was also playing in Seattle. They traveled the entire West Coast, then returned to Dallas, dropping off Darlene and her daughter, Debbie, who had accompanied Gene from Washington.

"The hottest of hot-rodders!" the movie trailer screamed. "The craziest of kittens, high school hellcats! Two terrific teenage movies and the rockingest, rollingest of cats—starring popular John Ashley, cute little Jody Fair, satellite-searing Gene Vincent, and that alarmingly charming Yvonne Lime, a kitten who has all the cats howlin'! Guys who've got what it takes, chicks who'll take all they've got—together in two movie theater treats, *Hot Rod Gang* and *High School Hellcats*!"

*Hot Rod Gang* was released on July 2 as a double feature, part of a calculated effort by American International and other film studios to cash in on the huge new youth audience for juvenile delinquency films. They were treading in turbulent waters, though; hand-wringing concern over juvenile delinquency had been mounting since the start of the decade. By 1955, when crime-fighting Senator Estes Kefauver assumed zealous chairmanship of the Senate Subcommittee to Investigate Juvenile Delinquency, the nation's parents, preachers, teachers, lawmakers, and law enforcers had reached the point of near obsession with what they deemed the toxic effects of film, radio, comic books, and television on American youth. The films included the 1953 motorcycle masterpiece *The Wild One*, featuring Marlon Brando as the brooding, leather-jacketed leader of a violent youth biker gang; *The Blackboard Jungle*, (1955), with its daring depictions of cultural and generational clashes; and *Rebel Without a Cause*, starring James Dean— one of Gene's favorite actors, who was tragically killed in a car accident just four days before the movie's release in 1955—as a sullen, unruly, and alienated teenager. They were all publicly derided as damnable factors in the startling new appearance, tastes, and behavior of the nation's youth, all components of the terri-fying new "seduction of the innocent."

For Gene, it was just good timing. He hoped the movie would help boost sales of his latest single, "Rocky Road Blues," to be issued on July 7 with "Yes, I Love You Baby" on its back.

All this partying was making Johnny thirsty. So he left the girls and the booze at the motel, jumped in the band's green Lincoln, and drove down the road a short way to the service station. A couple of ice-cold Coca-Colas on this late August night would do him just right. He pulled up next to the soda machine and fished out some change. He had enough silver to buy one soda, but he needed to change a bill to buy another. He looked around for some help. The place was all lit up like it was open, but there was no one in sight. "Hello?" he yelled. "Anybody here?" No answer. He honked the horn a few times, thinking maybe the attendant was out back. Still nobody. Johnny gave up, took his one soda, and drove back to the room.

They left the motel in Rochester, Minnesota, just after noon the next day for a gig in Marshfield, Wisconsin, then they headed for their next show in Mitchell, South Dakota. The car was in bad shape and seemed ready to quit on them at any moment, so they stopped in Minneapolis to get another one. They were going to leave their car and trailer at a parking ramp in Minneapolis, rent another car and trailer to get to the gig, then return for their ve-hicle later. Exhausted from their drive, the band dozed in the car, one guy leaned up against the other, while Thacker went to make the arrangements.

They were awakened by a loud rapping on the window. To the boys' astonishment, there was a swarm of policemen, gleaming guns drawn, surrounding the car. The cops dragged the stunned musicians out of the car, threw them against a wall, and ordered them to get their hands up. One of the policemen walked around to the rear of the car. "We got 'em now! They've got a machine gun!" he crowed, pulling Bill's bass guitar satchel out of the trailer. He flushed with embarrassment when he looked inside the bag.

The cops cuffed the boys, piled them into police cars, and took them down to headquarters for questioning. It gradually became clear during the interrogation that the cops thought the Caps had pulled off a murder. Specifically, the murder of a sixty-eight-year-old attendant at the service station back in Rochester, Minnesota. Apparently someone had seen Johnny leaving the station just before the body was found by a motorist stopping for gas. Gene couldn't believe it—he was both appalled and impressed by his band's new rap. "I was the first guy to ever be arrested for murder in rock 'n' roll who was white," he'd boast years later. After about an hour of questioning, though, the band was released. They hit the road for South Dakota once more.

After playing the Corn Palace in Mitchell, the band headed for Ypsilanti, Michigan. They had one night to make the eight hundred miles, and they were pushing the pedal to the metal the whole way. Rolling through Madison, Wisconsin, the fan went through the radiator, stranding the band once more. Gene, Johnny, and Butch chartered a plane to Ypsilanti, while Cliff and Bill stayed behind to get the car fixed. After they all met back in Ypsilanti, it was on to Monroe, then Jackson, Ann Arbor, and Sault Sainte Marie. Then they worked their way back to the green Lincoln and Minneapolis, where they played the Prom Ballroom with Dale Hawkins, whose "Suzie Q" had cracked the Top 30 in 1957, and Connie Francis, crooner of the 1957 Top 10 hit "Who's Sorry Now." To add to their transportation and legal troubles, Butch White decided to leave. Meeks quickly phoned Clyde Pennington, an old friend of his from South Carolina who'd already sat in on bass a few times in 1957, before Bobby was hired. He flew in immediately to take over on drums. The band picked him up and brought him to the Hastings Hotel, where they were staying for a few days.

Taking a break from their recent tribulations, one night Gene and Thacker went out on the town together, leaving the band back at the hotel. A teenage girl soon arrived, asking to see Gene. The fellows told her that Gene was out for the night. She insisted on waiting for the singer, so the Caps told her to wait in his room. They checked on her a little while later and were surprised to find her completely passed out. She had gotten into Gene's liquor. Always up for a practical joke, the fellows hatched the idea to trash Gene's room and make it look as if the girl had done it. The boys went to bed laughing, tickled with the knowledge that Gene was in for one hell of a surprise when he got back.

The next morning they were all rudely awakened by an enraged Gene. "Get that girl out of my room," he seethed, in no mood for a statutory rape arrest, then stormed down to the hotel lobby. After the underage girl was seen home, Gene assembled the band. He demanded to know what the girl had been doing in his room and how she got there. Gene didn't take their fumbling explanations well. He wanted to know exactly who was responsible for the prank. One by one he asked each band member if he liked his job and if he wanted to keep it. One by one each young man gave the same answer. Yes, he liked his job. Yes, he wanted to keep his job. Except for Bill. Bill said no, he wanted to quit. "I'm leaving now," he told Gene, "And please give me my pay." Incensed, Gene demanded he leave at that very moment. They began to argue, then the argument turned physical. Gene was knocked to the ground. Furious, he phoned the local police. One of the officers who arrived happened to be a musician, too, and suggested that Gene pay Bill for his services. Gene relented and gave Bill his money. Bill hopped a train to Chicago and joined up with Dale Hawkins. Grady Owen was quickly dispatched from Dallas to take his place.

They toured their way back to Los Angeles, visiting the Capitol tower on October 13 for the first day of a full week of recording. Though "Git It," backed with "Little Lover," was released on September 15, it had yet to crack the charts and Gene was hungry for another hit. He and Nelson fiddled with the formula once more, opting for a more rhythm and blues–inflected sound this time out. Jackie Kelso, from Johnny Otis's band, also on Capitol, was brought in to blow tenor sax, and Plas Johnson, who later gained fame as the embouchure behind the *Pink Panther* theme, added baritone sax.

They began with "Lonesome Boy," another Bedwell tune they'd demoed earlier that year at the Sellers Studios in Dallas. Gene and the band then moved on to Cliff's "You Are the One For Me" and "Maybe," written by Paulette Williams and Johnny Carroll. They returned the next day and knocked out a couple of Johnny Burnette numbers, "I Got to Get to You Yet" and the "Dream Lover"–esque "My Heart," then closed out the day with Cliff's tender, harmony-laden ballad "The Night Is So Lonely," which they also demoed in Dallas. They launched the following day with the Delmore Brothers' "Beautiful Brown Eyes," then covered Little Richard's 1956 hit "Rip It Up," Chuck Berry's '55 smash "Maybellene," and Huey Piano Smith's "High Blood Pressure."

First on the agenda on October 16 was Grady's "In Love Again," another song demoed in Dallas, then the foot-stompin' "Say Mama," a rocker written by Johnny Meeks and Earl Baughman, leader of the Circle E Ranch Boys back in Greenville, whose title had been changed from its original "Hey Mama." They worked out Gene's "Be-Bop Boogie Boy" next, and finished out the day with the Little Richard and Lloyd Price collaboration "I Can't Believe You Want to Leave," which Richard had waxed in 1956. The next day they tackled "Who's Pushing Your Swing," Cliff's "Anna Annabelle," and Joe South's "Gone Gone Gone." South's "I Might Have Known" started up the next session on October 20, followed by a new version of Gene's favorite "Important Words," the bluesy classic "My Baby Don't 'Low," and the pop gem "Over the Rainbow." For Gene's ethereal-sounding treatment, he had Cliff move to the celesta, the dainty, piano-like instrument heard in "The Dance of the Sugar-Plum Fairy" from Tchaikovsky's *Nutcracker*. Grady and Johnny swapped instruments for the tune because Grady was the only one who knew the guitar chords. They finished out the week with yet another Little Richard song, "Ready Teddy," and Gene's own "Vincent Blues," as well as an appearance on *Town Hall Party*, Los Angeles TV's answer to the *Grand Ole Opry*.

Capitol soon released Gene's fourth album, *A Gene Vincent Record Date*, comprised completely of songs from the spring sessions with Eddie, and another single, "Say Mama," with "Be-Bop Boogie Boy." Again, what seemed to all involved to be a surefire hit met with little success. Gene was frustrated. With no hits—and decreasing pay—to show for their tireless efforts, the band quickly disintegrated, each heading in his own direction. Johnny took it especially hard. He could've cared less about the money. He was in it for the glory and the good times and the being in a different city every night. He loved the thrill of it. He was a nineteen-year-old from South Carolina who was on an extended adventure. He would've done it for free.

Jerry Lee Merritt was in Centralia, Washington, halfway between Portland and Seattle, rehearsing with Clayton Watson and the Silhouettes, one of the earliest rockabilly bands of the Pacific Northwest. They'd been working with Bobby Darin on the road and the band was getting ready to head back out in a day or two. Gene Vincent walked in. Jerry almost didn't recognize him. Gene was dressed like Fidel Castro—he wore a goatee and was sporting an army cap and green fatigues. But Jerry knew exactly who the whiskered stranger was. He'd been a Vincent fan since "Be-Bop-A-Lula," and he was thrilled to be in the same room as his idol. Gene seemed friendly with some of the guys in the band and he hung around the rehearsal hall for a while, listening to Jerry pick. During a break he asked Jerry if he'd step outside and have a whiskey with him. They sat in Gene's tiny MG sports car and drained a couple of shots. Gene told Jerry about a tour he had lined up soon, and about how tired he was of playing with unpredictable, unreliable pickup bands everywhere he went. Jerry could sympathize and the two of them seemed to get along well.

"Hey, do you want to work with me when this here tour's over?" Gene asked after a while.

Jerry couldn't believe his ears. "Yeah!" he said, silently thanking his lucky stars for such an amazing opportunity.

Gene and Jerry played together all through that winter, gigging across the Northwest, hoping to breathe life into "Say Mama" and Gene's latest single, "Over the Rainbow," released in January with "Who's Been Pushing Your Swing" on its flip. Promoter Pat Mason found the dates for them; he'd turned out to be a real lifesaver. Gene had recently lost his big Dallas house to the IRS— Ed McLemore's Artists Service Bureau had not paid Gene's taxes, as he assumed they would, and they'd parted ways—and he and Darlene were, for all intents and purposes, homeless. They'd spent Christmas in Vancouver, Washington, with Lavonne and Milo Lund, good friends of Darlene's who took her in as a housekeeper after her first marriage. Not long after, they rented a house in Seaside, Oregon, where Pat Mason lived, to be closer to the only man who was finding Gene work.

But the big beat was waning. Gene could feel it slipping away every day, steadily losing steam like one of those cymbal-clapping wind-up monkeys drunken Jimmy Dean amused himself with at the start of *Rebel Without a Cause*. Elvis was serving his country in Germany. Richard was making things right with God. Chuck Berry was in jail for transporting an underage chick across state lines. Jerry Lee was taken down in disgrace, the American public not able to stomach his scandalous marriage to his thirteen-year-old cousin.

And then there was the plane crash. February 3, 1959. Buddy Holly, the Big Bopper, and Ritchie Valens—all gone in an instant. Gene was heartsick. He and the Blue Caps had performed with J. P. "The Big Bopper" Richardson, the disc jockey turned singer who had a 1958 hit with "Chantilly Lace," at a package show in Louisiana. And he thought the world of Buddy Holly and his fine songs, hits like "That'll Be the Day" and "Peggy Sue." Gene had met Buddy in Nashville in 1956 right after "Be-Bop-A-Lula" came out. He'd walked into the lobby of his hotel and there was this skinny fellow with glasses who looked kind of familiar sitting there. The fellow came up to him and said, "Excuse me, can I get your autograph?" Gene said, "Haven't I seen you someplace before?" And the fellow said, "Yeah, my name's Buddy Holly." He had a single out then called "Blue Days, Black Nights." Gene thought it was a fabulous record.

Rock 'n' roll was changing now. It was becoming soft, mushy, sickeningly sweet, like a rotted peach too long on the branch. The major record labels, bowing to increasing criticism of rock 'n' roll and its effects on youngsters, were throwing just about anything at the wall to see what would stick. In 1957 Capitol jumped on the calypso bandwagon, issuing Nat Cole's "When Rock 'n' Roll Comes to Trinidad" to compete with the hits of RCA's Harry Belafonte and Columbia's Tarriers and Terry Gilkyson and the Easy Riders. But teens turned up their noses at the soft island sound. So the majors tried again with folk, Capitol pushing the Kingston Trio. But rock 'n' roll's slyest enemy was what purported itself to be the music's staunchest proponent, *American Bandstand*. With the biggest names in rock 'n' roll out of the picture, the void was filled by the sanitized likes of Bobby Rydell, Frankie Avalon, and Fabian, recording for Dick Clark's Philadelphia-based record labels, as well as other crooning types like ABC-Paramount's Paul Anka and Atlantic's Bobby Darin, all of whom appeared regularly on Clark's show. These clean-cut and wholesome singers—enthusiastically boosted by the immensely pervasive and influential *Bandstand*—proved eminently palatable to the American public, and their flaccid, sugary pop tunes began to swamp the pop charts. Dick Clark, pulling down over half a million dollars a year through his *Bandstand* salary, ownership in music corporations, and gratuitous "composer's" royalties, did not appear bothered by the big beat's decline in the least. "I don't make culture," he would say later. "I sell it."

Gene and Jerry Merritt were on their way to Tokyo.

Pat Mason, along with Capitol and the company's Japanese counterpart Toshiba, had set it up. He'd called Jerry while Gene was up in Alaska on an extended gig and asked him if he'd like to go overseas with Gene. It took just two weeks for Jerry to get a passport and hightail it up to Anchorage, where Gene and Darlene were living with Pat's partner Whitey Pullen, also a rockabilly singer, and his wife. Darlene had, in fact, just given birth on April 27 to Gene's first child in Anchorage, a beautiful baby girl they named Melody Jean.

Gene and Jerry had a ball, drinking whiskey the entire way. They were just two Southern boys—Jerry originally hailed from Arkansas—with barely any education past junior high, living it up with the sophisticates in the first-class cabin on this fine June day. There was some kind of politician, they noticed—a senator or an ambassador or something—with his wife and entourage also on board. An amazing sight greeted them when the jet finally landed in Japan. Ten thousand people were lined up at the airport, cheering and waving flags. Gene and Jerry assumed that all the commotion was for the visiting dignitary. And so did the visiting dignitary. They started to get a little concerned, though, when they heard "Will Gene Vincent and Jerry Merritt please remain on the plane" crackling over the loudspeaker. Gene looked over at Jerry. "What did you do now, Jerry?" he heckled. "I didn't do nothing!" Jerry shot back. "Whatever it is, it's your fault!" They had no idea why they were being held on the plane. Finally they were allowed to leave. As they made their way off the aircraft, it dawned on them. The cheers, the flags, the thousands of screaming people— it was all for Gene.

Though that same month in America Capitol had released another single, "Right Now," coupled with "The Night Is So Lonely," and Gene's fifth LP, *Sounds Like Gene Vincent*, featuring material from the October sessions, Gene was a smash in Japan largely on the strength of "Be-Bop-A-Lula" and "Bluejean Bop," both of which had been released by Toshiba as 78-rpm records in 1956, then again as seven-inch singles in 1957. As the first American rock 'n' roll act to tour Japan, Gene and Jerry enjoyed deluxe treatment the whole way. Each was driven in his own car, flanked by geisha girls on either side, in a parade through downtown Tokyo attended by movie stars, models, and assorted other glitterati. And they were put up at the swanky Nakatsu Hotel, in the same luxurious suite where President Eisenhower once stayed, protected from zealous fans by a corps of police guards stationed in the hotel's hallways.

Their first gig was five dates at a huge theater in Tokyo. The venue sported eight balconies and could accommodate crowds of up to eight thousand. There were over a hundred talents on the package show, headlined by Gene and Jerry, who would hit the stage last to play a single song, "Be-Bop-A-Lula," accompanied by a twenty-five-piece orchestra. They were given roomy adjoining dressing rooms, where they spent most of their time between performances chatting with reporters and show folk. For five days they played one morning and two afternoon shows, drawing over twenty thousand shrieking teenagers a day. At the end of the day they were driven back to the hotel, just a block and half away, in separate limousines in hopes of detouring the thousands of eager kids who wanted to see, speak to, or touch their rock 'n' roll idol. They played other cities as well, including Yokohama and Osaka, sometimes performing three shows in a night, shuttling from stage to stage in an armored car with a police escort.

Gene became increasingly restless as the days went by, trapped in his hotel room like a fish in a bowl when he wasn't onstage. He called Darlene often, checking in on his newborn daughter. The police guards in the hallways and the sea of fans on the streets outside the hotel made it terribly inconvenient to even go out. So he and Jerry would amuse themselves, often working out material for Gene's next album. One afternoon Jerry played Gene a song he wrote in just five minutes in a bar in Yakima, Washington. It was called "She She Little Sheila." Whitey Pullen had heard it back home, thought it had hit potential, and casually said to Jerry, "Boy, I'd like to have a piece of that song." And Jerry had given him a co-writing credit, because that's just the kind of fellow he was. Gene really liked the song, too, and wanted to record it.

"That's it, I'm going home," Gene told Jerry one day. He wanted Jerry to go, too. "We can't, we've got this contract," Jerry reasoned. "They'll sue us!" But Gene departed anyway, disappearing on the next flight out. Jerry was left with no other choice. He finished out the tour himself, impersonating Gene. Amazingly, no one seemed the wiser.

Jerry had other reasons to stay in Japan. He was getting offers to appear in movies, and he wanted to see where they would take him. But he was soon receiving urgent telegrams from Capitol, and Gene was demanding that he return to Los Angeles so they could work on Gene's next album. Gene picked Jerry up at the airport in Los Angeles in a brand new convertible with a dent in it. "See what you made me do!" was Gene's welcome. He never mentioned a word about Japan. And Jerry never brought it up.

Gene and Jerry entered the Capitol studios on August 3, joined by musicians Ken Nelson supplied—bassist Red Callender, pianist Jimmy Johnson, drummer Sandy Nelson, Jackie Kelso on tenor sax, and the vocal trio the Eligibles on backing harmonies. Jerry came armed with his pal Whitey Pullen's Fender Stratocaster and they started with Gene's mid-tempo rocker "Pretty Pearly," then moved on to the pop chestnut "Accentuate the Positive," penned by Capitol founder Johnny Mercer, in a slow and swinging Jackie Kelso arrangement. Gene, who was on most of the record companies' mailing lists, had recently received a recording of the song by an obscure blues singer. He thought the record was excellent— he was sure the sole reason it wasn't a bestseller was because it was put out by a small independent label—and wanted to give the song a try. Next up was Jerry's "She She Little Sheila" and "Darlene," a low-down, honking-sax blues Gene wrote with some not-so-flattering lyrics. They reconvened the next day to get the novelty ditty "Why Don't You People Learn to Drive" down, as well as "Crazy Times," a Paul Hampton and Burt Bacharach tune, and the bluegrass favorite "Greenback Dollar." On August 5, they knocked out "Big Fat Saturday Night," the Fats Domino–esque "Wildcat," "Hot Dollar," and the romantic rocker "Right Here on Earth," and finished out the sessions on August 6 with Fred Rose's country classic "Blue Eyes Crying in the Rain," Whitey Pullen's "Everybody's Got a Date But Me" and "Mitchiko From Tokyo," a gentle rocker featuring Eastern motifs for guitar and sax and an intro sung in Japanese by Gene. The unique tune was co-penned by Bobbie Carrol, who also wrote "I Flipped," "Well I Knocked Bim Bam," and "Little Lover." The sessions had a different feel this time around. The studio musicians were all talented and professional, but the ragged exuberance, the sheer adventurousness, of Gene's recordings with the Blue Caps just wasn't there.

Jerry stayed with Gene, Darlene, and the kids at their new place in West Covina, a Los Angeles suburb, during the recording, and by the end of the sessions Jerry felt as if they were brothers. They'd gotten to know each other extremely well over the last year. Jerry loved Gene—he was so charming and charismatic, though in a shy and bashful kind of way, often calling fellows years younger than he was "sir." Gene seemed to be a very good father, too, Jerry noted while he lived with the family, treating Darlene's daughter Debbie as one of his own, always playing games and having fun with the kids. He was a real television buff—it was often difficult to drag him away from the tube—and he'd stay up all night watching Westerns and monster movies. Jerry thought Gene something of a genius as well, with his quick, creative mind always going at ninety miles an hour and his passion for weighty topics like politics and world governments frequently informing his conversations. He did have a hot temper, though, and carried a pistol, Jerry observed, though he was never violent. And he was extremely generous. When they were on the street and walked by a bum or a beggar he'd always go back and give 'em some money. He just couldn't pass anyone up—because that's the kind of fellow he was.

He was the best-hearted man Jerry had ever met. Sadly, his leg was always paining him; Jerry'd watch him wash down countless aspirins with beer or whiskey.

Jerry also saw that Gene could be one of the good ol' boys too, especially when they spent the day at Johnny Cash's big house over in Laurel Canyon. Gene and Johnny were good friends—they did a quick tour through Australia together a few months before the Japanese jaunt, along with Bobby Day, whose "Rockin' Robin" was a 1958 smash hit—and Jerry would often tag along on the visits. Johnny wasn't much of a talker, always watching TV, and as soon as Gene walked in, without even looking up, Johnny'd say, "They're in the usual place, Gene." Gene would go straight to Johnny's closet and pull out his western gun belt with its holster and pistol, strap it on, stand in front of a long mirror in Johnny's house, and practice quick draws for hours and hours. It was the dumbest thing Jerry'd ever seen.

Gene continued to travel around California, Oregon, and Washington, playing with Jerry and pickup bands here and there, or with Clayton Watson and the Silhouettes. On November 7, he and Jerry performed on the *Town Hall Party* television program in Los Angeles, and he often performed at the Garden of Allah in Niles, just outside San Francisco. He liked the place, since they booked both country-western and rock 'n' roll, bringing in top names like Jim Reeves, Rose Maddox, and Bob Wills on Saturday nights and Johnny Cash, Jerry Lee Lewis, and the Everly Brothers on Friday evenings. Gene would play both nights, altering his set accordingly. He got sixty percent of the door receipts, and with tickets priced at a buck and a half—the hall sometimes had three thousand people a night—the money was pretty good. Gene also liked the club's owners, Chuck Wayne and his wife Johnnie. Chuck was a disc jockey on country station KBSM in San Mateo and also had his own band, which he called Chuck Wayne and the Honeydrops on Friday night and the Chuck Wayne Country Band on Saturday. Chuck played guitar, and Johnnie would sing. Gene and Darlene grew very fond of the Waynes and stayed, along with Debbie and baby Melody, at their house on the weekends that Gene was playing the club. Gene even told them that he wrote "She She Little Sheila" for their little daughter of the same name.

Eighteen-year-old Ronnie "The Blond Bomber" Dawson felt bad for Gene. They were playing the big municipal auditoriums in places like Tulsa and Bartlesville, Oklahoma, St. Jo, Missouri, and other midwestern towns with a ten-piece all-black backup combo. Ronnie couldn't understand why a band like that was backing Gene. They didn't even have a guitar player, for pete's sake, Ronnie thought. So Ronnie ended up playing lead behind Gene for most of his stuff. He'd go and do his own show, including, of course, his single "Action Packed," which had actually been part of his prize for winning the "Big D Jamboree" talent contest ten times in a row the year before. He'd gotten a hundred dollars, a regular slot on the show, plus a recording contract. Then Gene would call him back out to play with him while he headlined the show. Of course, Ronnie wasn't complaining; he loved to perform and knew all of Gene's stuff. He'd toured with the Blue Caps one time—though their motel-trashing and wild drinking and carrying on kind of scared him—and he even demoed Johnny Meeks's "Hey Mama," which became "Say Mama," for Gene at the Sellers Studio back in Dallas in '58. But this tour was kind of pitiful. There was just no one there. Ten, fifteen people, maybe, at each gig. Gene didn't even really seem to care, though. All he could talk about was Europe. He kept saying over and over that that was the place where it was all going to be happening.

What was happening to the American music industry at the time was chilling. As radio emerged as a vital component of the making of a hit, record companies, greasing the wheels of commerce, began discreetly paying disc jockeys on the side. It started out as the simple giving of gifts—hi-fi stereo sets, free records that could be converted to cash—but by the late 1950s, an organized system of direct cash payments was put in place. The practice, dubbed payola, was first brought to the public's attention on November 19, 1959, when, in the course of a congressional investigation into the rigging of daytime quiz shows, the New York District Attorney's office served subpoenas on several record companies, ordering them to hand over their books for investigation. Heads within the popular music industry immediately began to roll.

Among the first to go was Alan Freed, rock 'n' roll's greatest radio friend and the most visible disc jockey in the business. Over the years Freed had amassed a small fortune from his generous thirty thousand dollars annual salary from New York's WABC radio, concert promotions, and record company kickbacks. Freed had moved to WABC when WINS refused to defend him against charges of inciting to riot after several people were seriously injured at a Jerry Lee Lewis concert in Boston. Not long after, Freed reached the apex of his own money-making with a Christmas show at the Broadway Paramount, grossing over three hundred thousand dollars from a twelve-day run. In November, when Freed refused "on principle" to sign a statement saying he had never received money or gifts to promote records, he was promptly dismissed from WABC as well as from WNEW, which aired his rock 'n' roll dance show on local television. Freed would die within a few years, steeped in alcohol and ruined by payola and income tax indictments.

Hearing dates were soon set for the House Legislative Oversight subcommittee of the Commerce Committee to investigate the misuse of free records, payola to disc jockeys and other radio station personnel, payola to record company A&R men, chart rigging through dealer payola, kickbacks at every level of the record industry, and conflict of interest between music and broadcast interests that used radio to promote their own product. Interestingly, though clean-cut Dick Clark enjoyed ownership in some thirty-three companies connected with the music business, including three record companies, a management firm, and a record-pressing plant, and at the time of the hearings held copyright to one hundred sixty-two songs, many of which he helped popularize on *Bandstand*, ABC stuck by the show's host, and the investigating committee simply ordered Clark to divest most of his music publishing and management holdings.

It was a cold, dark season for rock 'n' roll in America.

**III**

*Well, goin' pretty fast, I looked behind,*
*Here come the Devil doin' ninety-nine!*
*Move, hot rod! Move, man!*
*Move, hot rod! Move, man!*
*Move, hot rod! Move me on down the line!*

"HE'S ON HIS WAY OVER!" SOMEONE SHOUTED.

An urgent buzz of excitement swept like wildfire through the long, low building just off the runways of London Airport North. It was early, not even seven yet, on the frigid first Saturday morning of December 1959. But the hundreds of people—mostly young, mostly male, carefully clutching records or waving placards painted with slogans like "Our Wild Cat Gene"—shoehorned into the hut-like reception area would not be deterred. They were hungry for their first glimpse of the American whose music changed their lives.

The packed room was papered in large posters proclaiming "Welcome Gene Vincent—Rock 'n' Roll Idol of Millions. Hear His Latest Capitol Disc 'Wildcat.' " The company had strategically released "Wildcat" only the day before, paired with "Right Here on Earth." To one side, guitarist Joe Brown and his band were set up and anxiously standing by. Outside, the jet engines screamed in the cold. All eyes moved to the heavy door, which was flanked by executives from EMI Records, a sea of journalists and photographers, and a variety of British show business luminaries, including television producer Jack Good, singer Marty Wilde and his wife, singer Little Tony, and popular disc jockey Ray Orchard.

An ear-splitting din erupted as the door opened and Gene limped inside. The crowd burst into shouts and applause, the fans cheering a hearty welcome. Brown and his band launched into "Be-Bop-A-Lula." The teeming throng pressed in close around their idol. Gene beamed. He was right. *This* was is where it was happening.

He was quickly whisked away for a morning spot on the popular BBC radio show "Saturday Club," then sat for an interview with Ray Orchard for Radio Luxembourg in which he confirmed the rumor that he was contemplating giving up concert tours for life on a farm, and revealed that his greatest influence was his mother. He was then shuttled over to a London restaurant for a more formal reception, again attended by the Wildes, Good, Brown, record label people, the press, and a select few lucky fans. Gene was tiring after his long transatlantic flight and whirlwind morning, but he still managed to oblige the many admirers who appealed to him to sign their autograph books, record sleeves, and sundry scraps of paper. One girl tucked a tiny St. Christopher's medal into her idol's hand. "This is for you, Gene," she whispered. Touched by such a simple, sincere gesture, he looked up at her for a moment, then kissed her gently.

The Granada Theatre on the outskirts of London, in Tooting—the same theater where Jerry Lee had given his swansong performance just a year and a half earlier before being drummed out of the UK—was packed to the rafters the next day. It was the "Marty Wilde Show," but most everyone was there to see Marty's special guest, The Screaming End. After a quick introduction, Gene limped out onto the stage to a thunderous roar of applause. Despite the warm reception, he seemed a little uncertain, as if not quite sure the adulation was for him, and his mouth twitched nervously when he discovered that his microphone wasn't working. After a self-conscious moment to find another that was, Gene abruptly threw his iron-clad left leg over the top of the microphone stand, swiftly spun a full three-hundred-sixty degrees, and tore into "Be-Bop-A-Lula" like a ravenous beast ripping the life from its helpless prey. What the audience first thought to be a quiet and slightly befuddled singer in a red-and-black sweater was, to their stupefied delight, instantly transformed into the manically intense, verging on dangerous, performer they'd only seen on the silver screen and heard on his hit records.

Gene gripped his microphone like a gun, crouching low with the stand just a couple feet from the floor. He avoided looking directly at the audience, even when he addressed them, always keeping his head bent mysteriously over the mike or turned elusively toward the wings. At times he stood coiled, motionless, like a serpent waiting to strike. Then, quite unexpectedly, he'd whirl, pitch, and catch the microphone stand, then swing his leg around it in one continuous, instantaneous movement. It was pure magic. The audience was electrified. By the end of the second show a nonstop rumble of "We want Gene! We want Gene!" prevented master of ceremonies Billy Raymond from even getting a word in edgewise. In one single evening, Gene Vincent proved himself the wildest rock 'n' roller Britain had ever seen.

The television screen was dark, save for Joe Brown's guitar barely visible in the dusk at the left of the picture. As the words GENE VINCENT glowed briefly in the corner of the screen, the singer appeared in the background, cryptically folded over a microphone. He was dressed gloved-finger to boot in menacing black leather, the collar of his jerkin flipped up like a vampire's hood. A heavy medallion hung from a chain around his neck. His shadow, long and sinister, stretched out behind him.

The camera began to move in as, offscreen, Brown and his band sauntered into the low-down intro of "Baby Blue." The camera pulled away as Gene started to sing, the sweet husk of his voice contradicting the transfixingly frightening character on the screen. He walked brazenly toward the lens, his ghostly white face with its vicious glare consuming the entire frame. A vine of greasy curls tumbled over his pale brow, his threatening eyes smoldered in their sockets. He looked like a demon. On that Saturday night, with his third appearance on Jack Good's *Boy Meets Girls*, teenaged England was hooked.

Thanks in large part to American cultural exports, England was undergoing its own adolescent revolution at the time. Films like *The Blackboard Jungle* and *Rebel Without a Cause* addressed the universal struggle of teens around the globe: finding and maintaining one's identity in a hypocritical, antagonistic, and conformist adult world. American rock 'n' roll—despised by parents and poo-poohed by the BBC, thus all the more attractive to British kids—provided a sexy soundtrack, being beamed across Europe via Radio Luxembourg, in English only in the evenings. And as the dire financial straits that immediately followed World War II began to ease, British teens were, for the first time, able to make purchasing decisions of their very own. They bought blue jeans, 78s (a little later, 45s), and phonographs to play their records. And if they worked hard enough and saved carefully enough, even their own transport. The ride of choice: the British motorcycle, the finest in the world.

An entire youth subculture with the motorcycle as its axis began to evolve in Great Britain. The hand-built motorcycles with the evocative names—the Norton Dominator, the Triumph Thunderbird, the B.S.A. Gold Star—were a teenager's gleaming talisman of independence, affluence, and power. The black leather jackets sold as protective gear for bike enthusiasts quickly became the uniform of choice for young males, paired with blue jeans and, for the more misanthropically inclined, the metal-studded belt inherited from the Teds, the first identifiable postwar youth subculture. The Teddy Boys, named for their Edwardian-style dress—long drape coats faced with velvet, ornately embroidered vests, drainpipe trousers, skinny bootlace ties, and thick, crepe-soled shoes—was a group comprised largely of working-class youths, war babies brought up on rations, many without fathers, a deprived generation who acted out their disaffection with violence. Vandalism, gang fights, even murder, perpetrated by and amongst the Teds, had British authorities up in arms between 1953 and 1956, mirroring the concern over juvenile delinquency also reaching a fever pitch thousands of miles across the Atlantic.

The black leathers of the Rockers soon eclipsed the Teds, though it was certainly no relief to English parents. Brando's portrayal of the leather-jacketed Johnny in *The Wild One*, the bored and alienated youth whose motorcycle gang wreaks havoc on a sleepy midwestern town, awakened the rebel in many an English adolescent. Although the film was banned in the UK until 1968, British teens desperately drooled over their revered *Wild One* stills and posters and fashioned themselves after the coolest actor they'd ever seen. James Dean, who took Brando's disturbed but sensitive anti-hero to the next level with his three major motion pictures—*East of Eden* and *Giant*, in addition to *Rebel*—was equally revered.

The Rockers, mostly working-class youths themselves, wholly identified with Gene Vincent from America. He, too, was a motorcycle warrior—and had the limp to prove it. He, too, came from humble, blue-collar beginnings. And he stayed true to his rock 'n' roll roots, keeping the big beat alive as one by one Richard, Elvis, Buddy, and Jerry Lee had dropped out of sight. Greasy-haired and done up in black leather—a suggestion of *Boy Meets Girls* producer Jack Good—Gene Vincent was one of their dark and desperate own.

Gene resonated with French youths, too, who, during his Paris debut, not long after his British premiere, rushed the Olympia Theatre stage during his spot on the live radio show "Musicorama." In their zeal to be close to the man who stirred so much within them, they ripped Gene's new black suede jacket clean off his back. He went on to Germany after that, performing at U.S. Air Force bases, then returned to the UK to embark on a twelve-day tour as part of a variety package.

Adrian Owlett was agog.

All the lights had gone out in the Granada in Kingston. He could hear the heavy curtains being drawn back from the stage and then a gloriously high, clear voice singing, "*Weeeell . . .*" A tight spotlight quickly darted across the darkened stage, illuminating each musician's face one by one. The spot widened as it hit the owner of that beautiful voice, who was crouched down mysteriously near the drums. He was extraordinary, dressed in a bright green outfit with a stylish monogram, white socks, black shoes, and a shock of dark, greasy curls forming a shining fetlock over his pale forehead.

The audience exploded as Gene Vincent pummeled his way through "Rocky Road Blues," then, without a pause, barreled into the rollicking "Say Mama." The singer dropped to his knees with the mike stand stretched out lengthwise, then he tossed it high in the air, singing to the rafters all the while, still on his knees. Then he sprang up suddenly, shaking, stomping, and gamboling his way across the stage. He mounted the piano, then dove off it to the floor—never missing a beat. Adrian was stunned. The crowd was positively rabid.

The singer slowed down for a moment to explain the old folk story behind "Frankie and Johnny," then chatted briefly after the song, telling the eager audience that he had just toured the world and that England had given him the best reception yet, winning him rousing cheers and uproarious applause from his British fans. Gene hardly finished speaking when he broke into "Wildcat," dropping again to his knees during the sax break, then, placing his hands on his hips, shaking himself suggestively to the beat. Next he slid into his signature crouch, his left leg extended straight back behind him, before winding it down for the slower "Summertime." He moved to the edge of the stage for the song, crooning from a seated position, bathed in a moody blue light. The audience was, for the first time that evening, hushed.

Then it was straight into "Baby Blue," "Dance to the Bop" and "Dance in the Streets," Gene bucking and cavorting all the while. Next he told the crowd that he wanted to perform his favorite number for them. The lights were lowered as he tenderly sang "Important Words." As the tune ended he plunged right into "Brand New Beat." Again, the crowd was frantic, some girls shrieking, others crying, many fellows dancing in the aisles.

Gene drawled something about how much he had enjoyed the

show, and the crowd showed its approval with loud shouts and claps. Suddenly Gene swung his left leg in a full circle over the microphone stand and launched into "Be-Bop-A-Lula." By the end of the frenzied set, Adrian and the audience felt almost as drained as the singer, who staggered, exhausted, to the wings to seemingly ceaseless chants of "More! More! More!" and "Gene! Gene! Gene!" After a few moments, host Don Arden brought Gene back on. He seemed embarrassed at all the attention. He thanked the crowd again politely, then slid one leg backwards, jutted the microphone forward and belted out an encore of "Bluejean Bop," "Right Here on Earth," and yet another "Be-Bop-A-Lula."

The show ended at 11:20 P.M. At midnight there were still teenagers, inside the theater and out, shouting for more of The Screaming End. Adrian would never forget it.

Lawrence Morris Parnes, known not-so-nicely in the business as "Larry Parnes, Shillings and Pence," was England's crown prince of pop promotion. He broke ground for his kingdom in 1956 the day he discovered Tommy Steele at the Two I's Coffee Bar in London's Soho district; he quickly made Steele a star. Since then, Parnes had assembled an entire stable of golden boys, virtually interchangeable young singers he rechristened with new "power" show-business names: Billy Fury, Vince Eager, Johnny Gentle, Dickie Pride, and Lance Fortune. He created them—and profited greatly from them. He recognized that there was an extraordinarily lucrative business in setting teenage growing pains to music. And as the main supplier of talent for the massively popular TV music show *Oh Boy!*, which had every aspiring musician in the country glued to the television set every Saturday night, Parnes was enormously influential.

Realizing a consumer demand that needed filling, wily Parnes was one of the first operators to bring American pop stars to the UK In 1959, when he was unable to secure Elvis Presley, he'd thought of Gene Vincent. He was able to negotiate a fair price, fifteen hundred pounds a week, six shows a week, for four or five weeks. After booking Gene Vincent, Parnes got an uneasy feeling, though, that all would not be well and decided he needed somebody else on the bill. He'd been reading about an up-and-coming American singer and guitarist named Eddie Cochran, and he suggested him to the friend who was doing the negotiating for him. In just a few days Parnes had booked Cochran very reasonably, as well, two hundred fifty pounds a week plus expenses. He felt better.

Parnes never liked to leave anything to chance. Every tour was analyzed and strategized like a military campaign, with maps and charts and statistics on demographics and populations and attendance figures. After the first week of shows, his beloved numbers told him, he was sold out for the entire tour. Of course, having a pair of new records out from Gene—his single "Wildcat" and the long-player *Crazy Times*, which Capitol would release in the States in March—was a help. And a pair of singles in the *New Musical Express* charts, the UK's music industry bible, didn't hurt ticket sales any, either; both "Wildcat" and Eddie's "Hallellujah, I Love Her So" had cracked the Top 30.

In Scotland there was a happy reunion for Gene, Eddie, and Darlene. Darlene flew over with the kids and Gene hired a nanny to look after them in London so Darlene could accompany him to Scotland. Eddie arrived also, and they all took the train up for a week at the Empire Theatre in Glasgow. The show ran twice nightly, and also featured the Tony Sheridan Trio, Joe Brown, Georgie Fame, Billy Fury, and Billy Raymond. Clumsily christened by Parnes as "A Fast-Moving Anglo-American Beat Show," it was the first all rock 'n' roll program ever to tour the UK; when Buddy Holly and Jerry Lee Lewis had played these shores earlier, it had been as part of a variety package, like Gene's gig of a few weeks earlier.

Known in the concert business as The Death Place, Glasgow was a tough town to play. The crowds were typically unruly and would throw bottles at performers just for the hell of it, whether they liked them or not. It was usually singers with the sexiest images who were physically attacked; Glasgow blokes didn't go in for the pretty boys who made their birds all sweaty and moist. Billy Fury had a bad time; from the wings, whiskey bottles could be heard whizzing by, and his band eventually deserted him, leaving him standing alone on the stage. But the Americans made it through the week unscathed. Eddie closed the first half of the show, the crowd eating up his hits "Summertime Blues," "C'mon Everybody," and "Twenty Flight Rock," though the Scots disapproved loudly when he mistakenly chatted about being in England. Gene, who closed out the second half of the show, went over well too, his flamboyant, tough-guy antics—abusing the microphone stand, kneeling, crawling, and cantering across the stage—keeping the Scots transfixed.

In Glasgow, Darlene realized she was pregnant again. Gene was delighted and hoped for a boy. Darlene was not. She and Gene were already having problems, and with Gene on the road, there was no way she could ever be a real mother when living from a suitcase. After a few weeks, she flew back to the States, staying with the Lunds in Portland while Gene finished up the tour.

The show moved back down to England, playing the Empire in London, the Gaumont in Cardiff, Wales, the Hippodrome in Manchester, and the Empire in Leeds. The reception was the same everywhere. Screaming fans filled the theater seats during the concerts, then streamed from the halls afterward out onto the streets in search of their rock 'n' roll idols. After the shows, decoys who resembled Gene and Eddie would be sent out to distract the shrieking mobs while the musicians made their getaway. One evening Gene, Eddie, guitarist Joe Brown, and tour manager Hal Carter dashed to their car, only to find it locked. Hal frantically unlocked the doors and the group jumped into the car just as a throng of squealing teens surrounded the vehicle. While stopped at a traffic light, Gene, seated in the front passenger seat, was startled by fans who tried to open his door. As they pulled purposefully on the handle, he struggled desperately to pull the door shut. After a few moments of tug of war, the door flew open and a flurry of flailing arms and grasping hands gave Gene a going over. As the light changed Hal sped forward and Gene managed to get the door shut and locked. He was silent for a few hundred yards, then whimpered, "Eddie, Eddie—they got my pants!" Eddie and Joe, seated in the rear, leaned forward. They were greatly amused to see scrawny Gene left only in his underwear, leg iron, and cowboy boots. When they arrived at their hotel in Leeds, they laughed as he ascended the stairs to his room, trouserless, his leg iron landing with a loud *clunk* on every step.

When they weren't on stage, Gene and Eddie were busy making media appearances, frequently dropping by the *Boy Meets Girls* TV show and the "Saturday Club" radio show. Though they were kept occupied, Eddie was extremely homesick, phoning Los Angeles almost every day to speak with his mama. So when Sharon arrived, she was a welcome reminder of home.

From the moment she'd first laid eyes on him, Sharon Sheeley had made it her life's work to capture Eddie Cochran. Still in her teens, just getting the braces off her teeth, the willowy California girl was already an accomplished songwriter, having penned "Poor Little Fool" for Ricky Nelson and "Dum Dum" for Brenda Lee. She and Eddie shared the same management, and she helped out with some of his songs—joining Jerry Capehart with hand-claps on "Summertime Blues" and penning "Somethin' Else," and later "Cherished Memories" for Eddie. Since then her every waking moment was consumed with passionate thoughts of the handsome young singer with the strong jaw and deep-set eyes, and just how she could make him her very own. For nearly two years she relentlessly pursued him—showing up at all his personal appearances, spending all her savings on eye-catching fashions, and even bleaching her naturally very dark hair a very attention-grabbing platinum blond. They finally got together at a music business New Year's Eve party in New York City. After everyone else had left, they kissed for the very first time. It was just like in the movies; Sharon could hear bells ringing clear across Manhattan.

To Sharon, Eddie was the obvious star of the show. Apparently she wasn't the only one. Not long after she arrived, because of the terrific response he was getting from the crowds, Eddie was offered the option to headline. But when the idea of changing the marquee was broached, Eddie said absolutely not. He simply wouldn't hear of it. He loved Gene like a brother, he took care of him, looked after him. He knew that Gene wouldn't be able to handle it—that Gene emotionally could not handle the blow of having his best friend's name put above his. And Eddie didn't even care. It just wasn't that important to him.

Eddie and Gene loved each other as if they were brothers, Sharon knew. And they sure acted like mischievous little boys, getting themselves thrown out of hotels with their pranks. One night they'd collected all the shoes that hotel guests had left in the hallway to be polished and sent them down the laundry chute. In the morning, when Gene, Eddie, and Sharon walked through the lobby, the only ones in the whole building with shoes to wear, they were a dead giveaway. Other nights they'd have a few drinks, then go around at two in the morning knocking on hotel doors. When the sleepy and startled guest would open the door, they'd sing in giggling unison, "My old man's the desk man, he wears the deskman's hat!" Then, bang! They'd slam the door.

But Eddie was very protective of Gene, Sharon noticed. It got on her nerves sometimes. She and Gene just didn't like each other. It was obvious to her that he was very, very jealous of her relationship with Eddie. She could tell that he resented terribly that she'd come over, because she was taking his beloved Eddie's attention that he was so used to having all to himself. And she resented Gene. She flew thousands of miles to be with the love of her life, and she really wanted to spend a little time with him alone without having Gene around twenty-four hours a day. Sure, he had an incredible voice—his ballads could make you just weep— and his manic stage show was certainly unlike anything else out there. But it was getting harder and harder to distinguish the divine inspiration from the drunken abandon. Gene was just a miserable person, she thought. Always upset about something or another. And poor Eddie. He had to do quite a balancing act. He was torn between trying to keep her satisfied and trying to keep Gene from wallowing in his suicidal sorrows all the time.

And he played that leg like a violin, she thought. Gene would moan and groan and carry on, "Oh, my leg, my leg, my leg." But after one of their shows, as thousands of screaming girls—sweaty, moist, and besotted—descended on Gene, Eddie, and Sharon, who accidentally exited out the wrong stage door, Gene handily beat them all in the footrace back to the car. Sure, she knew that his leg bothered him. But there were plenty of folks who had handicaps. Just look at Ray Charles, she thought. It didn't make him an asshole.

On March 10, "My Heart" broke into the UK charts, climbing to its peak position at number sixteen on March 19, aided by Gene's two appearances on the "Saturday Club" radio show in early March and his TV appearances, with Eddie, on *Boy Meets Girl* in late February. Gene was pleased, though only with the chart success. He just didn't like the record. He felt he could have done a much better job. But he had the first-hand experience to know that it works both ways. You can cut a disc and think it's the greatest thing you've ever done. Then you discover everyone hates it. That's one of the things he found so fascinating—and so irksome—about the music business. His continual worry was to make sure that the public was getting what it wanted. There was always the nagging fear in the back of his mind that one day he might go onstage and find the audience didn't want him anymore. That one day he'd finish his act and maybe there would be no applause. He swore if that ever happened to him he'd quit immediately and buy a farm in Virginia. He started life as a poor boy, and he certainly wasn't afraid of a little hard work.

But for now, it was were back on the road with Parnes's Anglo-American package show, which stopped for a week each at the Hippodromes in Birmingham and Manchester and the Empires in

Liverpool and Newcastle. The ceaseless schedule was beginning to take its toll on Gene and Eddie. When Jack Good visited them at their hotel in Manchester, he found them both in bed. Gene was recovering from pneumonia and had a plaster cast back on his leg; he'd broken the iron brace. Eddie was suffering from insomnia and strained eyes. Good doubted that they'd be able to make the show that evening. He was wrong. They were superb.

As the Wildcats, on loan from Marty Wilde, launched into the first few bars of his act, Eddie crouched with his back to the audience. There was an audible gasp when, on the first words of "What'd I Say," he swung round to face the audience. He was wearing light tan leather trousers, a turquoise shirt, and a shimmering silver vest—and a pair of dark glasses. He looked fabulous. And outrageous. He used the glasses as a prop during that first song, making a great play out of pulling them off, like a stripper teasing a bar full of sailors. Making the most of his deep, dusky voice, at once irresistibly sexy and radiating total control, the charismatic Cochran moved gracefully, almost elegantly, across the stage, churning his guitar—innovatively strung so that all sorts of unheard-of bends were possible—like the wheels of a train. The audience was knocked out.

Then it was Gene's turn. Dressed in black leather from top to toe, his pale, feverish face pouring sweat, his huge eyes affixed on a hovering apparition only he could see, Gene was hell's very own angel, at moments singing with the softest, sweetest voice the audience had ever heard. Other times he was growling, snarling, and screaming ferociously into the microphone, its stand upturned over his head, the cords of his neck bulging and taut from his strain. During a guitar solo he held the stand by its base, plunging the microphone down dangerously close to the guitarist's amplifier. Recklessly bucking and flailing, swooping and raving, he drove the band, the audience, and himself unmercifully, providing for his fans the gloriously terrifying spectacle they had all come to see. Racked with pain, both from his chest and his leg, by the show's end, he was on the verge of collapse. The audience roared its heartfelt approval.

He only did what came to him naturally. To his fans, he was simply supernatural.

In the audience at the Liverpool Empire was a young fan named John Peel, along with his entire troupe in the Royal Artillery, whom he'd recently introduced to Gene Vincent's music. Also in the audience at Liverpool were four lanky teenagers with their hair greased back coolly from their foreheads—John, Paul, George, and Stu—who'd formed a local band of their own, the Silver Beetles, though they were still searching for a drummer. The scruffy lads loved Gene's music; the unbelievable "Be-Bop-A-Lula" was the first record Paul had ever purchased and they regularly included the song in their set list, along with other favorites they memorized from Radio Luxembourg, songs like Chuck Berry's "Maybellene" and "Roll Over Beethoven," Fats Domino's "Ain't That a Shame," and Eddie's "Twenty Flight Rock." As the insistent screams of the female fans threatened to drown out his two idols, young John Lennon yelled furiously at the shrieking girls to shut up. Gene's rawness on the stage, his untamed ferociousness, and his twisted, tortured beauty in his dangerous black leather impressed the lads greatly.

Keith Goodwin of the *New Musical Express* dropped by their flat at the Stratford Court Hotel in Oxford Street. The boys weren't feeling their best—Gene was still recovering from his pneumonia and Eddie had not yet beaten his insomnia. But the new record by Brenda Lee, the tiny teenage songbird from America with the big, bold voice, had put them in excellent spirits.

"It's been pretty tough these last few weeks," Eddie told the reporter as Lee's sultry single "Sweet Nuthins" reached its end behind him.

"But everybody's been real good to us," Gene added, "and that's how we got on our feet again so quickly."

Goodwin hardly settled into his chair before the two singers were back again at the record player, giving "Sweet Nuthins" another spin. Then another. And another.

"What a voice!" Gene enthused. "It's unbelievable for someone so young!"

"Listen to that drive," Eddie said. "Isn't she great?"

"So you're fans of this curly-headed, fifteen-year-old bundle of dynamite?" Goodwin asked.

"You bet," they said, almost in unison.

They chatted with Goodwin a bit, telling him of their immediate plans, that they'd be returning to America in a few days for a sorely needed ten-day rest. Then they'd be back in Britain for another string of one-night stands and then a summer-season stint at Blackpool, the coastal resort town.

When Goodwin probed further, Gene was noncommittal about his trip to the States. "I've got some business to attend to," was the simple explanation he gave the nosy reporter. He wasn't about to tell him of the painful parasite eating away at his insides, of his nagging certainty, though he didn't have any proof—and everybody, including Eddie, reassured him otherwise—that his wife was running around on him while he was away. He always denied to the press that he was married and if a reporter ever asked, "Are you likely to be soon?" he just laughed it off. But sometimes the anger would just boil up in him and he'd fret and fume and rail to Eddie in those bleak, black moments when the red-eyed rage would try to creep on him. Other times it would weigh heavy on his heart, and he'd turn dark and moody. But Eddie would always take care of him, quelling the fiery rage, chasing away the demons that taunted and terrified him, and protecting him from outsiders he didn't want around.

Eddie was more forthcoming. "Well, I have some TV shows and stage dates lined up," he said. "Also, I have to attend talks for a film which I'll be making later in the year. This is very important to me, since it'll be my first dramatic acting role."

The three chatted casually and at length on the merits of Ray Charles, Brenda Lee, Josh White, and other American stars, Gene and Eddie going about their daily business with the reporter firing off questions wherever he could.

"What do you think of British big-beat artists?" the writer wanted to know.

"Well, there's no denying you have some very, very good singers here," Eddie said. "But if you'd seen as many rock 'n' roll singers as we have, then you'd appreciate that it's very seldom we get really knocked out by an artist."

"Were you impressed by anyone in particular?" Goodwin asked.

Gene answered, "Yes, Wee Willie Harris," the rock 'n' roll clown partial to shocking pink, green, or orange hair. "He's real good. I liked him a lot. You see, he's different from the others and we have nothing like him in the States. I certainly got a kick out of Willie. And Joe Brown—he's great too," Gene added, though he didn't go in for the habit many of these British artists had of practicing all their moves for their act before they went onstage. That was just plain wrong. He never rehearsed or worked out his moves beforehand. Sure, it was a gamble, but that way every show was completely spontaneous, the way it should be.

"Yes, Joe is fine," Eddie agreed. "A good singer and instrumentalist, and very funny. I'm certain he would go down great in America. I also enjoyed Vince Eager. He's an exciting artist."

The reporter wanted to know how they found the British audiences.

"They were real good to us," Eddie said. "But I don't think they're quite as demonstrative as in the States. Over there, they often go nuts even when you're just announcing a number. But in Britain, they're somewhat more reserved and polite."

"I found that they went more for my wild rock songs than my ballads," Gene mused. "But on the whole, they weren't too different from American audiences. They scream a lot and clap and get excited just like Americans. I guess audiences are pretty much the same the world over."

"What did you think of the fans you met?" Goodwin asked.

"I loved them," Gene said. "They're very devoted and very friendly, and it was a pleasure to meet them. But so many of them just don't look like teenagers. They seem so grown up in the way they dress and act."

"I love them, too," Eddie agreed. "Their loyalty is amazing at times. For instance, we saw the same fans at theaters all over the country. They must have traveled miles to see us."

"Did they ask for souvenirs?" Goodwin asked.

"Well, yes," Gene said. "But most of them are happy just to shake your hand and have a little chat with you. I like that. Mind you, I gave away quite a lot of souvenirs. American dimes seem to be the favorite with the fans."

"And guitar picks," Eddie added. "I've handed out a whole stack of them. Shirts, too. Now and again, a fan asks for one of my shirts as a keepsake, and I don't like to say no. Also, on an average, we signed between two hundred and three hundred autographs each week."

"How about working conditions in Britain?" Goodwin asked.

"Right off, I must tell you that I've been far more tired here than in the States," Eddie said, picking up a pair of dark glasses. "Why? Probably because we've had so little time to relax. People are always calling on us between shows—not that I'm complaining about that—and when we're not working, we're traveling."

"Traveling, I would say, presents the biggest problem of all," Gene explained as he lathered his face with shaving cream. "Most of our journeys are by train. Now, I don't want to offend anybody, but I must say I don't like British trains. They're not comfortable, there's no way to relax; traveling just becomes boring and sometimes unbearable."

"What about theaters?" Goodwin asked.

"Fine!" Gene exclaimed. "No complaints there. We've played some good places and have always been treated very well."

"I agree with Gene," Eddie said. "But I would say that I prefer doing one-night stands as opposed to whole weeks at one theater. It's just that I like a change."

The reporter wanted to know what they thought of Britain as a country.

"Are you joking?" Gene chuckled, between strokes of his razor. "So much of our time has been taken up traveling that we really haven't had time to see the country. But seriously, I like it here, and would like to spend a lot more time in Britain in the future. I've thoroughly enjoyed myself."

Eddie, who had now donned the dark glasses and was strategically positioned in front of a small sun lamp, agreed. "More than anything else, I enjoyed the people," he said. "They're real nice and they've made us feel at home. On the other hand, I'm not crazy about your food. I miss home cooking a lot, and right now, I'm so homesick that I feel I just have to get back to the States for a few days."

"Anything you particularly want to do when you get back here?" the writer asked.

"Yes, there sure is," Gene answered. "I'd like to do more TV shows with Jack Good. He's the greatest guy I ever knew and he produces the best beat show of all. There's nothing to compare with Jack's show in the States."

Gene couldn't speak highly enough of Jack. He thought the man had more musical sense in his little finger than he could acquire in a lifetime. Gene had always been painfully shy, though he tried to hide it onstage. That's why he could never face an audience. It simply terrified him. Jack, with his kind words, sound advice, and unfailing support, gave Gene confidence.

One thing Jack hadn't changed, though, was Gene's aversion to onstage patter. No matter how much confidence Jack gave him in his musical abilities, Gene just couldn't speak onstage. He didn't know how to put his feelings into words, he was never sure of what to say, and if he did say something he always thought that people found him rather dull. So he made a rule for himself: keep your mouth shut. Of course, he always let an audience know how grateful he was for their applause and support. But he preferred to remain silent, so that he wouldn't goof up or dry up. And there wasn't anything Jack Good could do about that.

Ed agreed with Gene's praise for Good, giving "Sweet Nuthins" yet another spin. "I'd like to do some more programs with Jack. He's such a brilliant guy—frank and honest and enthusiastic. That's why he's such a good producer."

The car sped through the black April night, hurtling through the hushed firmament as its passengers, exhausted from their triumphant but tiring run at Bristol's Hippodrome, gazed out idly at the starlit countryside. Eddie was to Gene's left, sitting in the middle between him and Sharon, and theatrical agent Pat Thompkins rode in front with the driver. They'd be at the airport soon to catch the flight back to New York, then on to Los Angeles, and then home. Home. God, how Gene missed home. He couldn't wait to see his family again, Darlene—was she fooling around on him on the other side of the world?—and Debbie and little Melody. And he was looking forward to the small stuff, to sunny California weather, to late-night television and Westerns like his favorite show *Maverick*, to driving his own car, to not having to take the goddamned train everywhere. Thank God he'd been able to talk Eddie into hiring a driver for the journey to the airport, even though they all already had their train tickets. There was just no way he could've faced a six-hour train ride tonight. He simply couldn't do it.

The car's forward momentum felt good, and the monotonous hum of the motor and the sweet, soothing drink melting every pain and worry made him drowsy. His head swirled with narcotic imaginings and possibilities.

*A soft light gently pricked the darkness of the car's interior. It came from behind—another vehicle on the road, no doubt. But it was an odd color. It seemed almost red. The light quickly grew in intensity, soon bathing the car in a sickly crimson aura. Gene looked out the rear window and his stomach lurched. A giant car, a jet black machine, loomed directly behind him. A pair of smol-*

*dering orbs burned behind the darkened windshield. They were terrifyingly familiar. They gleamed—glowed, really—red as split blood.*

*"Faster, driver!" Gene commanded, his belly tightening into a burning fist of peptic protest. "Faster! Go! Go!"*

*But Gene was completely alone, powerless and small in the back seat. And the terrifying red eyes were following him, chasing him, terrorizing him just inches from the taxi's rear bumper.*

*Gene dove into the driver's seat, crying out in agony as he dragged the leg iron over the seat back, and grabbed the steering wheel. He stomped on the accelerator, giving it all he could give it.*

*The speeding car began to pitch and sway, heaved about by strong, dark winds. Through the windshield Gene could see that the car was on some sort of bridge, a downward-sloping trestle of massive stone and thick chains. Below him a volcanic lake fumed and boiled in a boundless pit, lofting arched, snaking waves of scarlet flame up and over the car.*

*His body trembling with adrenaline, Gene frantically twisted the steering wheel, trying to turn the car around, but the machine seemed to have a mind of its own. He was plunging down the bridge through the darkness—helpless, impotent—with the dastardly demon eyes gleefully supervising his blazing descent.*

*The cold rage seized him. It emboldened him.*

*Try to catch me, you bastard, but you will not win, Gene vowed. You will never win.*

*He grabbed for the handle and pulled on it. The door flew open. Gene leapt out as a colossal gust of fervid wind lifted the driverless car and cast it toward the angry abyss.*

*He was falling, falling, forever falling. It was dark, very cold, and silent. But he was unafraid. Gene looked up to see the glowing red eyes following his fall. He glared deeply into those horrid eyes shrinking smaller and smaller above him as he spiraled onward and downward. He began to laugh—loud, furious, victorious.*

*He landed with a thud, the grass a welcome mattress for his tortured, broken body.*

The grass under Sharon's cheek was cool and wet. She opened her leaden lids, and a dark and silvery world slowly circled into focus. Gene, that whining asshole, knelt beside her, rubbing his left shoulder. She was too tired, too drained, too confused, to hate him right now. She felt sodden, heavy. She tasted blood in her mouth, and it was warm and viscous and salty. She wanted to go home. Sharon tried to get up, tried to move. But there was nothing to move. She was completely numb. Oh God, something was wrong, she panicked, terribly, horribly, unspeakably wrong. She needed Eddie, her dear, sweet Eddie. Eddie would make everything all right.

"Where's Eddie?" she asked, her voice a hoarse whisper.

"Oh, he's fine," Gene drawled nervously, his eyes wide, trying his best to sound soothing. "He's sitting in the car having a cigarette. He's just shook up is all."

Sharon knew at that moment that Eddie was either dead or dying. If he wasn't, he'd be here at her side, not Gene. He wouldn't be sitting in the car while she was laying out here, in this field, on this lawn—where the hell was she?—bleeding to death. Oh God, Eddie, my true and only love, don't leave me, she prayed soundlessly, earnestly, shattered and unmoving on the damp grass. Dear God, please don't let him leave me. Her heavy lids drooped. A velvety darkness engulfed her.

She was holding Eddie's hand. She could barely see him through the blinding fog. He seemed to be sleeping. He looked so beautiful. Was it a dream? Perhaps they'd wake up soon. A stranger's face parted the murkiness. He was wearing a uniform. A siren screamed above her, and the lights were painfully bright. "Something told me you two were in love," the ambulance driver told her, "so I locked your hands together, miss." "Thank you," she whispered, then silently pleaded with God not to let her go back under. If she did, she knew, she'd never see Eddie again. For he was going to die. The velvet curtain dropped.

Gene hobbled painfully into the long, low, hut-like building, the same airport terminal he'd so triumphantly entered the December before. The scene this April 29 was entirely different. The room was virtually empty, save for a few chairs and a tiny table offering assorted hors d'oeuvres. There was no music. No cheering fans. No smiles. Just a white-coated waiter and a few photographers milling about. Gene, ashen-faced and swimming solemnly in his own thoughts, sat by himself as his American manager Norm Riley chatted with British promoter Larry Parnes. Gene had spent three days in the hospital in Bath after the crash, then flown home to nurse his broken collarbone and additional damage to his left leg. He felt dark and empty inside. Immutably hollow. Though he flew home with Eddie's body—"Eddie and I started out together, and we're coming home together," he told his mama on the phone just before he left England—he hadn't been able to bring himself to attend Eddie's funeral in Los Angeles. He just wanted to get back to work. So he returned to London just over a week later to resume the tour—without Eddie.

Soon Alan Vince, a young, artistically inclined fan who'd drawn an elaborate cartoon strip to be presented to Gene in a photo-op ceremony at the terminal, walked over. He was charged by a rep from the Capitol setup at EMI with the impossible task of cheering Gene up. Alan found himself a chair and sat down next to Gene, who was somberly studying the floor. There was an awkward pause.

"Go on, talk to him," the Capitol rep whispered in Alan's ear.

Alan thought for a moment, then asked about any forthcoming releases Gene might have coming up, hoping for the best.

Gene's face gave no hint of a smile, but he was able to muster some quiet enthusiasm about his music.

Yes, there was a new single on the way, he drawled softly. "It's called 'Crazy Times.' "

Alan would later think it a bit odd that Gene would use the word "we" when speaking of his music, as if he thought of himself as part of a group, rather than a solo singer. But at the time, he simply assumed Gene was referring to the Blue Caps, including his dancing backing vocalists the Brits had lovingly dubbed his "clapper boys."

Soon the photographers asked for the cartoon to be presented, and after being directed just where and how to stand, fan and fragile rock 'n' roll star were united under a hail of flashbulbs. Gene seemed pleased with the cartoon, which greatly pleased Alan. Before he departed, Parnes asked Alan if he was a member of Gene's fan club. He was indeed at one time, he explained to Parnes, but the club, run by a Capitol employee who simply didn't have the time or interest anymore, had recently shut down. "Then we'll have to reopen it, won't we Alan?" Parnes said. Alan blithely agreed, not sure if the promoter was joking or not.

Gene, limping badly, was ushered away to a car waiting to take him into London.

"I want to sing for you now Eddie's favorite song," a cheerless Gene Vincent announced, gently rubbing at his left shoulder, then launching into a high, haltingly doleful rendition of "Somewhere Over the Rainbow." It was all too raw, too fresh, too sad, for most of the girls in the audience at the Lewisham Gaumont, Gene's first gig since the fatal accident. Tears of teenage sorrow streaked their pretty English faces, and their lowing moans made a mournful accompaniment. Moods quickly brightened, however, when Gene, bedecked in a flashy new suit of Craddock tartan he'd picked up in Scotland, belted out a crowd-pleasing "Be-Bop-A-Lula." Despite his injuries, both physical and emotional, he was all over the stage, soaring around the microphone stand and mingling amidst the Beat Boys, his backing group featuring Colin Green on lead guitar and Georgie Fame on keyboards. Gene encouraged their many solos, urging them on to the same sort of musical daredevilness he so relished. By the end of the show, the exhilarated audience was as gleefully exhausted as the performers. And Gene, soaked in his sweat, was baptized in their raining applause and embraced in their glowing adulation.

It was immediately apparent that despite Eddie's tragic death— he survived only hours after the wreck, dying in the hospital from massive head injuries—Gene was still in peak form; two nights later, on May 3, Gene's epidemic onstage abandon incited a riot at the six-thousand-seat Liverpool Stadium. Parnes had almost canceled the show, thinking the youngsters would cause trouble because of Eddie's absence. But co-promoter Alan Williams talked Parnes into saving the date, padding the bill with popular local groups, including Gerry and the Pacemakers. The four thin lads— John, Paul, George, and Stu—who'd caught Gene and Eddie just a few short weeks ago at the Empire Liverpool were again in the audience, scrutinizing Gene's every move and intently analyzing the ruthless, reckless music that so provoked the crowd. After Gene's frenetic performance in the boxing ring that served as a stage, the place simply came apart. Gangs of youths began tearing seats up from the floor, hurling them across the stadium. Desperate to maintain order, Williams and Parnes scurried about the stage, stomping on upward-climbing fans' fingers to get them to fall back into the crowd. It was Liverpool's own beloved singer, the stuttering Rory Storm—whose drummer Ringo Starr would join John, Paul, and George when they landed a record deal with Parlophone in 1962 as the Beatles—who calmed the violent masses. At the height of the melee, he vaulted onto the stage and began to lecture sternly in his signature stutter, "S-s-s-stop it, you k-k-kids!" They listened, and stopped.

Alan Vince made it to the theater in Rochester just after Gene returned to rehearsals from nearby Chatham. He went there to find a music paper, which puzzled many of the musicians and local press people assembled there awaiting his reappearance. He opened the magazine to the hit parade, then hobbled quickly onto the stage. "Eddie's at number four!" he shouted to no one in particular, elated that his late best friend's current release, "Three Steps to Heaven," was swiftly climbing the charts.

It had been just over a month since Alan had last seen Gene at the airport. He had indeed taken over the operation of Gene's UK fan club—though he wasn't getting much cooperation from the record label, management, or the star himself—and it had been a nonstop few weeks for Gene, as well. On May 11, he entered the EMI studios at Abbey Road in London to make his first UK recordings. Accompanied by the Beat Boys, he waxed a rocking rendition of the classic "Pistol Packin' Mama," arranged for him by Eddie just prior to his death. They often performed it as a duet on the tour, and Eddie's hand in the final product—he loaned his signature intro motif from "Somethin' Else" to the tune—was unmistakable. Gene also cut "Weeping Willow," which he wrote under the pseudonym Debra Lynn and dedicated to his mother. As a child, he'd asked Louise why the willow cried. She told him it hurt because its creator, the Lord, was rejected by men and had to die on the cross. The extraordinary song showcased Gene's truly poignant phrasing and his remarkable range, despite the track's syrupy orchestral and vocal backing, supplied by the Norrie Paramor Orchestra and its chorus. The two songs were packaged as a single in early June, and by mid-month the disc had climbed to number 16 on the UK chart. The rest of the time had been taken up with one-night stands in Halifax, Chester, Wolverhampton, Romford, Brighton, and Wembley, an appearance on Italian television to perform "Bluejean Bop" and "Sexy Ways," and then another string of one-nighters through Rochester, Norwich, Ipswich, York, Glasgow, Southampton, Plymouth, London, Nottingham, Carlisle, and Sunderland.

Postwar England, even into the early sixties was still in an almost impoverished state, lacking many of the comforts of home in the United States. Air conditioning and heating were rare, fast or convenience foods were unheard of, the black-and-white TV service was limited to just two channels, and everything, including bars and hotels, seemed to shut down by eleven at night. Even finding a bottle of Jack Daniels was a major undertaking. All of this added to the anxiety and discomfort of young Americans who came to the UK to tour; Eddie would say, "Goddamn, I'm never going to get home! I'm going to freeze to death in this country!" The stress was taking its toll on Gene, too. Traveling from the gig in Ipswich, on the east coast of England, he caused quite a violent disturbance on the bus. He flew into a temper tantrum and was shouting abuse at everyone—band members and even tour manager Hal Carter, who'd been looking after him since the package tour with Eddie.

Hal wasn't too surprised. He'd never really liked Gene. Sure, he was a great performer, but he found Gene to be a stubborn, contrary, and selfish young man, prone to erratic behavior on the road. But this day, on the bus, he was shocked to see the singer storm up to the Beat Boys' young bass player, the sharp, pointy switchblade he called Henry tightly gripped in his hand, and slice the front of the kid's suit off with the knife. Another member of the crew, Henry Henroid, pulled Gene off. Hal chose to ignore Gene's antics, hoping he'd settle down, and chatted jovially with singer Johnny Gentle seated next to him. Something Johnny said made Hal laugh. In an instant, Gene flew down the aisle and put the knife to Hal's throat. "I'll teach you to laugh at me," he told Hal, a cold, red-eyed rage taking hold of him. "Gene," Hal pleaded, "we're not laughing at you. We're just having a conversation." Gene then ripped Hal's shirt with the knife. Hal was incensed. When they got to Dartford, just outside London, he made the driver let him off. He jumped out, the bus drove off, and Hal never saw Gene again.

Alan spoke with Gene for just a few moments before the first show in Rochester, but he was running through "Say Mama" with the Beat Boys and didn't have much time to talk. Alan needed to discuss fan-club business. So, as the singer requested, Alan went to Gene's cramped dressing room during the break between the two shows, where he found Gene relaxing in a small armchair.

Right away, Alan could see a marked change in Gene's personality. This wasn't the somber, unassuming Gene he'd met just a few weeks before. Although he still seemed introspective and moody, there was now a vehement restlessness about him. Gene was killing time before the second show by throwing a hefty knife at a door at the end of the dressing room. Jerry Keller, another singer sharing the dressing room with Gene, turned to Alan and said, "You want me to write an article for the fan club? I will, and I'll tell you a few stories about this guy!" "Okay, okay," Gene drawled with a quiet intensity, still flinging the glinting blade at the door. "I know I'm no angel."

Billy Fury strode to the center of the stage and introduced Sharon Sheeley. She hobbled toward him tentatively from the wings, out on a brief respite from months of recuperation in the hospital. Even with Eddie's entire body protecting her, her neck and back had been broken, her leg severed, and her skull crushed. It was a miracle she was alive, though without Eddie she hardly felt that way.

He knew, her Eddie. He knew about his imminent death in Manchester. He went through a silent change, so subtle that only those who knew him very well, as she did, picked up on it. When they'd arrived in town, he'd made her go to a record shop and buy all the Buddy Holly records she could find. He hadn't listened to a Buddy Holly record since his good friend had died. Eddie had been on that fateful tour, but was pulled off at the last minute to do the *Ed Sullivan Show*. In Manchester, he sat for hours in their hotel room listening to his late friend's records over and over on the record player. "Isn't that making you sad?" Sharon asked him. "Why are you doing this?" "It doesn't make me sad anymore," Eddie told her. "It's gonna be all right now." There was a sense of mystery, a feeling that he knew something that she didn't, that started there in Manchester.

Then one night, about one in the morning, Sharon was startled awake by the sound of screams. She tossed on her robe, dashed to the top of the stairs, and looked down. Eddie was pounding his fists on the hotel manager's door. When the manager opened it, Eddie grabbed him by the lapels of his robe and shook him violently, screaming over and over again, "I'm gonna die, my God, and nobody can stop me! Nobody can stop it!"

Now, the crowd roared with compassionate applause, rising to their feet to give her a standing ovation. Sharon began to cry. She couldn't deal with this. She couldn't deal with any of it. It was Gene's show—they'd turned the tour into a memorial to Eddie—but she just wanted to go home. She needed to go give Gene a hug, though, to just say hello and let him know that, no matter their differences, she loved him. They were, after all, uniquely joined by their cataclysmic sadness. Slowly she made her way to the dressing room. She was about to walk through the door when she heard Gene speak. He was all alone.

"Well, do you think I should wear the black leathers, Ed? Or do you think I should wear this blue shirt?"

Gene was talking to Eddie. It was as if Eddie was right there in the dressing room with him, just as he'd always been. Sharon's heart ached as she quietly shut the door and crept away.

Billy Fury came to Sharon's hospital room. He was crying.

"Gene's daughter died," he said through his sobs.

"No," she said in utter disbelief.

"Yes, he just got a telegram."

He told her about the show that June night at the Nottingham Theatre Royal, where Gene received a telegram informing him that his fourteen-month-old daughter Melody Jean had passed on. "My daughter has died of pneumonia," Gene choked, sorrowful tears streaming down his face. To Gene's horror, the packed audience, who came to share in his "Tribute to Eddie Cochran" show, laughed heartily at his announcement. They thought it was a joke. But when they saw that Gene was actually disconsolate, that this was truly a serious matter, the fans realized that he'd said "daughter," not "dog." Some of them began to cry. After asking to be released from his scheduled dates in Liverpool, Birmingham, and Cardiff, as well as from the contract for the summer season at Blackpool, Gene was to fly home a few days later to be with his wife. "I have not had a proper rest in months," he would whisper just before the curtain came down on his last show. "I must be left entirely alone, and then I can relax completely and think about things."

Sharon couldn't believe such a tragedy could befall Gene so soon after Eddie had died. As much as they didn't get along, her heart hurt for him; she wanted to ease what she thought must be his terrible suffering. So she carefully assembled all her St. Christopher medals and other spiritual and inspirational things that friends and fans had sent along with their get-well wishes and forwarded them on to Gene in London with a long letter telling him how heartbroken and sad she was, how sorry she was for his tremendous loss, and that she was praying for him.

A few days later, the news swept the country that Melody was very much alive and well stateside. Gene claimed that he was the victim of a hoax. Others, including Sharon, believed he sent the telegram to himself. "He put me through so much pain," she'd say bitterly many years later.

Gene was on the road again. It hadn't taken long. In June he flew back to Oregon, spending a relatively quiet summer at home with Darlene and the kids. He talked about finding another career, perhaps in radio, or maybe farming, though he still had two songs on the UK charts. By July's end, "Pistol Packin' Mama" reached number fifteen, and "Crazy Times" peaked at number twelve. In September, Capitol released "Anna Annabelle," from the last Blue Caps sessions, backed with "Pistol Packin' Mama," in the States. "Anna Annabelle" was released in November in the UK, with "Accentuate the Positive," from the *Crazy Times* session, on the flip. With the single's release, Gene was once again back on the concert trail in the States for a few select performances. In September, he was in California, and appeared on a local television show hosted by Black Jack Wayne, Chuck Wayne's brother. The birth of his son, Gene, Jr., on October 13 at Vancouver Memorial Hospital was a blessed event, but the singer was back on the road again in November, playing the Prom Ballroom in St. Paul with Wanda Jackson, then returning in December for a show with the Fendermen.

The new year of 1961 found Gene in Hollywood again, where his name was to be cast in bronze and terrazzo on the sidewalk at 1749 Vine Street, just across from the Capitol Tower. Official groundbreaking ceremonies would take place that February, and in the next sixteen months over fifteen hundred luminaries of motion pictures, television, radio, recording, and theater were permanently memorialized on both sides of Hollywood Boulevard from Gower to La Brea, and down both sides of Vine, from Yucca to Sunset.

Gene arrived at the Capitol studios in January for the first of two days of recording, though this time with no Blue Caps, no Eddie, no Jerry, not even Ken Nelson. Producer Karl Engerman teamed him up with the Jimmy Haskell Orchestra and its chorus, with Scotty Turner on lead guitar, to explore a pop sound more in line with what other chart-toppers—Bobby Rydell, Bobby Vee, and Neil Sedaka—were churning out. Turner was given the responsibility of choosing the material, and he met with Gene in his hotel room to sort through the options. Gene really seemed to like "If You Want My Lovin'," which Turner had penned with John Marascaldo, who'd co-written the Little Richard hits "Rip It Up," "Ready Teddy," and "Good Golly Miss Molly." But in rehearsals, most all of the other songs didn't seem to spark much enthusiasm from Gene. It seemed he was just loafing his way through. Turner became concerned. He was elated, however, when Gene entered into the studio and that red light went on. Gene let it all go, and delivered.

They were able to get eight tunes in the can at the end of two days, including the devious little ditty "Crazy Beat," with its jazzy bass and high-hat intro and exit, penned by Jack Rhodes, composer of "Woman Love," "B-I-Bickey-Bi-Bo-Bo-Go," "Red Bluejeans and a Pony Tail," and "Five Days, Five Days"; "I'm Gonna

Catch Me a Rat," another tune by Jesse Mae Robinson, who'd penned "Keep It a Secret"; "It's Been Nice," a collaboration of Doc Pomus and Mort Schuman, who'd supplied songs to Elvis Presley, Bobby Darin, and many others; and "Teardrops," by Dick Glasser, who also wrote "I Got It," in addition to Turner's "If You Want My Lovin'."

The long rest had worked wonders, Alan Vince thought as he and his brother walked with Don Arden and Henry Henroid into the small reception room in the main complex of London Airport as the sun was just beginning to rise. Gene's plane had landed before they arrived, and he was sitting at a small table, surrounded by reporters, photographers, and fans. Alan couldn't help but notice the remarkable change; the singer looked happy, rested, and fit. Dressed casually in a checked shirt and white leather jacket, Gene chatted easily with the reporters about his work schedule—ballrooms, one-nighters, and TV appearances in the UK, then a quick trip to the United States to appear in a film. Titled *State Fair*, it starred pop singer Pat Boone, with whom Gene played on his first tour of New York fair dates in 1956, though the two would never cross paths on the set and Gene's part would eventually be cut from the movie. He was asked if he was looking forward to it. "Well," Gene said, "I'm not over-keen on filming. I much prefer to sing and work for a live audience." When another reporter asked him why, he answered, "It's all those cameras and lights. They put me off a bit."

After speaking with Vince and his brother briefly about some fan-club business, he was hustled away to London. As the singer requested, Alan and his brother dropped by Gene's rehearsal with his new backing group, the Echoes, later that afternoon. The musicians were competent, Gene seemed comfortable, and after a quick run-through of his familiar songs, the session was over. Gene invited Alan and his brother to his hotel room later for a chat, since he had the evening free. He seemed a bit tired, but relaxed, when they arrived, resting on the bed as they sipped Cokes and chatted about Johnny Meeks, Elvis, Jerry Lee, and Eddie. During the conversation, he tried to ring up his buddy Little Richard, who was also in London at the time. Getting no answer, Gene left his name and number. Soon the phone rang and Richard was on the line. Gene seemed overjoyed to speak with his pal.

Leaving Gene's hotel, Alan thought how nice it was for all the fans—at least for the next three months until he needed to return to the States to shoot his new film—that Gene was back in England again. Even during Gene's absence, Alan received a deluge of letters from kids eager to join the club. The *Crazy Times* album held them over well until Gene could be with them again, and EMI just released another single to coincide with Gene's return. It was an odd choice though—"Jezebel," from Gene's very first album sessions in June of '56, with "Maybe," from the October '58 sessions, on the flip. No matter; Alan was just glad that Gene was back and seemed healthy and happy. Hopefully the nightmare of his last two visits to England was over.

The house in Niles was empty. Darlene and the kids were gone.

Gene and Darlene had been so happy to find the house several months earlier. They both liked the area. Darlene loved being near the Waynes, and Gene, whose leg was bothered by the cold weather in Portland, favored the milder climate and the security of living near a guaranteed gig at the Garden of Allah. Plus, he felt safe leaving his family in Niles while he was away in Europe. But Darlene had finally had enough.

She wanted a real marriage. She wanted to settle down. She hated life on the road. And with Gene's latest return to England, it had become painfully obvious to her that Gene would forever be on the road. She'd wanted to break it off with him for some time, but she was scared. He had that kind of split personality; one side was an angel, and the other side was the devil. She really didn't trust him—he'd get to drinking and get crazy. And she wasn't sure if he'd be crazy enough to use all those pistols and knives he had. She didn't want to find out. So while he was away those three months, doing even more shows and that damn movie, she'd decided to move herself and the kids into an apartment.

Distraught, Gene headed to the Waynes'. Johnnie Wayne knew it was hard on Darlene, raising the kids all by herself while Gene was in Europe. That's why Darlene and the children had come to stay with them when Gene first went over with Eddie Cochran. He seemed to be doing fairly well over there, so they'd found the house in Niles, right near the Waynes. Johnnie'd always thought Gene was a nice guy, though he did seem to have a bit of a temper. It didn't appear to Johnnie that Gene and Darlene argued any more than any other young couple, and Johnnie never saw him drink anything harder than a beer. He seemed to be a good parent and a good provider, though he wasn't much of a saver. And he was sure gone an awful lot. The Waynes phoned Darlene to let her know that Gene was back.

Darlene brought the kids with her to the Waynes. She and Gene talked for a few hours, but it was the same old story. He told her things would be different—just as soon as he got back from another string of gigs in England. Darlene's mind was made up. When a neighbor stopped by to visit with the Waynes, Darlene took advantage of the distraction, grabbed the kids, and left.

Gene was hurt, upset—and all alone.

Gene returned to England, now quite literally the "Mr. Loneliness" of the string-soaked single Capitol/EMI issued in February, coupled with "If You Want My Lovin'." He immediately embarked on a two-week tour, backed by the group Sounds Incorporated, which Henry Henroid had booked. Henroid was born Henri Henriod, the son of a Swiss father and English mother. He grew up in a tough area of South London before entering the Army for National Service, where he excelled at boxing and became a junior Army champion. After leaving the Army, he pulled espressos at the Two I's coffee bar on Old Compton Street in Soho, the same place Larry Parnes had discovered Tommy Steele. The owner, a former wrestler, soon put Henry—who stood just five foot nine, weighed only about one hundred forty pounds, but was as strong as a bull—on the road in wrestling bouts up and down the country. On his travels Henry had the opportunity to meet and associate with the fringe of showbiz, and eventually became acquainted with promoter Don Arden. When Arden became Gene's UK manager, Henry was a natural choice to look after the erstwhile singer on the road. Henry took his new duties seriously, even dressing the part, changing into a professional-looking suit every night, and would become a close friend of Gene's.

The six members of Sounds Incorporated, which augmented the fundamental guitar-bass-drums lineup with saxophones, keyboards, and flute, were thrilled to be accompanying Gene. They were huge Vincent fans since their school days. At their rehearsals, they found Gene to be quiet and unassuming. But they were amazed each night as a black-leathered lunatic with a maniacal gleam in his eye would take the stage, leaping atop pianos, smashing in drums, and busting microphones at every turn. For the band, the personality change was quite exciting; they never knew what to expect each time they performed. But it was also quite frightening.

On May 7, Gene and Sounds Incorporated filmed a spot on the *Thank Your Lucky Stars* television show. Adrian Owlett, who was utterly dumbfounded by Gene's performance at the Kingston Granada in January of 1960 and actually met Gene briefly after his show at the Guildford Odeon in May 1960, rounded up a couple of friends and showed up at the TV studio. As Adrian had hoped, they bumped into Gene and Henry on their way out. Adrian just wanted to say hello, but Gene invited them all to lunch at the Anglers Hotel in Teddington. There Adrian found Gene to be consummately charming, just as he was when they'd first met, and very attentive to him and his friends. At one point Gene slipped Adrian some money and asked him to go get him a bottle of scotch. Adrian was pleased to do it.

Gene Craddock, 1955, with unknown musicians. COURTESY PAT MASON

"Sheriff Tex" Davis (left), with WCMS radio personalities Ted "City Boy" Harding; Ted "Teddy Bear" Crutchfield, who would play briefly with Gene; "Country Art" Barett; and "Cornbread-fed Uncle Ted" Tatar. COURTESY WCMS

Gene and the Blue Caps in the WCMS studio rehearsing for their first concert to 1956. COURTESY WCMS

The 1957 Blue Caps
the Craddock house
Portsmouth, Virginia
Clockwise from top:
Gene Vincent, Johnn
Meeks, Bill Mack, P
Peek, Tommy Facene
and Dickie Harrell.

Gene Vincent, 1956. COURTESY WCMS

Gene Vincent at Matter's Ballroom, Decorah, Iowa, August 9, 1957.
COURTESY JOHN MATTER

ne and the Blue Caps on the *Hot Rod Gang* set, 1958. Tommy "Bubba" Facenda
ft), Grady Owen, Gene Vincent, Johnny Meeks, Paul Peek, and Juvey Gomez.

Gene Vincent, backstage at the Yakima Armory, Yakima, Washington, June 12, 195[
© 1988 LIGGETT TAYLOR

Gene (right) with Jack Mashburn (left), Carlos White,
and Bill Carter, 1960. RICKY QUISOL ARCHIVES

ne Vincent, 1961.

URTESY PAT MASON

Gene (left) with John Lennon.

ALAN CLARK ARCHIVES

y Fury (left), Jess Conrad, Gene Vincent, Joe Brown, Eddie Cochran, Adam
:h, and host Marty Wilde on *Boy Meets Girls*, England, 1960.

M THE COLLECTION OF TOMMIE WIX

Gene (left) and Jerry Lee Lewis, 1964. BEAR FAMILY ARCHIVES

Clockwise from left: Aynsley Dunbar, unidentified membe of Flame, Gene Vincent, unidentified member of Flam Bruce Johnston of the Beach Boys, Del Shannon, unknow Kim Fowley, and Rodney Bingenheimer at a party in Hollywood.
COURTESY KIM FOWLEY

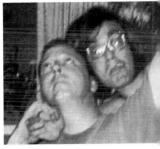

Gene (left) with Ronny We August 29, 1971, less than months before his death.
COURTESY RONNY WEISER

At the end of May, Gene flew to South Africa, where he had a hit with "Mitchiko From Tokyo," which, as a single, was only released there. He was backed by Mickie Most, a Decca recording artist from England, and his band on a two-week tour. Then he returned to the UK, where "She She Little Sheila," backed with "Hot Dollar," issued in May, had started a steady climb up the charts, eventually reaching number twenty-two.

He continued touring with Sounds Incorporated, who were getting used to his eccentric behavior. He took to riding with the band in the bus, rather than the big, private car he usually traveled in, making them stop regularly for what he said were Cokes. The band would later figure out it was scotch. He'd drink his liquor and then go to sleep, although he always had plenty of sleeping pills with him, just in case. In Gloucestershire, Gene collapsed on the pavement outside the concert hall. The band grew concerned as he lay there, stock still in his black leather, his eyes and mouth wide open. Then he smirked. The band picked him up, threw him in the back of the van, and headed on to the next show. It had become an increasingly difficult chore to get Gene onstage. Sometimes he would lock himself into the dressing room, and Henry would have to coax him out. Or if that didn't work, Henry would simply bang the door down. When Gene would finally emerge, the atmosphere was tense, like the entrance of the mad, stamping bull into the matador's ring. The crowd would give a bloodthirsty roar, and they'd open the wild beast's cage and let him out—for better or worse.

The phone at Bubba Facenda's house rang at three in the morning. His wife picked it up.

"Honey, it's Gene," she said.

"Gene who?" Bubba asked.

"Gene Vincent," she said, handing him the phone.

Bubba could tell Gene was upset. He was asking him to fly to England, to get all the old Blue Caps together and come on over.

Bubba could hardly believe it. It had been years since he'd heard from any of those guys, except for Dickie, who still lived in Portsmouth, as he did.

"Gene, I don't even know if Johnny or Paul or Bobby are still alive! I haven't talked to them since we went on that tour."

Gene started crying as Bubba told him it would be impossible for him to come over at the moment. He explained that he was now married, had a job that he loved as a firefighter, and that he just couldn't be there for him. In the back of Bubba's mind, like Gene's, he knew that as long as they were alive, one day they'd all get back together again. But that was not this day. Bubba tried to cheer Gene up, saying he'd heard that things had been going really well for him in Europe. He wished him the best of luck.

Bubba felt bad for Gene as he hung up the phone.

The King of Ballrooms was not well.

On May 3 Gene was helped off the stage at the Guildford Plaza, one of the countless British dance halls that booked Gene on the strength of his guaranteed massive draw. The singer was utterly exhausted. He'd been up since dawn and working all day as he and Sounds Incorporated recorded five songs for the "Saturday Club" radio show in London. When the shooting was finally completed that evening, he was immediately rushed to the ballroom to face the six hundred restless teenagers who surged screaming to the stage the moment he appeared. He launched into yet another wild performance—legs kicking, sliding, and bending, microphone whirling—but after just twenty minutes he could not continue. A few weeks later, at the Newcastle Magestic in June, he fell down a flight of thirty stairs and was unconscious for nearly an hour. He'd been rushing to his dressing room after being mobbed by teenagers who swamped the stage at the close of his fifty-minute act. In Glasgow in August, after the last show of a ten-day tour of Scottish ballrooms, Gene collapsed once again in his dressing room and had to be taken to the Glasgow Royal Infirmary. He rested there for two days, then insisted on leaving to fulfill his dates at Lydley and Rumford. He collapsed again.

"Gene is very sick," Arden told the *New Musical Express*, "and at one point near death. It is best that he should return to the States."

Gene flew out of London Airport just days before Capitol/EMI issued his latest recording with Sounds Incorporated, prophetically titled "I'm Going Home." The song would make it onto the charts, eventually peaking at number thirty-six. It would be his last charting single.

After a brief recuperation, the singer was back to work in the States, recording "Baby, Don't Believe Him" and "Lucky Star" at the Capitol studios in Hollywood with a band led by guitarist Dave Burgess, who was in the Champs when they'd toured with the Blue Caps. Then it was on to England, where EMI issued another odd pairing, "Brand New Beat" from the December 1957 sessions and "Unchained Melody," waxed in October 1956.

Gene was infuriated. "That record should never have been released," the singer fumed to a reporter. "It was made in 1956 for an album, but I had no say in it being released here. If I had, it would never have come out. It's a ballad and just isn't what the fans expect from me." He knew the British kids liked to rock; hell, that's what they were paying to see every night and that's why he could still pull in the crowds without any chart-topping hits. Sure, he thought every now and again about changing his style to something more pop-oriented—he was experimenting with new sounds on his latest recordings—but he knew that the fans, the true Black Leather Rebel fans, didn't want it. They wanted "Be-Bop-A-Lula," "Say Mama," "Bluejean Bop." And he wasn't about to let those fans down. They had long memories on this side of the Atlantic, he'd found, and they were the most faithful fans in the world. As far as they were concerned, he'd noticed, it wasn't what you got now, but what success you'd had in the past that counted. If he started to change his style now, he knew, they'd drop him quicker than that. He'd just recorded a couple of songs with Sounds at the Abbey Road studios, "There I Go Again (Whoops I'm Dreaming)" and "Spaceship to Mars," which he'd also just filmed for the new movie *It's Trad Dad*. They were both the type of songs his fans associated him with, he told the press, and he felt the backings and arrangements were terrific. He was hopeful his fans would go for them.

He'd shot his part in *It's Trad Dad* in December at the Shepperton sound studios. Written and produced for Columbia by Milton Subotsky—who'd also helmed the 1957 rock 'n' roll films *Disc Jockey Jamboree*, featuring Jerry Lee Lewis, Buddy Knox, Carl Perkins, and Fats Domino, and *Rock! Rock! Rock!*, showcasing Chuck Berry, Frankie Lymon and the Teenagers, and the Johnny Burnette Trio—the film was a bid to cash in on the UK's current "trad" jazz movement, a curious preoccupation with pre–World War I New Orleans jazz. The story followed the exploits of teens Helen Shapiro and Craig Douglas, who, when their coffee bar hangout lost its jukebox license because the mayor hated their jazz and pop music, rallied various disc jockeys to make things right. They crashed various radio shows, enabling twenty-seven musical performances to be included in the film. In addition to Gene, fellow Norfolk, Virginian Gary U.S. Bonds—who sang backing vocals on Bubba's solo "High School USA"—made an appearance, as well as Del Shannon, Chubby Checker, and various British trad bands. During his number, Gene sang, dressed in all-white leather, in an all-white studio, framed in the camera shot by a guitar neck being played on the left and the crook of a wailing saxophone's neck on the right.

He wore that white leather again in March, when he kicked off another British tour, this time co-headlining with Brenda Lee, at the Brighton Essoldo. Billed as the King and Queen of Rock, the pair, both backed by Sounds Incorporated, rolled out a show that was a throwback to the earliest, wildest days of rock 'n' roll. Lee, who last appeared in the UK three years prior, offered her throaty hits, including "Dynamite," "Dum Dum," "Kansas City," and

"Sweet Nuthins." Gene, whom Lee held in the highest esteem—he "was just wonderful, a wonderful entertainer and just a very sweet, gentle person," she'd say later—included Little Richard's "Lucille" and "Tutti Frutti" in his set, along with his early hits like "Say Mama" and "Bluejean Bop," later tunes like "Corrina Corrina" and "She She Little Sheila," the crowd-pleasing "Over the Rainbow," and his latest single "Lucky Star," which was released that month with "Baby, Don't Believe Him" on the back.

The show was a rousing success with fans and critics, though the music press continued to marvel at Gene's ongoing ability to attract full houses despite no smash hits in years. Calling his style "six years out of date," the wags noted that any other artist trying to get away with sticking with his old repertoire of familiar songs would surely be laughed off the stage. "Gene's fans take him as seriously as he takes himself," one magazine wrote. "He is devoted to the life he leads and is completely carried away when he has a mike in his hand and a rockin' band behind him." His perpetual draw was credited to his live show, "an excitement that has to be seen, as well as heard, to be properly experienced."

One night, at a party after a tour stop at the Granada in Tooting, Gene—who'd returned to his black-leather stage gear after just a few performances—met Margaret Russell, a twenty-one-year-old beauty who worked as a showgirl at Murray's, a nightclub in London's West End. She was a friend of Henry's from his days managing the Two I's coffeehouse in Soho. Soon, she and Gene were inseparable. In May, when Alan Vince, after doing some fan-club business at the EMI offices, called on Gene at his London apartment not far from Marble Arch, Margie was there. It was one of Gene's rare days off, and he invited Alan to go to lunch and go shopping with them. Margie said little, but Gene seemed relaxed and fit. And very happy.

After gigging on the Continent briefly—he did not yet have a current British work permit—Gene was back at Abbey Road on July 3 with the Charles Blackwell Orchestra and Chorus for his third

British recording session, produced by Bob Barratt, Norrie Paramor's assistant at EMI. Gene got along very well with Paramor, thought Charles Blackwell was an extremely talented man, and didn't really mind not recording in the more familiar Capitol tower. He always felt that working in a new environment could produce something from an artist that he didn't know he had. Something just a little different, like the twist version of "Be-Bop-A-Lula" they came up with at Abbey Road. They also got "King of Fools," "You're Still in My Heart," and "Held for Questioning" in the can. He was pleased, but he wasn't necessarily relying on any of the records he cut in Britain becoming a chart winner. He only really needed them to sell well. It always helped, of course, to have a hit in the charts simultaneous to a tour, but he felt that it wasn't really necessary if one was a name artist, as he was. Hits didn't give guaranteed drawing power, he thought. He never totally ignored the charts. But he thought it was stupid to rely on them as a reflection of an artist's popularity. Because here he was, without any major hits, ready to embark once again on a tour of one-nighters through seashore and summer resorts in Italy.

Margie accompanied Gene, but the affair that started so seemingly happily turned tempestuous. Outside the venue after one of the Italian shows, Henry was having trouble getting paid by the promoter. Inside the bus, Gene and the feisty Margie began to argue, and it turned violent. As Henry and the members of Sounds Incorporated tried to break up the ugly lovers' brawl, Gene caught his left leg on one of the seats and broke it, unbeknownst to the others. Outside, the promoter watched wide-eyed in amazement at the violent goings-on. Sure that he was dealing with a busload of psychopaths, he immediately handed over the money.

The next gig, across the Appenine Mountains, was a night's drive away. As the rest of the band and crew dozed and the Italian bus driver flew along the curves and hairpin turns, Gene suddenly awakened in excruciating pain. His leg was so badly swollen that it had burst the seams of his trouser leg. "Henry," he drawled quietly. "He's broken my leg, Henry." They found a hospital, where Gene's leg was set in a cast. The rest of the band drove on to the show, leaving Henry and a crew member to accompany Gene. Henry suggested to Gene that he might just cancel the next gig, but Gene insisted that he wanted to perform. So they rented a car and rushed off to catch the bus. Soon they pulled into an all-night restaurant so Gene could use the bathroom. A few minutes later, Gene hobbled out on his crutches, the restaurant's owner giving chase behind him hollering, "Polizia! Polizia!" Gene had swiped a bottle of whiskey, tucking it under his arm. Dumbfounded at Gene's ability to sniff out liquor—even in the Italian mountainside in the wee hours of the morning—Henry paid off the owner and hustled Gene back into the car.

They finally caught up with the band at the next town. Henry checked Gene into the hotel, then went to the venue to check on the sound system. Suddenly Margie ran in. "Quick!" she shouted. "Get back to the hotel!" Henry dashed to Gene's room. Gene was sitting in a bathtub full of hot water, prying his new cast off with a coat hanger. Infuriated, Henry dragged him from the tub. As the porous plaster began to dry, it started to shrink, squeezing the afflicted leg in a chalky death grip. Gene was in agony. Henry rushed him back to the hospital to have his leg refitted with yet another cast. That night, Gene performed sitting on a stool.

Gene and Margie flew to Germany after the Italian tour was complete, to be joined by Sounds Incorporated at the newly opened Star Club in Hamburg, a haven for both Germany's rowdy rockers and arty existentialists. But the band took the train from Italy and did not arrive in time for opening night. Instead, Gene was backed by the Beatles, the British group who'd opened up for him once at the Cavern Club in Liverpool in the summer of 1961. Since then the kids had recorded with Tony Sheridan, backing him on his single "My Bonnie," which had done reasonably well on the German charts. Gene liked the band, who took to wearing black leather, just like their hero, and enjoyed working with them on the stage with its skyscraper set. Like the Italian tour, the two-week run at the Star

Club was marked by increasing antagonism between Gene and Margie, Gene eventually accusing almost every member of the band and crew, including Henry, of sleeping with Margie.

Despite their near-constant feuding, Gene and Margie moved in together on their return to England, renting a modern, semi-detached, three-bedroom house in Welling, Kent, in August. Gene was troubled because as an American citizen, he'd already played the number of weeks allowed by his yearly working permit; he would have to wait until next March before he could legally tour Britain again. Not being able to work in Britain also handicapped promotion of his new record, "King of Fools." Television engagements scheduled behind the disc had to be canceled because they were also forbidden by the permit.

Setting up a home base in England was not easy. He was still receiving a pension of $127.10 a month from the motorcycle accident he'd had while on active duty, and though the government money was inconsequential compared to his show-business earnings, it did give Uncle Sam some say in where he lived. He was able to get permission to live in England for the moment, though.

Gene certainly didn't feel his healthiest, either. He'd just recovered from a bout of flu he'd picked up during the tour of Italy and the short residency in Germany, and he was putting a lot of energy into the new house, since he would be off again in a few days to spend four weeks in Israel, followed by a tour of France.

"I'm dying, I'm dying," Gene murmured over and over at the hospital in Haifa.

Within their first week of shows in Israel, Henry had received a frantic phone call at the venue from the backing band's keyboard player. Gene was dying, he told Henry, and he'd already called the ambulance. Henry hurried back to the hotel. The ambulance arrived and Gene was whisked away on a stretcher. At the hospital, the doctors could find nothing wrong with the singer. They were appalled at Gene's self-centered behavior. The police were called and Gene narrowly missed being charged with misuse of an ambulance. Henry canceled the rest of the Israel tour. In France, Gene instigated a brawl with the hotel staff in Paris and battled yet again with Margie. Henry took to calling her "Rocky" because of the racoon-like black eyes she sported regularly.

While he was at home resting from the tour through France, which was hailed as one of the country's most successful ever by a rock 'n' roll artist, Gene learned that his application to work in Britain had finally been approved. His manager and agent, Don Arden, immediately set about booking dates for him, planning around an operation on Gene's leg scheduled for December.

Arden put Gene back out on the road on November 21 for a jaunt through the UK with Adam Faith, whom Gene first met when they'd appeared on a television show together. They opened at the Rialto in York, and finished up on December 9 after a three-week run at the De Montfort Hall, Leicester. Gene changed his look somewhat for his latest outing, replacing his trademark black leather jerkin and heavy-metal medallion with a black leather jacket, neat black tailored trousers, a white shirt with a frill front, and a fly-away bow tie. He was backed by the Echoes for the tour, while Sounds Incorporated finished up their own stint in Hamburg. Gene's pals the Beatles, with whom he'd become quite friendly during his summer run in Hamburg, broke into the British charts that month with their debut single "Love Me Do." The group's "Please Please Me," with its singular harmonies and contagious beat, would vault to number one not long after. It was to be the start of an unparalleled run of fifteen consecutive chart-toppers and a Beatlemania epidemic of international proportions.

Here she was, married just moments ago at the registry office in Dartford, Kent, to Gene Vincent, rock 'n' roll singer extraordinaire at the peak of his career. And how were they celebrating? With a drink at the nearest pub. A goddamn drink.

Margie had accepted Gene's insistent marriage proposal, which came with a gift of a white miniature poodle, after his return from yet another tour. The January jaunt had come dangerously close on the heels of the operation on his leg at St. George's Hospital on Hyde Park Corner in London. He'd actually seemed to be taking some sort of stock of his life then. With fatherhood an almost certain reality again—Margie told him she was pregnant and he seemed thrilled—Gene planned to write his memoirs while recuperating, dictating his life story into a tape recorder to be written into a book for publication later in the year. But it never happened.

And now here they were, celebrity newlyweds, able to afford the most lavish of celebrations, hunkered down in a dank corner pub. Drink, Margie thought. This is what dominated our lives.

Gene's drinking was beginning to soil his professional reputation as well. During a tour of France a few days after his marriage, Gene and Henry were invited to dine with top executives of Pathe Marconi, the French distributor of Gene's records. Gene arrived at the elegant Paris restaurant very drunk. He further amazed the Pathe brass by pounding on the table and demanding, "Gimme my money! Gimme my money!" Henry and Don Arden—who one day had even had to send some of the fellows from Sounds Incorporated over to the house to break up yet another row between Gene and Margie—knew something had to be done. Desperate, they took Gene to a doctor on Harley Street who claimed he could cure him of his alcoholism by giving him a drug that would make his body reject alcohol. Gene was fed intravenously while he slept for days. Not long after he awoke, though, Henry found him stone drunk once more. "I did it, Henry," he boasted with booze-soaked pride. "I fucked them doctors. I ain't sick!"

In April, a month after Capitol/EMI released *The Crazy Beat of Gene Vincent*—comprised of the '61 sessions with the Jimmie Haskell Orchestra, plus some unissued Blue Caps cuts—the doctors who'd operated on Gene's leg ordered that he stay off of it for at least a week. Gene and Margie flew to Majorca, off the coast of Spain, for a brief holiday, and then it was back to work, with a stint in Paris. They were greeted at the airport and at the Hotel Napoleon by thousands of adoring fans, and every night in his hotel room Gene boozily basked in the attentions of the French celebrities who would stop by to pay homage to the Black Leather Rebel.

Back at home in England, despite the birth on May 29 of his second daughter, Sherri Ann, Gene continued to drink. Just prior to his pals the Beatles reaching number one on the UK charts in May with "From Me to You," Gene's contract with Capitol had expired. And it was not renewed. Margie convinced herself that Sherri Ann's birth would mean they would finally settle down, but Gene continued to perform. She watched as his wages began to drop. And the less he earned, the more he seemed to drink. A virtual twenty-four-hour patrol of Gene and his access to alcohol was imposed prior to shows, but Margie watched him get around it with the ingenuity of a dedicated drinker. He'd simply pay, on the sly, various groupies and hangers-on to fetch him small, flat flasks of whiskey that he could slip into his pocket or stuff down his cast. To everyone's dismay, he'd grow progressively drunker all day.

Ritchie Blackmore was in the back of the band van with the rest of the Outlaws. Gene was sitting up front. They were traveling to a gig, one of the countless live shows and media appearances they'd done since they'd first starting backing Gene several months ago, taking over from Sounds Incorporated, who'd landed their own record deal with Columbia.

Ritchie, who in '69 would join organist Jon Lord to form the heavy metal group Deep Purple, was pleased to be playing behind Gene Vincent. The young guitarist, who'd also worked with Jerry Lee Lewis, had always enjoyed Gene's music—particularly the early hits like "Be-Bop-A-Lula," "Bluejean Bop," and "Lotta Lovin' "—and was especially impressed by the articulate technique of Gene's first guitarist Cliff Gallup. Like most other aspiring British rock 'n' rollers, Ritchie admired Gene, and he found him to be professional and very polite. He was aware that Gene was drinking while they were working together, though Gene kept it pretty much to himself. And Gene could be a lot of fun, often taking part in the practical jokes the band would play to pass the endless hours on the road. Like today.

When the van pulled to a stop for a moment, Ritchie hopped out, pulled out his trusty slingshot, took aim, and fired. He jumped quickly back into the van. His aim was true and the woman whose back had served as Ritchie's bull's eye was none too happy about it. She turned to see Gene, who'd observed the whole thing, laughing heartily in the front seat. Thinking she'd found her culprit, she marched right up to his open window, reached inside, and slapped the famous rock star right across the face. Ritchie didn't think Gene was too pleased. But he and the band thought it was hysterical.

Gene felt as savage as any man can when people tell him his wife's been having an affair. The cold rage, the darkling heart, seized him again, taking over. That's why he pulled the Luger on Margie when he returned to their London home from his gig at the Star Club in Hamburg. But he could never have pulled the trigger, he knew. He could never have murdered her. He loved her too much. He did it just to scare her.

And he did just that. Fearing for her and Sherri Ann's lives, Margie phoned the police for help. They found the gun, loaded with five cartridges, tucked away under a mattress when they arrived. The revolver, plus another pistol, was confiscated, and Gene was fined twenty pounds for keeping guns and ammunition without a license. He was given a year's conditional discharge for assaulting his wife. In court, Gene's counsel explained that while the singer was appearing on the Continent, "other parties" made remarks to him about his domestic affairs. "As a result," the lawyer said, "certain domestic difficulties arose, which resulted in the conduct you have just heard of."

Gene and Margie had already made up by that time, though, and he hobbled out of court on crutches, his wife by his side, to attend a BBC recording session. "I hope my fans remember my name is Gene Vincent and not Gene Autry," he'd say of the incident later. "While I was in the United States Navy I was a crack marksman," he boasted. "I have a collection of guns at home in New Mexico and the guns in this case were given to me by friends in Germany for that collection. I guess I just brandished one in a moment of temper."

It had been more than a year. Gene hadn't been in a recording studio since the July 1962 sessions at Abbey Road with the Charles Blackwell Orchestra that had produced the twisting "Be-Bop-A-Lula '62." After his October tour through France and Belgium—twenty-five cities in twenty-eight days—Columbia, his new record company home, put him into the studio right away. On November 14, they paired him with the Bill Shepherd Orchestra at the Olympic recording complex in London to wax a poignant version of the Arthur Alexander single "Where Have You Been All My Life," "The Beginning of the End," written for Gene by Bob Barratt under the name Dwayne Detroit, and "Temptation Baby," composed by British producer Joe Meek for the pop music movie *Live It Up*. Meek, who wrote most of the film's music, helmed sessions, some of them hit-making, for acts like the Tornadoes, Heinz and Screaming Lord Sutch, and Gene's pals in the Outlaws and Sounds Incorporated. Both groups also appeared in *Live It Up*, along with fair-haired Heinz, who landed a key acting role as well. Gene shot his brief part in the film, singing "Temptation Baby" to a shapely chick promenading around a steel-tired traction train engine, the following month.

Later in November, Columbia brought Gene back to Olympic, this time with the Ivor Raymonde Orchestra, to record three pop numbers, "La Den Da Den Da Da," a contagious reworking of the 1958 Dale Hawkins tune "La Do Dada," the twisting "Humpity Dumpity," a nursery rhyme novelty written by Raymonde himself, and Joy Byers' "A Love 'Em and Leave 'Em Kinda Guy."

Then it was back on the road, Gene joining Duane Eddy for a

tour, stopping at London, Liverpool, and Manchester. Al Casey, who'd played with Sanford Clark when the singer had toured with Gene and the Blue Caps in the fifties, was now with Eddy, who was also joined on the tour by Little Richard and the Shirelles. One night Al and Duane ended up over at Gene's residence, a pleasant but modest flat. To their surprise, Gene dragged out a collection of Nazi memorabilia—pictures, iron crosses, and other artifacts. He seemed quite proud of it, causing Al to wonder whether Gene actually ascribed to some ultra-right wing philosophy. But Gene didn't mention any political leanings, so Al concluded he just collected the stuff because it was probably hard to come by.

The American musicians were shocked to hear the news that their idealistic young president, John F. Kennedy, had been assassinated on November 20. Gene took it especially hard, limping all the way down to the embassy to see if there was anything he could do. It seemed to Duane that Gene thought World War III was going to break out. "Well, I'll have to go home, because they'll want me to go back in the Navy," Gene told Al, who was a bit taken aback by Gene's patriotic fantasy. They had to talk him into finishing the tour and not catching the next flight out to the States.

One of the wildest musical spectaculars ever seen on television, one reporter called it.

*Whole Lotta Shakin' Goin On*, a Granada TV production that aired in March, kicked off with a set by the British group the Animals, who would later find international fame with their "House of the Rising Sun." Gene, clad from head to toe in shiny black leather, came next. And Jerry Lee Lewis, pounding his piano with both hands and feet, closed the program. It was all shot in front of a live audience, and by the show's end, the fans were positively frantic.

Vincent and Lewis. He couldn't have come up with a more appropriate pairing, producer Johnny Hamp thought. As far as technique went, the two rock 'n' roll legends had no masters.

Almost every modern beat group and singer modeled themselves on performers like Vincent and Lewis. The network had received sixty thousand letters requesting a repeat of their Little Richard special; he expected an even bigger response to Gene and Jerry Lee.

Gene knocked out five songs on the show, backed by the Shouts, his new touring band. They'd blazed their way through France and Switzerland just a couple of weeks earlier, causing a riot in Lausanne when zealous fans uprooted their seats in protest of the iron curtain that was dropped to deter them from jumping onto the stage. He did "Lula," of course, and his screaming take on the 1962 Ray Charles hit "You Are My Sunshine." He and the band had just put the tune to tape a few days before, along with a remake of the Clovers '56 single "Love Love Love" and Sammy Turner's 1959 hit ballad "Lavender Blue." "Say Mama" went over well on the show, and he finished up with "I'm Going Home (To See My Baby)" and Richard's "Long Tall Sally." Gene didn't bother with either sides of his December single, "Temptation Baby" and "Where Have You Been All My Life," or his February release, "Humpity Dumpity," backed with "A Love 'Em And Leave 'Em Kinda Guy." None of the songs had charted. There just wasn't any room on the charts anymore for a solo singer, it seemed, what with the Rolling Stones breaking through with "I Wanna Be Your Man" at the end of 1963, the Beatles landing yet another hit with "I Want to Hold Your Hand" in January, and the Stones finally making the Top 10 with their remake of Buddy Holly's "Not Fade Away."

No matter. There was always the road, always another show. Always another screaming audience a little further round the bend, like the package tour of the UK starting the very next day. Just him and his old buddy Carl Perkins—with the Animals as the headliner.

It was beginning to feel like a treadmill, all forward momentum but never really getting anywhere. Back into the studio in April with the Shouts to wax covers of three of Richard's songs, "Slip-pin' and Slidin'," "Long Tall Sally," and "Good Golly Miss Molly," plus the silly "Shimmy Shammy Shingle," and "Private Detective," released as a single in August with "You Are My Sunshine." Then into the studio with the band again in June to record Richard's "Send Me Some Lovin' " and "Hey Hey Hey Hey," Sam Cooke's "Another Saturday Night," the Jimmy Hodges classic "Someday," Dale Hawkins' "Susie Q" and a modern-day "Baby Blue." Back out on the road—France in March and May with the Shouts, Scandinavia in October, the UK with assorted pick-up bands in between. Pills and booze for the leg, a few misadventures on the concert trail, like the time he'd pulled a gun on the Shouts in a hotel room for laughing at his song idea. "I've got something that's bigger than all of you lads," he'd bellowed, then reached into his suitcase, and pulled out a gun. It seemed to be a starter pistol—but the band wasn't about to ask. Then the release of his first full-lengther for Columbia, *Shakin' Up a Storm*, in October, comprised of all of the Shouts sessions from that year. And still no hits.

Spinning wheels, forward momentum, but never really getting anywhere.

Dickie Harrell was on the phone.

He had heard that Gene was in the hospital for his ear. It had gotten worse during the tour of France and Germany with the Puppets. One night in Bremen he'd even had to be rushed to the hospital because of the blood coming from his ear, accompanied by excruciating pain. It was some kind of infection, pretty serious, in fact, so he'd gone to the Royal National Ear, Nose, and Throat Hospital on Gray's Inn Road in London for an emergency operation.

Gene was glad to hear from his old buddy. For years after Gene had first gone to England, there was talk of the Blue Caps coming over to join him. But the equal exchange—one British band had to go to America for every American band that went to Britain— had never been worked out. Gene wanted someone, anyone, to come over, and, besides Bubba, asked both Jerry Merritt and

Johnny Meeks at various times to join him. Jerry had to decline because of marital problems, and Johnny, well, he had gotten some film work and was happy in Los Angeles. Gene still held out hope that maybe one day the Blue Caps would come to England, and it would be just like old times. The good times.

"I wouldn't mind coming over and just traveling with you for maybe a week or so," Dickie told his friend, who sounded very lonely.

"That'd be nice," Gene said. "Then I'd have somebody to talk to."

But it never did materialize.

Blackpool was terrific, Adrian thought. Gene, who'd landed a three-month summer season gig at the resort, was in great form and the audiences at the town's South Pier Theatre, where he was backed by his new group, the Puppets, absolutely loved him. Adrian, who'd read in the papers early in the summer that Gene was seriously considering the leg amputation that doctors had been recommending since his accident in 1955, had sent him a friendly letter in Blackpool. Soon he received a reply, a letter signed by Gene but written in another's hand. A few days later Gene himself called, inviting Adrian out to Blackpool and the roomy four-bedroom house he rented for the band and himself—and Jackie.

The marriage to Margie was over. While visiting his family in the States over the New Year holiday, Gene had flown down to Mexico to obtain a divorce. He "really loved that girl," Gene told Adrian in Blackpool, but things had just not worked out. But Gene appeared happy now, and pretty Jackie Frisco obviously loved him deeply and took very good care of him, Adrian observed. The story Adrian pieced together of their romance was that they'd met in South Africa in the early sixties, backstage at one of Gene's shows with Mickie Most, who'd had hits with his own versions of Chuck Berry's "Johnny B. Goode" and Ray Peterson's "Corrine Corrina" before returning to England to become the Animals' producer.

Jackie was Most's very young sister-in-law. Gene told the star-struck girl then to come back and see him when she was sixteen. And she had.

Gene did fourteen shows a week at Blackpool, just four songs a show, "Bluejean Bop," "Dance to the Bop," "The Last Word in Lonesome Is Me," which always brought a rapturous hush over the boisterous vacationing crowds, and "Be-Bop-A-Lula." He added "Pretty Girls Everywhere" for the BBC's live broadcast of the "Saturday Club" radio show on August 7. Gene had done another live spot a few months earlier in March, performing "What'd I Say" and "Whole Lotta Shakin' Goin' On" at the Cavern in Liverpool for French TV, and "Be-Bop-A-Lula" in Cannes in April for another French television broadcast.

Sundays in Blackpool, Gene performed a charity show for youngsters with cerebral palsy and other afflictions, for whom he'd become a sort of hero. Over the years he occasionally visited hospitals and restorative care centers to meet and speak with seriously injured patients. Adrian witnessed one show at the Woolwich Odeon where there had been a party of handicapped kids at the front of the auditorium. Gene stopped the set, rolled up his pant leg, told them the story of his injury, and urged them to always follow their dreams despite their disabilities. The crowd reaction was nearly atomic.

Gene's own leg was still a constant source of pain, Adrian noticed, and the over-the-counter pain relievers he'd been taking when they'd first met had been replaced by a considerable reliance on prescription pain killers. His drinking habits had changed, too, Adrian observed. When they'd first met, he was drinking scotch. Now he'd moved on to Red Martini, at least four bottles a day in Adrian's estimation. Hidden away or left out in the open, bottles were everywhere. Gene must have known he was an alcoholic, Adrian thought, but he simply referred to himself as a "man who likes to drink." He seldom appeared to be drunk, though, Adrian marveled, and concealed his intoxication well. He was obviously used to drinking and had an extraordinary threshold before keeling over like some of the lesser drinkers who visited the house.

Though other artists playing Blackpool—Gerry and the Pacemakers, Manfred Mann, and P. J. Proby—would regularly drop by to party or play poker, at which Gene was a master, Gene often seemed to prefer the company of "ordinary" folks. He'd take the bus down to the South Pier, sometimes stopping off at Uncle Tom's Cabin, a huge, virtually featureless barracks-type pub, for a chat and a drink. He seemed to like the fact that he could be completely incognito there and enjoy his pint in noisy surroundings like everyone else. Later he'd walk down the pier, signing autographs, or pop into the pub next to the theater for a chat with the bartender. He'd been like that since Adrian had known him, actually. When he was on the road with Henry, one of his favorite stop-over places was the Busy Bee, a truck stop. Gene insisted on going there and spent many hours with the truckers, just shooting the breeze or eating egg and chips, though he never really ate much, no matter where he dined. Gene was a star, Adrian was well aware, but he retained a very human touch as well.

## IV

*Well, thought I was smart, the race was won,*
*Here come the Devil doin' a hundred and one!*
*Move, hot rod! Move, man!*
*Move, hot rod! Move, man!*
*Move, hot rod! Move me on down the line!*

"YOU'RE NOT GOING TO BELIEVE WHO'S OVER HERE," BUBBA FA-cenda's mama told him over the phone.

"Who?" he asked.

"Gene Vincent."

She was right. He didn't believe it. After so many years away, Gene was back at his parents' house just a street away. Just like old times.

"Gene's over there?"

"He sure is. Do you want to talk to him?"

Gene got on the phone. So it really was him.

"Gene!" Bubba said. "Damn, you're not but a block away. Come on down!"

Gene showed up at Bubba's doorstep within minutes. He had Jackie with him, a kind of cute girl, Bubba thought, with short dark hair. They sat and talked awhile, catching up on each other's lives. Gene couldn't believe that Bubba had been the Tommy Fa-cenda of "High School USA." Bubba explained that since his first name was also Eugene and he didn't want to seem as if he was trying to imitate Gene, he'd used his middle name, Tommy, on his record. Gene thought maybe it had been one of Bubba's cousins up in New York.

Gene didn't tell Bubba, or the reporter for the Portsmouth newspaper who interviewed him while he was in town, that he'd had to leave the UK suddenly, that he owed a lot of people a lot of money, including the tax man and his ex-wife Margie. And Gene didn't tell Bubba, or the reporter, that those people were eager to do whatever they needed to collect. He kept things upbeat with both, telling the reporter that he'd just finished a tour with the Beatles—"We were friends before they became famous and we're still friends," he said—and that, in fact, he was on his way to Hollywood to record a song that his friend Paul McCartney wrote for him.

It was a pleasant enough visit with his old pal, but Gene was itching to leave after about an hour.

Gene just couldn't go through with it.

He and Jackie had driven to Albuquerque, New Mexico, where his parents and sisters were now located, and he'd checked himself into the Veteran's Administration Hospital there. Osteomyelitis was eating away at his leg, day by excruciating day, leaving dead and black the shrunken bone behind it, visible beneath the gaping wound that would never, ever heal. He'd nearly made the crucial decision, to have the dying leg off at last, to finally rid himself of his tyrannical companion, the cursed splinter of a limb that had thwarted his every move for an entire decade. But on the eve of the operation, he had second thoughts. Maybe something else could be done. New things, miraculous new procedures and treatments, were being done with new drugs every day. Maybe a cure would come for him one day soon. Perhaps he should wait just a while longer.

He fled the hospital clothed only in his gown, still the tortured captain of his own pain.

Jerry Merritt loved having Gene out at the Yakima farm. He'd called Jerry before the holidays, after he'd returned to Los Angeles from a two-month stint in South Africa, where he and Jackie visited with her family, relaxed on the beach, and Gene had attempted to teach her nephews how to send smoke signals. He'd also purchased for one of the boys his very first penknife. Since then Gene had been in the studio with his old friends Al Casey and Dave Burgess. Burgess, of the Champs, was now a head honcho at Challenge Records, and they were working on tracks for a new Vincent album. Some of the other Champs, fellows who'd joined up after "Tequila" reached number one, were in the studio, too: Musicians like guitarist Glen Campbell, who would go on to enjoy a wildly successful career as a country singer; drummer Dash Crofts and sax man Jimmy Seals, who would sell millions of records in the seventies as the pop-rock duo Seals and Crofts; and David Gates, a backing vocalist and arranger, who two years later would form the multi-million-selling pop group Bread.

They got a few songs down, "Bird Doggin'," by Keith Colley, Seals' "Love Is a Bird," Dave Burgess' "I've Got My Eyes on You" and "Words and Music," which he co-penned with Jerry Fuller, who wrote "Travellin' Man" for Ricky Nelson, and Fuller's "Ain't That Too Much." They also did the Carl Belew and W. S. Stevenson tunes "Lonely Street" and "Am I That Easy To Forget." But they needed more material.

So Gene had phoned Washington, saying, "Jerry, I'm comin' up there. Write me a couple of songs." And Jerry did. The first, "Born To Be a Rolling Stone," aptly described his wayward pal, who was always "movin' round without a home." So did the second, Jerry thought, "Hurtin' for You Baby"; Gene was always having so darn many women problems. Gene came up to Washington not long after to pick them up, and, to Jerry's delight, accepted a four-night engagement at Yakima's Chieftain Hotel in January. It was great to see his old pal again, with his new hint of a British accent, conservative short haircut, and grown-up cardigan sweaters. It was great fun playing music together again and just fooling around in the hills, sightseeing in the valley. Gene was relaxed and seemed to enjoy the time off from being a European rock 'n' roll star. One day they went into the little grocery store near Jerry's home in the foothills. Gene was wearing a Greek fisherman's hat that John Lennon had given him. Jerry was hugely impressed and told the girl behind the counter, "John Lennon gave him that hat." She looked at the both of them like they were crazy.

Gene had seen his buddies the Beatles just that summer in Blackpool, he told a reporter with the Yakima newspaper. "They're the same," he said, "just the same. John still wears dirty jeans and an old hat and he still looks unshaven. The only difference is he now looks that way from the back seat of a chauffeur-driven Rolls Royce." He also told the reporter about his latest passion, a forty-foot, tri-hulled sailing yacht, purchased, he said, because "from now on I'm going to do my traveling in a slow, see-the-country manner and quit beating my brains out trying to break my own traveling record." Gene told the reporter of his plans to sail back home to London from Los Angeles after he finished the gig at the Chieftain Hotel.

Though Challenge had just released "Lonely Street," coupled with "I've Got My Eyes on You," on both sides of the Atlantic, plus a four-song EP in France, Jerry wanted to use some of Gene's more familiar material in the radio commercial for the Yakima show. He gave his old pal Del Worrell, whom he knew was a huge Vincent fan and had all of Gene's singles, a call. Del was willing to loan him some records, so Jerry asked him to drop by their rehearsal at the hotel. When Del arrived, Jerry introduced him to Gene, telling the singer what a big fan Del was and how he was loaning some of his precious records for the radio spot. They chatted a bit about Del's favorite Vincent songs.

"What happened?" Gene asked after a while, indicating Del's limp. Del also wore a brace on his leg and walked with a cane.

"Well, I had polio when I was a youngster," Del said.

"Boy, if you ever need an operation or anything, you contact me," Gene said sincerely. "I'll be glad to pay for it for you."

It was a nice gesture, Del thought. He was touched. Later he would learn that he was probably making more money that Gene at that time.

Del was there at Gene's first night at the Chieftain. It got off to a rocky start when some idiot tossed an egg out onto the floor. Del was embarrassed for Gene. Gene covered well, though, limping over to the egg, singing all the while, then kicking it out of the way. The crowd offered an ovation. Gene then introduced Del to the audience as his own personal friend, and dedicated "Greenback Dollar" from Gene and Jerry's *Crazy Times* album to him. Del was thrilled. They chatted again between sets. Del noticed that Gene was sipping wine and that his eyes were very glassy, though he didn't seem intoxicated. He wondered if Gene might've been taking some pills. But he seemed pretty sharp, mentally alert. And that voice was still pure magic.

For Gene's continental fans, his two year absence from any European performances hardly seemed to matter. They greeted their idol on September 11, 1967, at Orly Airport eagerly waving placards, and thronged to his concerts throughout France and Switzerland where he was backed by the French band Le Rock 'n' Roll Gang. Gene had changed quite a bit since his last visit; he was heavier and his leather wardrobe was a little different. But his frantic live show was still the same, selling out many of the venues. The tour, promoted by an enthusiastic but inept French fan, was soon marred, though, by disorganization. Gene was provided no interpreter and most all of the musicians and club owners could not speak English. In Lyon, Gene—who knew no French—demanded of the promoter—who spoke almost no English—his return-flight ticket to the United States before he would take the stage. But there were a few high points. In Geneva, Switzerland, on October 6, Gene gave an interview—with the aid of interpreters—to Radio Suisse Romande before performing to a capacity crowd at the Salle de la Reformation. The next night, after a show in the small town of La Chaux de Fonds in the Jura mountains, Gene was able to unwind a bit. He sampled the staple meal of the Swiss, cheese fondue, opting to dip tomatoes in the sauce instead of the traditional cheese, which his dinner companions found to be a delightful improvement on the age-old dish. He also chose to drink beer instead of the more customary white wine. He enjoyed himself so much at La Chaux de Fonds that he stayed another night and gave a spontaneous performance at a local nightclub. Gene continued to tour France through the end of October, then returned to Los Angeles.

Disc jockey Jim Pewter was shocked when Gene arrived at his West Hollywood studio in April 1968 for a taping of his Armed Forces Radio Network rock 'n' roll show, heard in thirty countries. He'd always been a big fan of Gene's. He'd even seen Gene and the Blue Caps perform twice at the Prom Ballroom between 1956 and 1958 in his hometown of St. Paul, Minnesota. Gene and the band, in fact, had inspired many a young Minnesotan back in those days to pick up a guitar, plug in an amp, and start up a rock 'n' roll band of their own. Pewter had marveled then at Gene's incredible show; he and the Caps sounded just like their Capitol recordings. Gene had been in top from vocally, and the Caps were the best self-contained rock 'n' roll band Jim and his buddies had ever heard.

Now, just ten years later, he didn't even look like the same Gene Vincent. His face was much fuller and he appeared much older than his years. Jim could sense that he had endured a lot of pain, a lot of stress. He was still very polite and soft-spoken, Jim noted when Gene called to arrange the interview, though he now spoke with a slight British accent. The two seemed to hit it off once the tape started rolling.

"Oh, yes, I remember," Gene said, smiling, when reminded of his shows in St. Paul in the late fifties.

"And you're back and you're working," Jim clarified for his listeners. "Things have been exciting during the past three years. You were telling me about England—"

"Yes, sir. I've been to England quite a few times, actually. I lived over there for about four years—"

"Yeah," Jim said softly, encouraging Gene to continue.

"And I met quite a few of the rock 'n' roll fans over there. And they're very enthusiastic, I must say."

"Yeah, the rock revival is starting all over again as far as music of the late fifties."

"Well, it seems that way, actually, yes. Here in the United States—I told you I just come from Minneapolis—gee, we just packed 'em in down there."

"Oh, you did a show there?"

"Yeah, yeah. And, well, I've been to quite a few places, and everything's been just great."

"Do you still call the group the Blue Caps?"

"Uh, no, usually I'm just by myself with a supporting band, you see," he replied, his enunciation sounding vaguely British.

"Gene, you've picked up an English accent," Jim said.

"Um, many people's told me. I was hoping I wouldn't, but I suppose I have."

"No, it sounds fine," Jim reassured him. "When I talked to you on the phone, you know, I didn't recognize you. But after living there for a few years, it shows."

"Well, I didn't know that," Gene chuckled. "I'm sorry."

"Where are you from originally?"

"I'm from Virginia," Gene said. "I had a Southern accent before."

"We're gonna go back, Gene, and bring a record on the turntable that brings back memories not only to the people listening, but the summer of '56 was the first summer I bought a guitar, after 'Be-Bop-A-Lula.' "

"That's a compliment, thank you very much."

Jim spun the song. "How did it start for you?" he asked when the song ended.

"Well, 'Be-Bop-A-Lula' was entered into a contest, actually, that Capitol was having, you see," Gene said, repeating the story he'd told over and over again since 1956. "And I was entered into the contest by the radio station I was working for at the time, and it won."

"Then you cut the record—"

"Yes sir."

"And how long did it take, Gene, before it was on the charts, nationally speaking?"

"Well, we cut it at the radio station—it was about two weeks, really. And I think those were the longest two weeks I've ever waited for anything, you know. I just kind of sat around. Nothing happened. And then a disc jockey up in Baltimore, he picked it up, started playing it, and then about a month after that, why, it went."

"It's still happening."

"Yes, it is," Gene smiled.

"It's a classic. You're listening to the 'Jim Pewter Show.' Gene Vincent is here, and he gave me a picture album. Wow, this takes me back. Prom Ballroom, and there's a line of about a thousand people waiting to get in, in St. Paul. And a picture of Gene Vincent with Red Foley. Here's Melody Mill Ballroom, Dubuque, Iowa, a teenage dance show. Oh, the crowds, Gene. Remember?"

"Yes."

"And it's still that way, you know?"

"Well, like I was just telling you, I just came from Minneapolis, and it was packed every night. And the stuff I done, uh, was actually rock 'n' roll, the old stuff. They didn't want to hear my newer stuff."

"You still do, like, 'Lotta Lovin' '?"

" 'Lotta Lovin',' 'Be-Bop-A-Lula,' yeah."

" 'Dance to the Bop?' "

"Yeah. Yeah. And 'Bluejean Bop,' they want to hear that."

"Yeah."

"It was amazing, you know. I was just real surprised."

"You know, Jerry Lee Lewis, every time he appears in the Midwest, around that area, there's a strong following."

"Yes. Jerry's, well, he's quite a good friend of mine. We played in England, as well. We did a television show that went down quite well there."

"Mm-hmm. More pictures here. The movies, too, I remember.

*The Girl Can't Help It.* Little Richard and Fats Domino. Eddie Cochran was in that, wasn't he?"

"Yes, he was."

"Yeah, we'll be talking about Eddie just a little bit later."

"That was his first movie, I think."

"You did about how many pictures, Gene?"

"Oh, mercy. I've done about four."

"Four?"

"Uh-huh."

"This is exciting. *Ed Sullivan Show*, Everly Brothers, and here's a picture with Buddy Knox, Jimmy Bowen. Is that Sonny James?"

"Yeah, that's Sonny James on the end there."

"Uh-huh. Do you remember where these were taken?"

"Oh, yes, I remember it. I just seen Buddy Knox about three or four weeks ago."

"I've been trying to contact Buddy. He's back in, where? Georgia?"

"Yeah. I have Buddy's number if you want it."

"You know, 'Over the Rainbow' is another song that was very popular, uh, to people I knew."

"Yeah, well it was more popular in England than it was in the United States, actually, for record sales, but I think I've got a copy at home, I'll try to get it to you."

"Okay, fine. Gene, I want to talk about a young man that you knew. He was your friend. Eddie Cochran."

"Ah, yes, Jim, he was more or less like a brother to me. We hung around together and we went almost every place together. And when we were in England, why, you know, we traveled almost constantly together."

"Was this in the early sixties, Gene?"

"Ah, yes. Uh-huh."

"When did Eddie pass away?"

"Well, me and him were coming from Bristol, England, to London. And, the way it happened—I was supposed to pick up some suits, and Eddie had his girlfriend with him and we hired a car, you see. And we thought we hired a taxi. But on the way back, the car skidded, and he was killed and I was busted up."

"You were in the same car?"

"Yes. Uh-huh."

"I remember reading about that."

"Uh-huh. And that was a real tragedy. I was very upset about it for a long time."

"Now, you were doing shows with Eddie?"

"Yes. Uh-huh. Me and him were on the same show."

"You know, if Eddie was alive today, Gene, he would be very happy to know that his recordings are still being played."

Gene paused for a few moments before answering. Jim could tell that when Eddie died a little part of Gene had died along with him. "Well, I hope wherever he's at, he knows that they're being played because he was a very fun-loving fellow, a very good fellow. I think if you could've met him you'd have liked him very much."

"I just saw Eddie once—and I saw him in a movie, I remember—but, live, it was only once, around 1958."

"Was that in Los Angeles?"

"No, that was in Minneapolis."

"Minneapolis."

"Yeah, yeah. Eddie played his own lead guitar, didn't he?"

"Yes. He was a fantastic lead player. Actually started with the lead guitar before he ever started singing. He played for, gee, many record sessions, at Capitol—"

"Oh, you mean like he was a studio musician?"

"Oh, yes, at Capitol and with many, many recording studios around Hollywood, yeah."

"Mm-hmm."

"And, well, like I said, he's a very fun-loving fellow. And I've never seen him mad. Never."

"You know, you were telling me a story—getting back to the beginning of rock—about Elvis Presley and Carl Perkins, and it really surprised me."

"Ah, yes. They heard about this rock 'n' roll, you see. And Carl was on his way to do the *Ed Sullivan Show* and Carl had an accident, hurt him quite bad, that killed his brother, I think, and I think it broke his neck. Somehow, he got out of that and, well, they needed somebody to fill the Ed Sullivan thing. So they got Elvis Presley."

"What year was that, about?"

"Gee, that was about 1955. That was before, you know, I was going. I was singing, but I wasn't popular at that time."

"I know Carl Perkins still does country music, Jerry Lee Lewis came out of the roots of country, and you did a little bit, you did some country, didn't you?"

"Definitely."

"Sure. And I know Buddy Knox did. How about Eddie Cochran?"

"Eddie's always had a love for country. You know, he always done a lot of it when me and him were just together. But as far as his doing it on stage, I never heard him do one on stage. But I'm sure that if he got the right tune that he would've done some country."

"Of course in the late fifties they called it rockabilly."

"Yeah, rockabilly, yes."

"Gene Vincent, what's on the agenda for you upcoming in the future? Anything special?"

"Yes. They've asked me to go back to England on tour again, which I'm not quite sure I can do as yet, 'cause as you know, I'm in the hospital with my leg. But I have a new record coming out soon. I don't know which label it's going to be on, but I was talking to you about it the other day."

"Yeah, when I get a copy I'll be giving it some airplay."

"I sure hope so."

"Yeah."

"And Jim, may I take this little bit of time to say it's been a pleasure meeting you and talking with you."

"Well, it's great being with you, Gene. It's like a dream in a way, because I remember seeing you in the late fifties in St. Paul. And the memory of Gene Vincent stays in your mind. Because you are, you know, one of the leaders, one of the heavyweights of pop-rock."

"Well, thank you very much."

"And then I pick up *Billboard*: Gene Vincent, 'Be-Bop-A-Lula,' is selling again—"

Gene chuckled softly.

"Along with Bill Haley, old Chuck Berry records, Conway Twitty, and early Elvis is coming back again."

"Well, I don't know whether you've heard this song out by Elvis Presley called 'U.S. Male'?"

"Yes, I heard it—"

"That's fabulous and that's pure. That's the pure stuff like he used to do."

"Gene, I have to say goodbye."

"Jim, it's been my pleasure."

"Continued success, you know, on the tours and everything—"

"Thank you very much."

"And if you ever see any of the old rock artists, say hello."

"I sure will."

"And we're going to close with a tune called 'Hi Lili, Hi Lo.' And this was recorded where, Gene?"

"It was recorded in Hollywood, on Challenge Records," Gene said. It was part of the easy country rock sessions of early '67 he'd done with Dave Burgess, Al Casey, and the guys from the Champs. They'd gotten Jerry Merritt's two songs down—"Born To Be a Rolling Stone" in a harmony-layered, Mamas and Papas arrangement, and "Hurtin' for You Baby"—plus the Merle Haggard hit "I'm a Lonesome Fugitive" and Keith Colley's "Poor Man's Prison," in addition to the lilting "Hi Lili, Hi Lo," the old German folk song, sung by Leslie Caron and Mel Ferrer in the 1953 movie *Lili*.

"Hmm. And it was overseas in the record shops?" Jim asked.

"Yes. It was released in France. It's not been released in the

United States yet," Gene said. All the Challenge sessions, in fact, packaged as the simply titled *Gene Vincent* album, had been released in France and the UK a few months earlier, as had Capitol/EMI's greatest hits collection *Best of Gene Vincent*.

"Oh, it hasn't?"

"No."

"Well, let's give it a spin. Gene, I hope I can get overseas sometime and see you perform, and maybe even over in Minneapolis or St. Paul sometime, I might be back there."

"I sure hope so."

"We'll keep in touch."

"Yes, sir."

"You're looking good, I can't believe it."

"Oh, thank you very much."

Jim wound up the show with Gene's melancholy waltz.

Jim was elated. Gene Vincent had just signed a contract with Playground Productions, the production company Pewter ran with his fiance Judy Felice. Though EMI re-released "Be-Bop-A-Lula" and "Say Mama" in the UK in May and Gene was still signed as a songwriter to Gene Autry's Central Songs publishing company, Gene's contract with Challenge had expired and he was looking for an American record label. He seemed impressed with Jim's knowledge of the music business, which included a stint working with Robert "Bumps" Blackwell, Little Richard's manager, Pewter's own Midwest hit, "Little Girl," in 1959, and interviews with some of Gene's pals, contemporaries and idols like Alan Freed, Buddy Holly, Little Richard, Ray Charles, and Muddy Waters.

And Gene really liked "Story of the Rockers," the song Jim wrote especially for him not long after their interview in April. Gene invited Jim and Judy over to his apartment on Cahuenga and Yucca in Hollywood so that he could hear it. There they met Gene's wife Jackie, and the four of them got along very well. Gene listened to Jim's demo, which he cut with three session players at Fidelity Recorders, just up Yucca. When the song finished, Gene said he would like to record it, then pulled out his guitar and sang a song he wrote with Jackie called "Pickin' Poppies." Jim thought it would make a great flip side.

Now he was ensconced in the Hollywood Sound Studios this July 25, along with Judy, producing a Gene Vincent session. His plan was to record these two songs, then try to place them with a company that would promote Gene back onto the national music charts in America. Jim was thrilled to have this opportunity to bring back a true rock 'n' roll legend.

Gene was comfortable in the studio, and Jackie seemed right at home too, contributing ethereal, almost hallucinatory-sounding backing vocals on "Pickin' Poppies." With seasoned musicians— led by arranger, sax, and flugelhorn player John D'Andrea—like lead guitarist Al Casey, rhythm guitarist Louis Morell, bassist Joe Osborn, drummer James Troxel and pianist John Hammond, plus three other horn players, recording was a breeze. Jim was pleased with the results. And hopeful that he had a hit on his hands.

Could that really be him? Ronny Weiser wondered.

It was the address on Franklin that the information operator had given him when he'd asked for a Eugene Craddock. He'd made the call as soon as he'd raced home from Aaron's Record Shop, just after the store's owner sold him a couple of Gene Vincent import albums and casually mentioned to the flabbergasted college kid that Vincent was in town, living somewhere in Hollywood. The address on Franklin, in fact, was just a few blocks away from the apartment on Hayworth Street that Ronny shared with his parents and brother.

Had he been living so close to his idol, the rock 'n' roll cowboy who so mesmerized him from the very moment he laid eyes on a friend's *Gene Vincent and the Blue Caps* album at school in Como, Italy? The greasy, curly hair, the agonized expression, the sharp black shirt with the square pearl snap buttons—it was America. It had moved him down to his first pair of imported American Levi's. Gene Vincent's mystique had conquered him before he'd even heard a single note. And when he did—well, it was hard to describe the voice that made him shudder, made him shiver, and completely captivated his mind, body, and soul, even now, after his family had finally migrated to America, the promised land.

He was disappointed, though, when they arrived in Los Angeles in 1966, to find that the American soundtrack was no longer Presley and Vincent, Little Richard and Fats Domino. It wasn't the tough American with the black leather jacket and the sideburns and the pompadour heading to the local honky-tonk on a Saturday night. It was a bunch of sissies. Guys looking like girls. Their music was not soulful. It didn't have any guts, it didn't have any drive or feeling. Later, when a pack of hippies grabbed a college friend's record player and chucked it out his dorm room window, Little Richard still spinning on the turntable, Ronny knew it was time to take action. He started a rock 'n' roll fan club and a fanzine he called *Rollin' Rock*, and dreamed of the day he could release all the wild, juicy, sexy, crazy, earthy teenage rock 'n' roll platters he wanted on his very own record label.

The guy in the red convertible that had just pulled into the garage sure looked like Gene Vincent. Could it possibly be him? Ronny was trembling—wow, he was actually trembling, he thought to himself—as he approached the heavyset man getting out of the tiny sports car. This could not really be happening, he thought. Gene Vincent is not human. He's a myth, a dream, an idea, a concept, a fantasy. Gene Vincent is a god. He can't actually be made of flesh and bone like the rest of us. But here he was.

"Hi, um, Gene?" Ronny stammered, nervously clutching the current issue of *Rollin' Rock*.

Gene smiled and nodded.

"Er—my name is Ronny Weiser," he continued, his heart pounding ten miles a minute. "I'm president of the Hollywood Rock 'n' Roll Fan Club. And the Gene Vincent and Little Richard Fan Club. And—can I talk to you?"

Gene smiled again and, to Ronny's immense surprise, invited

the kid inside. In the kitchen he pulled out some snacks and a couple of cold Cokes from the fridge, then politely asked Ronny all about his magazine and the fan clubs and his classes at UCLA. He listened intently to Ronny and was very friendly. Ronny could hardly believe it. Gene Vincent, interested in what he was doing, in his life, in his work. They talked and talked, mostly about rock 'n' roll, which Ronny could easily tell was Gene's biggest passion. They seemed to connect. There was a magic about him, Ronny thought, that made you happy, but kind of sad at the same time. When Ronny finally walked out of the apartment, he was in a daze. He wondered if he was awake or in a dream.

Jim Pewter didn't know what he might find. And it scared him.

Gene had called around two in the morning. He sounded really on edge. He told Jim that he should come out and see him. He said he had a terrible argument with Jackie about her family. He said he had a gun. And he said he was going to use it.

Jim quickly jumped into his car to make the hour's drive from Hollywood out to Gene's new home in Simi Valley. By the time he reached the suburb, a dense fog had settled amongst the hills.

The front door to Gene's modest two-story house was wide open as Jim pulled up. He could hear Gene's dog barking. He ran inside and called Gene's name, but got no answer. With his heart in his mouth, one by one he checked the rooms downstairs. They were all empty. Then he moved upstairs. When he got to the master bedroom, he found Gene passed out on the bed. A pistol lay across his chest. Several empty beer cans were scattered across the bedclothes.

Jim let out a relieved breath, then woke Gene up and made some coffee. Gene, a bit groggy and drowsy with drink, thanked Jim for coming over. They talked for two hours over coffee, just as they had from time to time over beers in Hollywood. Gene dragged out his scrapbook and regaled Jim with stories about the Beatles and his good friend John Lennon, whose favorite song, Gene reminded him, was "Be-Bop-A-Lula." He told Jim of Lennon's eternal passion for the details behind the voluptuous echo on "Lula" and "Woman Love." He showed Jim loads of photos in the scrapbook of him and the Beatles together. He also hinted to Jim that he thought Brian Epstein, the Beatles' manager who died of an apparent accidental drug overdose in August 1967, was murdered because there were sinister forces that wanted to take over the Beatles' business interests. Jim didn't know about that one. He thought perhaps Gene's drinking, combined with the various medications for his leg prescribed by the local Veterans Hospital and an improper diet, might again be playing havoc with his friend's moods and memories. Eventually, Gene brought out his guitar and sang some of his old hits for Jim. When they both began to tire, Jim asked Gene if he thought everything was going to be all right. Gene assured him it would, that it was time for him to get some sleep.

Leaving Gene's home, Jim looked up at the street sign shrouded in fog at the end of the block. A chill shinnied up his spine. Gene had purchased a house on Cochran Street. Driving away, it dawned on Jim. It was Eddie who'd sent him to Gene.

Jim discarded Gene's gun in a dumpster near a gas station several miles from Gene's house. Then he headed back toward Hollywood, eerily comforted in the knowledge that Eddie had used him to pull Gene out of another crisis—just as Eddie had always done when he was alive.

Adrian Owlett had taken the demo tape to every major record company in England. Nobody was interested.

It was a competent enough demo. Gene had recorded the four songs on his own, and the pop-rock material was certainly in tune with the sound of the day, with its bleeping electric piano on "Rainyday Sunshine" and echoing backing vocals on "Green Grass," a tune Jerry Merritt wrote for Gene. And it showed Gene could still rock 'n' roll, with the singer sounding soulful, even a bit funky, on "Mister Love," and playful on Chuck Berry's 1956 hit "Roll Over Beethoven." But all doors seemed to be closed to Gene in the land where he'd reigned king just a few short years ago. Gene just couldn't understand it. Adrian felt awful for his friend.

He flipped on the radio. John Peel's "Top Gear" show was on. He had a band called Family on, and they were doing some sort of tribute to Buddy Holly. Adrian snapped to attention when Peel raved on about Holly and the old rock 'n' roll, and then mentioned his love of Gene Vincent.

Jim Pewter met Gene at the Guys & Dolls Club on Santa Monica Boulevard. From '65 through '68, Jim sang lead and played rhythm guitar there with a combo on Friday and Saturday nights. Gene had called and wanted to get together to discuss an offer he'd just received. Over several beers, Gene laid out the situation. BBC disc jockey John Peel, apparently a die-hard Vincent fan, had heard a four-song demo Gene recorded in May. And even though EMI U.K. just released *Best of Gene Vincent, Vol. 2* that February, Peel wanted to make an album for his fledgling Dandelion label, which he ran with partner Clive Selwood of Elektra Records UK. Kim Fowley—the rising young star who'd produced the 1960 chart-topper "Alley-Oop" by the Hollywood Argyles and 1963's Top 10 hit "Popsicles and Icicles," written by David Gates and recorded by the Murmaids—was to produce. Fowley was an acquaintance of producer Bones Howe, who was recording Gene's youngest sister, Piper. Working under the name Piper Grant, she was trying to launch a singing career like her older brother. She'd put a plug in for her currently hit-less brother, and Howe had passed the word on to Fowley. Now Gene wanted out of his production contract with Jim and Judy's Playground company, a deal that required a minimum of four masters to be recorded with six options of one year each. Jim had added a clause—and Gene had agreed—that one recording during the first year would have to reach either the *Billboard* or *Cashbox* Top 100 for the other options to be picked up.

Jim thought about all the work he and Judy had put into Gene so far. After the July session, Judy had made the rounds of the record companies with the tape. She was turned down by Dot, Liberty, A&M, Tetragrammaton, and several other labels. Not one to give up easily, Jim then had two hundred copies of the "Story of the Rockers" and "Pickin' Poppies" single pressed up on his own Playground label. These he sent out to various disc jockeys in the hope of sparking some radio airplay. The response was less than remarkable, though its extremely limited pressing would eventually make the Playground single one of Gene's most rare and valuable records.

Now, less than a year after their July 9, 1968, contract was signed, Gene was asking Jim to release him from their production agreement. He wanted Jim to become his manager instead. It was a lot to think about. Jim would have to discuss it with Judy.

Gene called Adrian one August night nearly in tears. The sessions with Kim Fowley were not going well. Gene liked Fowley all right, he told Adrian, but not as a producer; he didn't seem to understand what the singer wanted. There was some dope being passed around among the musicians and the nonstop stream of assorted groupies, scenesters, and hangers-on who dropped by the studio unannounced, Gene told Adrian, and they had some newfangled ways of recording that were confusing. It wasn't like the old days, when making a record came easy, when it was fun. It was just too much, Gene lamented.

For Fowley, the whole scene was wrong. The wrong musicians, the wrong studio, and the wrong songs. His original concept—as he'd explained to Gene over cheeseburgers at an L.A. drugstore after he was recruited for the project by Elektra, Dandelion's U.S. distributor—was to take Gene to Malaco, an up-and-coming studio in Jackson, Mississippi. Inspired by the rawness, the sheer danger of Gene's early work, as well as the lowdown swamp funk gaining popularity with groups like Creedence Clearwater Revival, Fowley wanted to put Gene Vincent back in the deep South, the milieu from whence the fallen rock 'n' roll god had emerged. Put him in touch with his roots. Let him soak up that undefinable supernatural energy that existed only in the South. Let him dabble with the Dixie voodoo. Then they'd make a real rock 'n' roll record—mean and greasy and full of fire.

The idea was quickly nixed by the label brass. Why spend the money on an out-of-town studio—plus transportation and accommodations for Fowley, Gene Vincent, and musicians—when the label had its own boutique recording facility right there in Los Angeles? So here they were, holed up in the Elektra studio with its incense burners and hippie-dippie decor and session-crashing carousers like those guys from the Doors and their blond and tan surfer-girl girlfriends.

The whole thing was the antithesis of Gene Vincent, Fowley knew. And the record was not going to be great, he also knew.

From the start, they'd had trouble nailing down a guitar sound that would please Gene. They even brought in Blue Cap Johnny Meeks for a few days. Red Rhodes, who was hired to play steel guitar, had given his friend Johnny the call.

Johnny had joined the Champs not long after the Caps disbanded—he could still remember Dave Burgess waking him on the bus to tell him that Gene and Eddie had been in a wreck in England—plus he'd done some movie appearances and a stint in the service. Now he was just playing music on the weekends, working during the week as a tour guide at Busch Gardens in Los Angeles. He was happy to help out his old buddy, so he immediately arranged for some time off and went down to the studio.

It wasn't a good scene, Johnny thought when he arrived, and it certainly wasn't the Blue Caps. There were probably ten, twelve, fifteen people there just hanging around, though Johnny didn't know any of them. And there were five or six people actually being paid to work the session who seemed to have no knowledge at all of the Blue Caps or Gene or what he wanted or what his music was like. They were just musicians, playing their instruments, who were put all together in a studio and were expected to come up with another smash hit like "Be-Bop-A-Lula." It just didn't work.

Linda Ronstadt, a versatile vocalist, recently turned solo, who'd had a Top 40 hit with the Stone Ponys' "Different Drum" in 1967, asked if she might attend the recording sessions, since she respected the great Gene Vincent. Gene allowed her to hang out. Gene was also pleased to meet John Sebastian of the Lovin' Spoonful, who dropped by the studio with his dog one day.

After Johnny left and there were still more tracks to do, Gene finally decided to use the guitarists that were there—Rhodes on steel, plus rhythm guitarist Mars Bonfire, who'd coined the phrase "heavy metal" with his Steppenwolf song "Born To Be Wild," immortalized that year in the biker movie *Easy Rider*, which represented to hippie culture what *The Wild One* had to the adolescents of the fifties.

Gene was much better at the country stuff—laid-back tunes like Ernest Tubb's "Rainbow at Midnight," the old spiritual "Circle Never Broken," and Hank Williams' "I Heard That Lonesome Whistle," which he dedicated to "Mr. John Peel and Mr. Adrian Owlett, who's been so kind to me"—than the rock 'n' roll, Fowley was quick to realize. And he knew exactly why. Gene was in there with people he didn't know, and who didn't really know him. Along with Rhodes and Bonfire, there were Fowley's friend Skip Battin, a very capable bassist who would later join the Byrds; Jim Gordon, a fine drummer who would go on to play in Derek and the Dominoes with guitarist Eric Clapton; and Grant Johnson on keyboards, a kid from the Canyon who actually had more rock 'n' roll attitude than any other player at the session, and whose piano solos, consequently, would figure prominently in the final product. All talented guys. But the connection, the synergy, just wasn't there.

And the songs weren't either. Fowley had hoped to hook Gene up with some fabulous songwriting guitar player down in the deep South, set them both out in a rowboat in the middle of a bayou with a bottle of whiskey and some fried chicken, and see what kind of hot, swampy magic they'd come back with. Instead, it was, "Well, Gene, what songs do you know that you feel like recording?" So he'd come up with "Rockin' Robin," the old Bobby Day hit, and "White Lightning," which he used to do with Eddie Cochran. And, if another "Lula" retread wasn't bad enough, the Dandelion folks also gunned for a redo of "Lotta Lovin'."

But the main reason there was no blood, no guts, and no glory on the rock 'n' roll tracks, Fowley knew, was that they weren't in any danger. There wasn't any madness. There was no voodoo. Here was an overweight, obviously unhealthy, aging rock 'n' roll star—when they'd first met, Fowley assumed Gene was at least fifteen years older than he was, though they were only four years apart—and they were stuck here in artsy-fartsy purgatory. Well, we're going to fail at rock 'n' roll, Fowley thought not long after the sessions began, but we might be able to salvage a passable country record, albeit a "Gene Vincent as a Sunday school teacher singing in the minister's parlor" kind of country record.

And Gene was difficult to motivate. He just didn't feel like singing every day. There was a certain window of opportunity, Fowley learned, entirely dependent on the pain in the man's leg and the amount of medication he'd taken to alleviate the ache. Sometimes he was just too irritable. Other times he would be just irritable enough to channel that edginess into his performance, like on the fiery but strained "Sexy Ways." And other times he was mellow enough to do a ballad. So they did the slower stuff when the meds had set in, after the pain had been numbed. And for the rockin' stuff, Gene seemed to use the pain as an engine, as a kick-start to get him going. His leg seemed to be a relentless reminder to get things done. But he was always a professional in the studio, Fowley noted. He always had the material memorized, and he always sang on key. He could always be counted on to just deliver.

In the UK, Peel had neither the time nor the money to go out to Los Angeles and supervise things, and, in accordance with his strict laissez-faire policy toward Dandelion artists and their productions, he offered no creative input, other than his idea—utterly ill-advised, he would admit later—to redo "Be-Bop-A-Lula" one tired more time. He just let Gene get on with it the best he could.

––––––––

When Tom Ayres was asked to take over the management of Gene's affairs, he agreed without giving it another thought. Their mutual friend Kim Fowley had introduced them, and since Ayres and Vincent were both from the South, everyone thought they'd get along well. And they were right. Ayres produced and managed the Sir Douglas Quintet, the zesty Tex-Mex, blues-rock combo deemed by some the greatest studio band in the world, and was pleased to be working with another fine talent.

Gene was operating out of southern California at the time, but he jumped all over the world, hopping from club to club across America and jetting back and forth to Europe. Tom could tell it was wearing on the man. So he devised a kinder performance schedule for Gene, and envisioned a less frantic, more country kind of sound for his new singer. Tom arranged some shows for Gene at some local colleges, which he really seemed to enjoy. They'd show his films, he'd answer the kids' questions, and then he'd give a brief concert, just thirty minutes or so. It was fun for Gene, and he could actually make as much money doing that as he could doing a nightclub show, which often required an entire day's worth of travel and rehearsal before he ever hit the stage. The intimate atmosphere at the college shows suited Gene; he loved talking with the kids. He always appreciated his fans, Tom noticed.

Jim Pewter had declined Gene's request that he become Gene's manager. He simply had too many other irons in the fire. But he would finally get "Story of the Rockers" and "Pickin' Poppies" into commercial release in 1970, as a single on the Forever label, a division of Century City Music Corporation in Los Angeles, where Jim was general manager. But again, Gene's single would fail to chart.

Gene and Tom and Rodney Bingenheimer, an aspiring actor friend of both Tom and Kim Fowley who'd dropped by the Dandelion sessions at Elektra, were in Toronto, Canada. Gene was to play a large rock 'n' roll revival festival there, along with the Doors, Bo

Diddley, Little Richard, and Jerry Lee Lewis. But ticket sales were way off and the promoter wasn't happy about it. "Well, get the Beatles," somebody joked. A call was made.

The next day, September 13, John Lennon's Plastic Ono Band arrived: Lennon, his wife Yoko Ono, guitarist Eric Clapton, bassist Klaus Voorman, and drummer Alan White. Rodney picked them up in a limousine at the airport. They were given a motorcycle motorcade all the way to the venue. Lennon was not feeling well— he had the flu—but he brightened the moment he saw Gene. The two chatted and traded autographs backstage. Fowley, who was acting as consultant and master of ceremonies on the show, had arranged for a group to back Gene, the Alice Cooper Band. Cooper had stopped by the studio while Fowley was mixing Gene's album and mentioned that his band did all of Gene's songs. So Fowley had set it up. It was an emotional gig in front of the massive crowd at the Varsity Stadium—the largest audience Gene had played to in years—and he broke into tears during "Be-Bop-A-Lula." He wasn't able to finish the song; Lennon came out and hugged him reassuringly.

The stars loved Gene, Tom noticed. Elvis Presley, Bob Dylan (who actually bought a Blue Cap as a youngster so as to better emulate his musical hero), Del Shannon, the Beach Boys, Melanie—they thought that Gene hung the moon. They dropped by his shows from time to time, and when they got around Gene they were simply speechless. It was usually the only time they ever saw Gene, actually, as he rarely went out. Tom and Gene would go out rambling, pub crawling, occasionally. But Gene was from the old school, Tom was quick to pick up, from an era that adhered to the adage that "foolish names, like foolish faces, are always seen in public places." Of course, that leg was always bothering him. But he'd hobble right along, and he never complained. He took pills the doctors gave him, codeine, for the pain, but it didn't take a doctor, nurse, or any medical technician to look at that leg and know that he was in bad shape. Tom wondered how he could even walk on it—it would actually bend like rubber. Gene would visit the doctors, his home away from home, it seemed, and he would call up and say mournfully, "Tom, they're gonna take my leg. They're gonna amputate it." Tom would say, "Gene, that's the most wonderful thing that could ever happen to you." And Gene'd wail, "How can you say things like that?" Gene was of the belief—he was into Eastern religions, Buddhism especially—that when you die, you must die all in one piece. And so he always refused to have the damn thing removed.

One thing about Gene, Tom noticed from the very first moment he started working with him, that no matter what happened or what the deal was, there'd be a misunderstanding. Or some freak accident. Or something. One night they were on the road, Gene, Tom, and Rodney, all in Tom's big Cadillac. At about two or three in the morning, they stopped to get gas. Tom put the nozzle into the hole in the back bumper, after folding the license plate back, and set the pump. Gene had gotten up out of the back seat—he'd been drinking wine—and hobbled around to the back of the car. Just as he got to the back bumper, the pressure in the nozzle caused it to backfire and fly out of the hole. The nozzle landed on Gene's healthy foot and drenched him with gasoline. He fell to the pavement. "Now you messed up my good foot!" he screamed. After he calmed down a bit, he went to light one of the cigarettes that was forever dangling from his mouth. Luckily Rodney jumped in and stopped him, saving him from being blown to smithereens.

Another time, Tom and Gene were at the Paramount Hotel in San Francisco, going up to the tenth floor. As they got off the elevator, they passed a young, skinny guy with a mop swabbing the floor. The young man turned around and said, "Gene Vincent, you don't look like you used to." Gene jumped about ten yards, flat-footed, across the marble floor, then screamed back, "You don't look like you used to either!"

The tour got off to a rocky start. And it didn't get any better. For one thing, Gene arrived too damned early.

In September, Henry Henroid had received a transatlantic call from his old charge in the States. He was looking for work. He sounded desperate. Henry told him he would see what he could do—he knew it wouldn't be easy to sell a hitless rock 'n' roll singer to European venues—but that it would take some time.

Gene had arrived just a few days later. He called Adrian, with whom he and Jackie had kept in frequent touch during their self-imposed exile in the States, to pick him up at the airport. On that same day, Adrian received a telegram from Jackie, who had walked out on Gene the day he'd returned from the Toronto Rock 'n' Roll Festival. Gene had left for England just two hours later. She begged Adrian to take care of Gene, said that she loved Gene more than life itself. Though Gene didn't talk about it, Adrian assumed the two were having problems and that was why he'd come to England ahead of schedule.

Adrian took Gene to his house, where he stayed for a week. Adrian was delighted to see his old friend again. He had put on some pounds—he now had a visible paunch—he was sporting mutton-chop sideburns, and his hair had thinned a bit, but he seemed to be the same old Gene. His style standards had slipped a bit, Adrian noted; he was no longer wearing the smart Italian fashions he wore when they'd first met. But he was still generally neat and fairly tidy, and though he dressed casually most of the time, he still looked good in whatever he was wearing. And he still enjoyed going to the local pubs, especially down at the Weir Hotel, with its walls of beaten copper. Gene would sit and admire their warm gleam and tell Adrian there was just nothing like the Weir in all of Los Angeles. He liked all the English beers, but scotch whiskey with water and ice was his favorite when they were out. He'd sit and drink and smoke his Capstan cigarettes—full strength, at least one hundred per day, in Adrian's estimation—and just seem to bask in the easy warmth, the relaxed spirit, of an English country pub. Sometimes they went out for a bite to eat, though Gene's drinking always took precedence over food. Gene enjoyed a good curry once in a while, or Mexican food, and they ate Chinese regularly, which Gene really loved. His appetite was always small for food, but he enjoyed the ethic of eating out in nice places. He also liked to watch television when he could, especially *Star Trek*, and he also enjoyed English programs like *Dad's Army* and certain game shows, particularly those whose concept had originated in the States.

It wasn't long before Henry learned of Gene's arrival; Gene had run into Tom Jones and his publicist Chris Hutchins on the flight from Los Angeles, and Hutchins tipped Henry off that his artist was back in England. Henry was not pleased. He wasn't ready to launch the UK tour yet and wanted Gene out of the country. Though Gene's one-time UK manager Don Arden and Henry were not even on speaking terms anymore, Arden believed that he still had a valid contract with Gene, Adrian was sure, and they all knew that Arden wouldn't be shy about enforcing it. So Henry quickly phoned some old acquaintances, called in some favors, and slapped together a last-minute tour of France for Gene.

It was a disaster from the moment Gene landed in Paris and the airline lost his luggage. On many of the dates the scheduled backing bands never arrived, and whatever local band was available—always unrehearsed and unfamiliar with the material—would have to stand in. It was often miraculous that Gene, worried about being ripped off, would even make it to the stage, now that he was in the habit of demanding his money in cash up front. The few times he gave in and did his show without prepayment, the promoters promptly stiffed him. And then, on an overnight train from Lyon to Paris, he was robbed.

By the time Gene returned to England on November 5, utterly frustrated, he was incognito no more. Dandelion released his new single, "Be-Bop-A-Lula '69," with "Ruby Baby" on the flip, on October 24. The music papers ran stories on the new album, titled *I'm Back and I'm Proud*, on John Peel's label. A cavalcade of greasy-haired, motorcycle-riding rockers made their way to London Airport to greet their hero. A BBC camera crew was also on hand to shoot the whole thing.

They were making a documentary, an hour's worth of following

Gene from rehearsal to road to gig called *The Rock 'n' Roll Singer*. They captured most of the first four days of the tour to promote the single and the forthcoming album due for January release. They were at terminal C-24 as Gene landed, capturing the excited chatter of the rockers, who remained steadfast and true to the pop iconography of the fifties, despite their mid-sixties seaside rumbles with the Mods—those rock 'n' roll–shunning, scooter-riding sissies—and despite the current onslaught of drug-addled hippie culture. The television crew was at the exasperatingly abysmal basement rehearsal with the totally unprepared Wild Angels, the backing band for the UK tour, who had to hurriedly learn "Be-Bop-A-Lula '69" just minutes before a BBC TV performance, which was ultimately canceled because Gene and the band arrived late. They followed Gene as he limped alone through the chilly streets of London at night, smoking cigarettes with his collar flipped up against the cold. And they were there when Gene's BBC TV spot was renewed; he and the Angels went on right after the grocery prices update, Gene clad in his trademark black and handing in a fine performance in front of a live dancing audience, though he was now a far softer, much rounder, less mobile version of his former rock 'n' roll self.

The camera crew even traveled in the van with Gene and the band, documenting the idle conversation. "It's the same goddamn thing as the Gestapo," Gene explained emphatically about the current state of American government to the boys during the ride to the television studio. "The same identical thing. Only Hitler ran the Gestapo, and the CIA runs the president. The president don't run the country anymore. It's the goddamn secret police. And that's just about what's wrong with the students and everybody else in the United States today. They know it. Who runs the CIA? The president don't know who runs the CIA, he don't know. Nobody knows. It's secret. It's a secret police." Later, as they headed toward an overnight gig at the Isle of Wight, Gene chattered away, "The Japanese are fantastic people. Give 'em a beer can, man, and they'll give you a car!"

Over the four days the film crew caught Gene battling the soul-numbing tedium of life on the road—sorting out improper hotel accommodations, finding ways to pass the endless hours spent in transit, and the now perpetual struggle for payment. "This is the hard part," he sighed at one point as he loitered in a dark corner of another featureless nightclub. "Waiting. Waiting to rehearse. Waiting to get on."

Yet, at each gig, he always delivered, exiting the stage utterly sweat-soaked and completely breathless. His time-seasoned voice still burned with the urgency of his early hits during all of the performances of "Whole Lotta Shakin' " and "Say Mama" and "Long Tall Sally." Slower, country-tinged tunes like "I Heard That Lonesome Whistle" he now burnished with a bittersweet melancholy, a wistful sadness that would mesmerize even the packed houses at the London Palladium and the popular Speakeasy toward the end of the tour. The crowds, mostly comprised of drape-coated, string-tied, hardcore rockers, still demanded encore after encore in appreciation of his talent and heart. Gene absolutely shone that evening at the Speakeasy, Adrian thought, in front of the sold-out crowd jam-packed with stars. John Lennon and Yoko Ono, George Harrison, John Entwistle of the Who, Peter Frampton, and Georgie Fame, who jumped onto the stage to take over on piano—it was a glorious night for all. A triumphant cap to an otherwise pretty irksome comeback tour, Adrian thought.

When Tom Ayres phoned Neil Bogart with the news that he now had Gene Vincent and the Sir Douglas Quintet, the vice-president and general manager of the Buddah record company, who'd performed with the Quintet once or twice years before down in Texas, just couldn't resist. "My God," he said, "I'll take it. Let's get in the studio and get started."

The sessions, waxed for the Buddah subsidiary Kama Sutra, went well. Gene seemed at ease in the studio, and so did Jackie. Of course, that wasn't too surprising. Music was in her family. Besides her own vocal career—she'd waxed a couple of singles for

Decca in England back in '63—her brother-in-law was Mickie Most, the Phil Spector of the United Kingdom, who produced the Animals, Herman's Hermits, and just about everyone else. Jackie's backing vocals on the Dandelion tracks, in fact, were mentioned in *Rolling Stone* magazine, part of a package review of Gene's three new releases, *I'm Back and I'm Proud*, Capitol's newly issued *Gene Vincent's Greatest*, and Capitol/EMI's *The Best Of Gene Vincent, Vol. 2*. Though all three albums received guarded kudos, the story—topped with a large portrait of a thin, young Gene up top and captioned "Gene Vincent, 1956–1970"—looked eerily like an obituary.

When multi-instrumentalist Chris Darrow, who'd worked with the Sir Douglas Quintet previously and was hired to add fiddle to the Cajun-flavored "Danse Colinda," arrived for the session at the Sound Factory, all he found was some fat guy with thinning hair fiddling around in the corner. He was dressed in workman-type clothes and wearing sturdy black shoes. Must be the janitor, Darrow figured.

Darrow scanned the studio, looking for the passionate hellion whose freewheeling hits he grew up on, whose *The Girl Can't Help It* was still Darrow's favorite movie of all time. Darrow was proud to have been asked to play on the album. He would have shown up just to hang around the great Gene Vincent. I wonder where Gene is? Darrow thought to himself. Soon, the fellow in the corner turned around. Darrow was stunned to see that it was Gene Vincent. It hit him hard.

After they talked for a while, Darrow found Gene to be a very sensitive guy, a sweet man. He gave the young fiddle player the impression that he was also kind of a sad man, though, a tired soul with deep and heavy thoughts. It seemed to Darrow like Gene's wife was the one who was in control, the one running the whole show all the time. Gene looked like he was in love with his wife. But Darrow got the feeling that perhaps the poor guy was just living his life for her. Maybe it was the way he looked, or maybe it was the way the lines in his face cut. There was just a darkness, like a cloud, that seemed to surround the man.

Musically, though, Gene didn't seem to have lost a thing, Darrow was pleased to discover. Gene and the three Sir Douglas members had been practicing at Tom Ayres's house for a couple of weeks, and he seemed restless and ready to roll. He paced the studio, surveying and fine-tuning the equipment setup, like having engineer David Hassinger—who'd recorded number-one hits by the Supremes, the Monkees, and the Jackson Five, and the Stones' "Satisfaction"—move a microphone inside the bass drum to achieve a richer sound, or boost a mike's sound level. He rarely used sheet music—he seemed to know all the songs—and seemed to favor the slower, country ballads. The longer, jam-heavy affairs—like "Slow Times Comin'," full of meandering guitar solos and instrumental grooves—he had his doubts about. It always seemed to be Gene who'd sense that a take was not going well; he'd be the one to stop the band and make corrections.

Jackie was good for Gene, Tom Ayres thought. She took good care of him. She grieved a lot about Gene's drinking, and acted almost like a mother to him. When they were going out on the road, she would fix Gene a thermos of hot soup for the ride. They'd climb into Tom's big Cadillac, Gene always dozing in the back seat, and rocket down the highway. Gene did club dates here and there, but the rock 'n' roll revival shows—like the one in March, after the recording sessions, with Little Richard, Bo Diddley, and the Drifters at the Felt Forum in New York City—were the highest profile gigs.

Gene stopped by Tom's huge house almost every day, just to check in and see what was going on. A lot of people—musicians, friends—lived there, hanging out or working in the home recording studio, and Gene was friendly to them all.

Gene got along with everybody, Tom marveled. Sure, if you got hard or got pushy with him, well, look out. He'd get real pushy back. But deep down, he was as gentle as a kitten. He could be hard to handle at times, but if you leveled with him, he was a good guy. The kids really seemed to dig him, especially the precious few who knew what he was all about. Sometimes Jim Morrison from the Doors would come around, stopping by a bar down on Santa Monica Boulevard. In the daytime they'd all meet there, drink, and just sit around. Jim would always want to know from Gene what it was like to be a real rock star. He was a rock star in his own right, what with the Doors' huge hit "Light My Fire" and their monster-selling, self-titled psychedelic album debut in '67, but he didn't have Gene's legendary status. And he wanted it, it was easy to tell.

It was another nightmare of a tour.

It had been booked by a rank amateur; Henry Henroid had washed his hands of Gene after the last troubled European jaunt. He knew that if Gene didn't get off the road, they'd all have a dead man on their hands. And he didn't want to be a part of that just to earn a few bob. Henry'd simply had enough of the lunacy—the drinking, the tantrums, the unpredictability.

Without Henry along, just about everything that could go wrong did. Gene's British backing band, the Houseshakers, were given the wrong directions to the second gig of the French concert junket; Gene was forced to give a less-than-stellar show accompanied by a local jazz band. The following morning on their way to Paris the band came upon the car hired to transport Gene sitting in the grass at the side of the road. The driver, a strapping, surly Frenchman nicknamed "Gorilla," had nearly fallen asleep at the wheel; Adrian had talked him into catching a brief nap off the road. "I don't want to travel with that nut," Gene, visibly shaken in the backseat, told the band. "He's going to kill me!"

Gene opted to travel instead with the Houseshakers in their van and his mood brightened. Wearing a pair of enormous sunglasses, he cracked jokes and passed around pictures of Jackie. Trouble returned, though, at Lon-le-Saunier when Gene refused to go on without being paid first. When the impatient crowd heard the news the angry fans tore up boxes and papers and set fire to them inside the hall. A full-scale riot broke out; the band holed up inside the venue until they could exit safely. When things had settled some, the musicians made their way to the van. The air had been let out of the tires. They were forced to abandon the vehicle and hitch rides to the hotel.

After receiving word that the tires had been fixed, the band returned to the venue the next morning with hopes of driving back to Paris. They arrived to find the van, and all of the musical equipment inside it, gone, taken as a ransom by the tour's promoter to force Gene to continue the tour. Outraged, Gene decided they would take the train back to Paris and enlist the aid of the British and American embassies for the return of their property. At the train station, members of the tour promoter's family stood across the entrance to the station, blocking the musicians' way. "You can't go," they warned Gene and the band. "We've taken your gear and you'll get it back when you do the next show."

"We're not working for nothing," Gene countered angrily.

"You owe us," they said.

"No, you owe us," Gene argued as the band members chimed in. The two groups bickered back and forth.

Then the promoter's family linked arms in a laughable show of force. Gene and the band pushed defiantly through the feeble barrier and boarded their train to angry shouts of "We'll sue you! We'll sue you!" On the train, Gene grew introspective on the few hours' journey to Paris, opening up to Houseshakers leader Graham Fenton about very personal memories he had of Eddie and his sorrow over the fatal crash. Graham could tell that Gene had never gotten over it, that it greatly troubled him still. When they arrived at their hotel in Paris, the van full of equipment was waiting for them, returned by the promoter who feared Gene and the band would go to the police.

The cutting short of the tour didn't help matters much as far as Gene's finances were concerned. Gene was always short of money anyway—Adrian watched him blow it on booze and guns and knives for his collection and the heavy supply of painkillers he had to purchase in France, where there was no National Health Service. Adrian noted that somehow though, through it all, Gene still had that magic. That voice was still beautiful, and the crowds that did get to see him paid their respects with ovations.

He spoke of Jackie quite a bit in France to the band and to Adrian, but Adrian wasn't quite sure how to gauge Gene's feelings. He'd seen Gene constantly "falling in love" on the road. He was charming and liked the ladies—and they liked him. But he was also fairly ruthless, Adrian thought, and could regard a groupie as just that. The poor girls would see a future with him, which, of course, there was not. Adrian didn't think he was better or worse in the groupie department than any of the other major artists on the road. The temptations were simply there, and sometimes Gene availed himself of them.

Gene also took advantage of the full spirituality smorgasbord as well, Adrian noticed, coopting whatever religious notion he might gather from a chance conversation. Once he announced to Adrian that he was a "doctor of metaphysics," whatever that meant. And while he professed to be a Buddhist, Adrian doubted that Gene had any concept whatsoever about the faith and felt he was probably just drawn to the karma element of it. The "doctor" did play around with basic human physiology, though, putting people under so that they might have an out-of-body experience while unconscious. He would simply apply pressure on the jugular vein, which cut off the blood supply to the brain momentarily. It was extremely dangerous business, Adrian knew, and he shuddered to think what might happen if one day he should actually kill someone in error. Adrian thought Gene's dabbling with religions and spirituality was only token, although he'd seen how upset Gene was when his mother and sister became involved with the Tony and Susan Alamo Christian Foundation, a religious sect out in Los Angeles.

Gene was all done up in a tight leather suit—leather shirt and leather trousers—and he just didn't look quite right, Bill Kirchen thought. The rednecks at the Oakland Coliseum, who were really there for the headlining Merle Haggard, the "Okie from Muskogee," didn't seem to know what to make of him, either. It hadn't been two decades since the man's first hit, but to Bill, his band Commander Cody and His Lost Planet Airmen, and the fifteen thousand filling the Coliseum, Gene seemed from an impossibly far ago piece of the past.

He was a hell of a nice guy, Bill thought, and though he'd put on a little weight, after all those years he still had a fabulous voice and could still rock like crazy. He recalled their recent rehearsals in the dirt-floored basement of the funky Commander Cody house in Oakland. Tom Ayres had gotten them together. Gene must've been pretty down on his luck to stay at some obscure local band's creaky old house rather than at a hotel, the guys thought. They were to back Gene for a few gigs in the Bay Area: an outdoor folk festival at San Francisco State, a show at the Longbranch Saloon in Berkeley, and the opening slot for Haggard. Gene brought a well-dressed woman with him. She seemed affectionate toward him and also appeared to function as a sort of caregiver. But she didn't seem much into sitting in basements with dirt floors with a bunch of hippies. She actually seemed kind of appalled at the situation. But Gene had no problem hanging out in the cellar with them, balancing the mike stand on a musty mound of earth. He seemed to like just going over tunes. And he seemed to get a real kick out of finally running into people who actually knew his old records.

He'd recently returned from England, Gene had told them, and he seemed a little insecure, a bit nervous, about his ability to still pull off a good show. It was kind of odd because Ayres had booked him three nights on the rock revival series at Harlow's in New York City a few months before, and the show received fa-

vorable notices from *Billboard* and *Cashbox* and even aired on
Mike Douglas's TV chat show. But he had some very pop material
that he was trying to get across, tunes from his forthcoming album
*The Day the World Turned Blue*, his second for Kama Sutra, that
he'd just waxed at the Crystal Sound Studio in L.A. with his old
pal Al Casey on guitar. Bill thought the songs were a bit unseemly
for someone who'd made his mark with such a distinctive rock 'n'
roll sound and image, who sang like a bird, yet had a real nasty,
bad boy, crooked-teeth vibe. Gene wanted to do his "heavy" new
material like "Sunshine" and "High on Life" and seemed to figure
erroneously, Bill and the rest of the band thought, that the hip
scene would really groove on its meaningful content. But there was
no way that a fifties Southern greaser trying to sing to San Fran-
ciscan hippies about peace and love was ever going to work, the
band knew. So they'd encouraged him to do some of his old stuff,
practically twisting his arm to sing rocking classics like "Woman
Love." He'd politely protested, saying he'd be arrested in Oakland
if he sang that song.

You wish you could get arrested, Bill thought; Gene certainly
had some rather unrealistic views. It was kind of sad. He was so
nice, he was a real sweet guy. But he just didn't seem to be focused
on what he was up to. Bill could tell that something was wrong,
but what it was he just didn't know. Gene just didn't seem to have
it together. It wasn't because he was drinking or smoking pot or
indulging in any of the other drugs of the day—like the PCP some
jerk dosed the band with at the Longbranch—Cody rhythm guitarist John Tichy pondered. Gene hadn't consumed any mind-
altering substances, legal or otherwise, that John had seen during
their time working together. Sure, he offered some lame patter
about pot at the folk festival, but John was sure that it was just
to pander to what Gene believed were the tastes of the several
hundred in the audience that day. It actually came off as pretty
pathetic, John thought.

Even when Gene stuck to what he knew best, it didn't work

out so well. Gene had run through Jerry Lee Lewis's "Crazy Arms" downstairs in the basement, and the band had all said, "Oh, man, do that! You sing that great! Yeah!" It was a nice country shuffle, well-suited to his style. But he'd said, "Oh, I can't do that because I always get the words mixed up. I always say 'blue ain't the way for the word that I feel' rather than 'blue ain't the word.'" So they'd said, "Okay, fine," shrugged it off, and moved on to other material. But sure enough, there at the Coliseum on that fine December day, the song showed up on the set list as the opening tune. And sure enough, as advertised, Gene blew the lyrics. The singer cringed.

Marcia Avron, an American chanteuse Gene once performed with and who'd recently taken up residence at Gene's house in Simi Valley, was a know-it-all, Adrian thought. And she seemed to know just how to push Gene's buttons. Gene was obviously smitten—buying her countless dresses and boots and other things—and thought she could do no wrong. Adrian figured Gene had told her that he was big news in England, which, sadly, he was not anymore.

Adrian found Gene's most recent infatuation to be a very disruptive influence on the latest tour. For instance, coming back from a gig in rural North Wales, Gene quite suddenly demanded pizza, at Marcia's insistence, Adrian was convinced. As he and the band well knew, pizzas were virtually unknown in the UK, especially at that late hour, and getting anything to eat at midnight on a Sunday evening in North Wales was a definite impossibility. The request started quite a row, with Gene eventually becoming woundingly offended that Adrian did not care to eat with him and his girlfriend when they finally found a food-selling service station on the M1 highway. Gene, well drunk anyway, was outraged, and instead of keeping him calm, Marcia seemed happy to influence him to be a complete bastard, Adrian thought. Over the years he'd learned how to keep Gene compliant and relatively easy to work with, even when he was drunk. Marcia obviously didn't have a clue. The nonsensical scene pissed everyone off and relations re-mained strained between Gene and Adrian.

Graham Fenton of the Houseshakers, the backing band on the tour, was asked to drive Gene in his roomy '59 Chevy to the next gig in the southeast of the UK. After the show Gene decided he wanted Chinese food. It was late, and, as in Wales, finding some-thing—anything—to eat at that hour was nearly impossible. Gene grew angrier and angrier—huffing and puffing and spluttering—as their fruitless search continued. Marcia, alarmed, blurted out, "Gene, it's your—" Still in distress, Gene quickly clamped his hand over her mouth, but Graham thought he could make out the word "ulcers." Thinking Gene might be having a seizure of some sort, Graham sped to the local hospital. As he pulled up to the hospital gates, Gene, delirious, began to curse and bellow, "If you take me in there, the tour is finished!" Marcia tried to calm him and pleaded with Graham to take them back to their hotel in London. Graham was extremely worried about Gene, but followed Marcia's wishes.

Graham knew that he didn't have enough gas to make it all the way to London, so he drove into the only gas station he could find that was still open. The automated pump would only take pound notes. He and Houseshakers manager Earl Sheridan checked their pockets for cash. Neither had any. Reluctantly, Gra-ham woke the dozing Marcia and explained the situation. She roused Gene, who roared angrily, "Hey, man, you've got a gas gauge that tells you when your fuel's running out! What's the matter with you?" Gene opened up his case, threw a handful of pound notes at Graham and snapped, "Just get me back to the hotel, will you?" All the way to London Gene mumbled delirious accusations of assorted "goddamn bastards" ripping him off. After dropping Gene and Marcia off, Graham returned home to find that Gene had vomited blood on his car's backseat. Graham hoped his obviously ill friend would be okay.

Gene arrived the next day in high spirits for a BBC radio taping. It was as if the events of the last night had never happened. Later he pulled Graham aside and said, "I'm really sorry about your car. I'll pay for any cleaning." Graham turned him down. He was just relieved to see that Gene was well.

Tensions heightened again after the radio tapings for "Top Gear," John Peel's show, and "All Our Yesterplays" in London. Against Adrian's advice, Gene recorded a new version of "Say Mama," plus "I'm Movin' On" with the Houseshakers for another label, B&C Records. They were assembling an album called *Battle of the Bands* and wanted a name artist aboard to help sell it. Adrian didn't want to see Gene endanger his contract with Kama Sutra. But Gene didn't seem to care.

Gene was received well at his next several gigs, pleasing the screaming, stamping crowds of mostly old rockers and their girl-friends with encore after encore. But at the Fishmonger's Arms in Wood Green, Margaret Russell turned up—with her lawyer. Gene was served with a court order for payment of back alimony. After the next show in Kingston, Gene was handed another writ, this time from Inland Revenue demanding payment of back taxes. Adrian admired Gene's grace under such pressure. He coped with the hassles by simply being charming. On the surface, he seemed totally unconcerned because he thought he was in the right, and he believed that right would always prevail.

They were cramped in the August swelter of the small bedroom at 1264 Hayworth Avenue in Hollywood. No rehearsal. No band. Just a ten-dollar microphone, a hundred-forty-dollar Akai tape recorder, Gene on his acoustic guitar, and Ronny, Jackie, and three of Ronny's friends to give him encouragement at the Weiser family apartment.

Ronny liked the Kama Sutra records okay, the Quintet's *Gene Vincent*—which came out in July 1970 in the States and in the UK in early '71 under the title *If Only You Could See Me Today*—and the newly released *The Day the World Turned Blue*. Gene had waxed that disc in October 1970, teaming up once again with Al Casey on guitar. Tom Ayres helmed the sessions, which, for the most part, featured Gene doing more of the same: recycling his favorite artists' songs—Gene Allison's "You Can Make It If You Try," Carl Perkins's "Boppin' the Blues," "Looking Back," a Brook Benton tune Nat King Cole had turned into a hit, and Don Gibson's "Oh Lonesome Me"—with a largely toothless, country-rock-tinged sound.

Those albums were fine, Ronny thought. But they were kind of bland, kind of gutless. He wondered if there wasn't something else that could be done. The new stuff just seemed to be lacking some of that original sound from the fifties. That rawness, that recklessness, that primitivism. So he asked the singer if he could record a little something for the fans, a few tunes he could put out on his new Rollin' Rock record label. Gene said he didn't mind.

Ronny suggested that Gene try "School of Rock 'n' Roll" by Gene Summers. The singer gave it a couple of attempts, but he couldn't get it to work.

"Well, do what you like," Ronny told him. Practically without effort, Gene rolled out Buddy Knox's "Party Doll," Sam Cooke's soulful "Bring It On Home," the sweet ballad "The Rose of Love," and Little Richard's "Hey Hey Hey Hey," one take each, one right after the other. His voice was still beautiful, but now tempered with a transfixing world-weariness.

Ronny had seen Gene at least once a week when he was in Hollywood, and they had become good friends. Weiser dropped by his place or met up with him at radio appearances or his occasional shows at clubs, like during his week in May at the Brass Ring, where famous fans from Clapton to Beatle George Harrison sat in, or other nightspots in the valley. He apparently was still finding work in France and England, so he'd be gone for a month, sometimes six weeks at a time. But he always seemed kind of depressed. He wanted to have a real rock 'n' roll band to back him up, but he just couldn't find people who really knew what it was all about, except maybe Billy Zoom, the rockabilly fanatic who played flute and electric piano for Gene before joining L.A. punk band X on guitar. And he wasn't happy about the whole scene that was happening in America, the hippie thing. He was very much against illicit drugs, he had no sympathy for the anti-American undercurrents, and he seemed deeply distressed at the course popular music was taking.

He was feeling pressure to become a straight country artist, he confided to Ronny, or to turn hippie himself and record music similar to what groups like Led Zeppelin or Jefferson Airplane were doing. He didn't want to do either. "I always sang country music, and I always will sing country music," he told Ronny, "but I'm not a Nashville artist. I'm a rock 'n' roller, and I will always be a rock 'n' roller. I'll never betray rock 'n' roll. I'd rather die. And when I die, throw me at sea in my black leather suit." Becoming musically colorless, like the stuff he saw coming out of Nashville lately, was boring to him. Even Hank Williams had R&B influences; that's why Gene admired his music so much, Ronny figured.

They were always talking about music, mainly rock 'n' roll. Ronny tried not to talk about anything too personal, like his leg. He could see it was constantly hurting his friend. Gene showed it to Ronny once. It was an open, ugly wound, and Ronny quickly tried to forget it. Gene liked to chat about his favorite rock 'n' rollers, folks like Carl Perkins, Wanda Jackson, Elvis, Little Richard, and Chuck Berry. He also liked Brook Benton, Sam Cooke, and Fats Domino. And he was a big friend of all of the living legends. One night, Gene and Ronny were at a Little Richard show at the Whisky. When Richard found out that Gene Vincent was in the crowd, he brought him right up onstage and they did "Be-Bop-A-Lula" together. Ronny never forgot it.

They also talked quite a bit about the Blue Caps. Gene wanted to get back together with the Blue Caps very badly, and he was always trying to figure a way to do it. He talked a lot about Eddie, too, telling Ronny all about his best friend. He believed they'd go on forever, he told Ronny, doing rock 'n' roll music and being the idols of young people all over the world. Ronny was careful not to ask about the accident—that was much too personal, he thought—and Gene never brought it up. Ronny knew it had affected the singer very badly, very strongly. It still seemed very fresh in his mind.

Ronny tried to talk about positive things. That's just the kind of guy he was. But he knew Gene was lonely, and that he felt like a fish out of water in groovy Los Angeles at the height of the hippie movement. It seemed there was nobody around who even knew who Gene Vincent was, except for Manny down at Aaron's Record Shop. He was completely forgotten. Yet it was only ten years earlier that he was selling millions of records. It was depressing. The great Gene Vincent playing in front of a dozen people at some cheap dive in the Valley for a lousy forty bucks. Still, his friend always struggled to give the best show he possibly could, whether there were twelve or twelve thousand in the audience. But he was typically backed by a bunch of hippies who had no idea what his music was about. It was the lowest point of Gene's career, Ronny knew. Gene was obviously despondent about it. He was in mourning for the Gene Vincent he once was.

The phone rang in the promotions offices at Monument Records in Nashville. "Bill, this is Gene."

"Gene-o!" Sheriff Tex Davis exclaimed in surprise.

"I got a problem," Gene said. He sounded down, real down. Desperate, even.

"What's the problem?" Bill asked.

"I need a record label."

"Oh, you got one," Bill told him without a moment's hesitation. Gene was stunned. "I do?"

"Sure, you're on Monument Records," Bill said. "If you wanna be on the label."

"I'd love to be," the singer answered.

"Gene, give me your phone number, I'll call you back."

Davis had been appointed Monument Records' head of national promotion in 1967, and helped to make hits out of singles by Kris Kristofferson, Larry Gatlin, Charlie McCoy, and countless others.

After he hung up the phone, he went into Fred Foster's office, the label's owner, and told him of the out-of-the-blue conversation he'd just had with Gene Vincent. Foster was enthusiastic. He was a great fan of Vincent's music and wanted to sign him to a multi-album deal. The first album would be all new material, Foster planned, and then an album of rerecordings of Vincent's classic hits could be made later. Foster thought he had some viable production ideas for the singer that might break some new ground for him. He was excited at the prospect of working with such a fine vocalist.

Davis rang Gene back. The singer was ecstatic and wanted to get into the studio immediately.

"That's fantastic," he told Bill. "But look, I got a big tour planned in Europe—forty dates. Why don't I drop into Nashville and we'll cut the album? And then you can go to work on it while I do the forty dates."

Davis didn't think that was such a good idea. "No," he told Gene, "you're down now. You couldn't sing with your heart. There's no way you can do anything now, you're feeling so bad. You hate yourself. You go over there and let the fans give you that feeling again. The pizzazz you always had. And then come back here with that pizzazz and we'll just kill 'em."

"That's what you want to do?" Gene asked.

"Yeah, Gene," Bill told him. "That's what I'd like to do."


It was the strangest thing, Jerry Merritt thought. Gene was on the phone. Out of the blue, he said, "Jerry, you got any fishing poles?" Gene didn't fish. They'd never gone fishing before.

"Well, yeah," Jerry said, puzzled.

"I'm comin' up there," Gene told him. "I'm gettin' out of this mess and we're gonna go fishing."

Jerry hung up the phone and turned to his wife. He was upset. "Something's wrong with Gene," he said, an uneasy feeling crawling over his skin. "I don't know what it is. But something's wrong."

The man was very ill. Adrian could tell. Gene seemed fairly lucid and relatively happy sitting on the bed in his hotel room in Ealing, London. His mood seemed positive. He seemed very anxious to make up with Adrian after their falling out from the last tour eight months before. But he was talking utter nonsense. He described to Adrian how Capitol re-signed him and that a new album would be forthcoming. He described his ten-year-old son as a naval officer, just as he himself had been, he said. He spoke of these things as if he honestly believed they were true, as if these fantasies were, in fact, his reality. It was sad.

Adrian knew that he was in the presence of a man who was soon to die.

The guy was weird from the moment he came into the Radio London studios in Hannover Square, disc jockey David Simmonds thought.

It all happened very quickly. Steve Bradshaw, host of the Radio London program "Breakthrough," was offered an interview with Gene Vincent. As he didn't know much about the rock 'n' roll singer, he asked Simmonds to do it. Simmonds had seen Vincent onstage back in the early sixties, so he agreed. Vincent showed up about a half an hour later. He'd changed quite a bit since Simmonds last saw him. He didn't look like an old man, because he wasn't old, Simmonds knew. Rather, he looked like a man who was not well.

When Gene had landed in England just days before, he was met at the airport with yet another writ over nonpayment of back alimony. He appeared a few days later in the High Court in London and was ordered to pay six hundred pounds to Margie, who had finally gotten a divorce in 1970 on grounds of cruelty. A taping for the Johnnie Walker radio show on the BBC—five songs with the band Kansas Hook—went reasonably well. But he was fired from his engagements at the Garrick Club in Leigh and at the Wookey Hollow Club in Liverpool when it became obvious that he was in no shape to perform. A British doctor, alarmed at the condition of his liver and his gastrointestinal ulcers, strongly urged him to go home and enter the Veterans Hospital. *Immediately.*

He hardly seemed fit to speak. Even before the interview started, Simmonds would ask him a perfectly ordinary question, like "How are you?" and Gene would look at him as if he'd just insulted his mother. And he complained to the disc jockey that he was in pain all the time because of his leg. He was a very strange character, Simmonds thought. He'd go from being quite charming to being very difficult. He seemed to be a troubled soul, and Simmonds never knew how much of it was an act.

"When, in fact, did you start?" Simmonds began the interview, simply enough.

"Twenty years ago," Gene said. "I started with a song called 'Be-Bop-A-Lula.' I started with three fellas in the South, which names were Carl Perkins, Elvis Presley, and myself. Now Carl Perkins was booked to do *The Ed Sullivan Show*, 'cause he heard about this music and they didn't know too much about it. Unfortunately, Carl had an accident which killed his brother and broke his back, so they said, 'Well let's get this guy called Gene Vincent.' But I was in the hospital with a broken leg, so they got Elvis Presley. Elvis is a fine singer and a good man and I cannot say nothing against him. He is the one to me that is one of the biggest what you might call rock 'n' rollers of them all."

Simmonds was incredulous. "Now you claim," he asked disbelievingly, "with these two other people, to have started rock 'n' roll?"

"Yes," Gene answered.

Simmonds couldn't believe it. "Is that right?" he asked Gene.

"No, no," Gene answered. "What we started was a thing called rockabilly. You call it rock 'n' roll." The singer laughed. "That's the difference. It changed over the years, you see."

"Okay," Simmonds granted him. "What is your definition of rock 'n' roll then? And who started it?"

"My definition of rock 'n' roll is a rather soul-type singing from the heart," Gene said. "We can put this across, we have the ability, and we know when people want it and when they don't."

"You're saying it's soul?" Simmonds prodded. "You're saying that the original rock 'n' roll was black and rockabilly was white?"

"No," Gene said. "Rockabilly come from hillbilly music, really."

"They're white folks—" the interviewer said.

"Oh, are you going to bring color in?" Gene pounced. "I didn't know we were bringing color in."

"But you said rock 'n' roll is a sort of soul music," Simmonds said. "Now this is black, isn't it, originally?"

"Yes," Gene said, "but Americans, white people, have souls, too. You got a soul, ain't you?" Gene laughed.

"Okay. You still haven't answered my question, then. Who started rock 'n' roll and when?"

"Well, I'm tellin' you, we started what you call rock 'n' roll. We called it rockabilly then, and what you're singing today is what we started, us three people. Now rock 'n' roll can be termed in many different ways. Probably you have your own term of it. But what you call, what the papers and what the pop people today call rock 'n' roll, we started."

"To me, rock 'n' roll is people like Jerry Lee Lewis and Carl Perkins and Gene Vincent and Chuck Berry and Little Richard," Simmonds said. "But I wouldn't have included you in the original three, because for a start the other two came from this small label in Memphis, Sam Phillips' Sun label, and they were into it before you were with Capitol. Is that right?"

"No," Gene said. " 'Cause Sun wasn't started then, Capitol was."

"Capitol had been running a long while but wasn't into rock 'n' roll."

"That's right," Gene said. "That's true."

"But would you agree with me that rock 'n' roll started with Sam Phillips' Sun label? He was recording—"

"No, not really, no," Gene interrupted. "Can't say that. Sorry.

I know Sam well and Sam picked up on something that was already happening. It was already into it when Sam picked it up. But Elvis's first song was—a lot of people don't even know his first song, that's the way Sam picked him up. And I know how—"

"I think it was 'Kentucky Moon,' " Simmonds interrupted, "wasn't it?"

"No. 'Blue Moon of Kentucky.' "

" 'Blue Moon of Kentucky.' That was his first song, then?"

"Now will you stand corrected, sir?" Gene sneered. "Will you stand corrected?"

"You're trying to beat me under this table, aren't you?" Simmonds laughed at Gene's combativeness.

"That's it!"

Simmonds continued, "His first hits were with old blues songs by people—"

"No, sir," Gene interrupted. "No, sir. His first hit was played on the radio called 'Blue Moon of Kentucky.' So many people called in saying 'Gee, what a great new sound' that Sam picked up on it. But a lot of people were doing it before that, especially Carl Perkins. We played Memphis, and a lot of people think that 'Blue Suede Shoes' was put out by Elvis Presley. It wasn't. Carl Perkins done it. And we were playing Memphis one night—me, Carl Perkins, and Elvis. And Carl came out and done 'Blue Suede Shoes,' and Elvis came after him and started doing 'Blue Moon of Kentucky,' and they started cheering for Carl Perkins. Elvis came backstage, put his foot on his guitar, smashed it, and said, 'I shall never play with another rock 'n' roller again.' And from that day to this, he hasn't."

"You're putting him down for this, aren't you?" Simmonds asked.

"No, I'm not, no," Gene said. "When the man says something, he means it. He's a good man, I like him. He's a friend of mine, I know his wife—"

"Then why would he have done this?" Simmonds pressed.

"Maybe he was just annoyed, I guess," Gene said. "But when

you're supposed to be one of the biggest singers around and they cheer for somebody else, you tend to get annoyed."

Simmonds changed the subject. "Now, I remember you ten years ago playing with Jerry Lee Lewis at the Fairfield Halls. I think you were going to come back the next year, but the people who ran the Fairfield Halls decided not to have anymore rock 'n' rollers because—"

"I think it was Golders Green, wasn't it?" Gene interrupted.

"No, no."

"Sorry, sorry."

"It was definitely the Fairfield Halls in Croydon," Simmonds said. "And way down the bill was a fellow called Mickie Most, playing the guitar on his back, who had just come back from South Africa. And today I'm told he's a millionaire, producing records for all sorts of people—"

"Actually, Mr. Most is my brother-in-law," Gene broke in.

"Is he?"

"Right."

"I'm pleased to know it," the interviewer said. "And a young gentleman with blond peroxide hair called Heinz. Do you remember Heinz?"

"Right."

"He was booed off the stage," Simmonds recalled. "He was terrible."

"You say he was terrible," Gene jumped in. "Now listen, anybody who pays to see somebody who gets up on the stage, and who is even on the bill in the first place, is not terrible. And I stand to say to you that that's not true."

"You mean that no performance can be bad?" Simmonds asked in disbelief. "Surely that can't be true?"

"It's true," Gene asserted. "To you it might be bad. To me it might be good."

"I'm just saying that the majority of the people there that night—"

"Yes, but who are you to judge anybody's music?" Gene piped up.

"I have paid, I've paid to get in—"

"Right," Gene said. "And you can also get your money on the way out."

"No, no," Simmonds disagreed. "Once I'm in, I'm going to stay there for the duration of the performance. And if I think a man is bad, I think I'm entitled to hiss or boo if I want to, or clap if I think he's good."

"But who is bad?" Gene asked. "Who are you to say what's bad or is good? You've just tried to bring color in, you try to hit me with about nine different things and I gotcha every way. You're no judge of music. You don't read it, you don't talk it, or you don't live it. I do. Now politically, business-wise, husband-wise, I might be a no-good son-of-a-gun. But there's one thing I can do. I know my music. Can't mess me up on it, baby. Try it!"

"Now, you know I'm not trying it," Simmonds backed off. "I started by criticizing somebody else called Heinz."

"Right, but you don't criticize no musician."

"And you defend him," Simmonds said. "How do you know I'm not a musician myself?"

"If you were, you wouldn't say that."

"As it happens, I am," Simmonds said. "Do you want me to play the piano? It's on the left-hand side—"

"Well, you can play the piano, but can you play it well?"

"Well, I don't know, I mean, who is to judge? According to you, nobody can judge a musician."

Gene laughed. "Now you just said it, I didn't say it. To me you might be the worst piano player in the whole world. But to you, you might be very good. Or to somebody else you might be very good."

"Yeah, but if I then inflict myself on a paying audience, I must accept that if the audience does not like me, that is that," Simmonds argued.

"Look, look," Gene said. "All I do is, I am paid to do a show. People pay to come and see me. If they don't want to come and see me, they don't have to pay. Right?"

"Right."

"You dig?"

"Whilst we're into your own act, I also remember ten years ago, your own act was fairly wild. You came on to 'Be-Bop-A-Lula' and of course everybody went mad and you also used to dress in black leather, as I remember, in those days. Do you still wear this gear?"

"Yeah, I wear black leather," Gene answered. "You know, I'm a different type of person, I guess, than any other man. I drink, smoke, cuss, and go out with women. I suppose no other body does that. At least they won't admit it. I suppose you don't."

"Oh, but I do!"

"Right," Gene said. "At least you admit it."

"Oh, yeah," Simmonds said. "The fact that you wear black leather is only part of it. You also seem to use your affliction, too, in your stage act—the fact that you wear a leg iron. I remember this at the time as being—"

"I only have one leg now," Gene lied.

"You only have one?" Simmonds asked, dumbfounded, as Gene had just told him off-air that his leg pained him constantly.

"Yeah."

Simmonds went on. "At the time you used your—"

"No, it was painful," Gene said. "Putting my weight on one leg so I can hold it there and do the act for my audience that I should do, that they paid to see. When my audience pays to see something, I must give them my best, no matter how I feel. Sometimes the pain is bad. When the weather's nice, it's pretty good. You can check my record at Naval Headquarters at Grosvenor Square. I was also ordered back from Mildenhall by the 48th Technical Air Force 'cause my leg was so bad. And my records are there for you to see."

"So you're saying that in fact you played on really when you shouldn't have been playing?" Simmonds asked.

"That's right," Gene told him. "And I shouldn't be here now."

"Yeah," Simmonds said, not sure what to believe. "The audience, because of the gear you wear, do you think you attract a certain sort of audience? Rockers, for example?"

"No, sir, I can please my audience."

"But you must know, over the years, the sort of people who come to see you. Is there one group that stands out? Kids on motorbikes?"

"No," Gene said. "The older people. We draw a lot of older people, about forty, now. They like me and I like them and we get along quite well together."

"But what about young kids, too, in their late teens?"

"Well, the young kids now don't come and see me anymore, you know. It's the twenty-ones and twenty-twos, let's say up to forty, you know."

"And what sort of music are you into now, Gene?"

"Same thing I do," the singer said. "I do exactly what they want me to do."

"I mean, you still play the old rock 'n' roll numbers?"

"I try to put in some of the newer ones," Gene said, "which they sometimes won't accept. So I change immediately."

"Now, other old rock 'n' rollers, like Jerry Lee Lewis, have, in a way, changed with the times. Now Jerry Lee has left behind his 'Breathless' and 'Great Balls of Fire' days that you were into when he was into his sort of music. And now he plays more country music, because that way he knows he can keep abreast with changes. Why haven't you done this?"

"Oh, I'm getting ready to do it now," he said. "But actually I love rock 'n' roll and I was in it from the start. And, really, there is not that much difference between country and rock 'n' roll, there's really not that much difference. And Jerry Lee, to me, is doing what he done in the fifties."

"He was playing country music before he went into rock 'n' roll," Simmonds said. "He's really come full circle."

"That's true. Right."

"Do you play country music?" Simmonds asked.

"Yeah," Gene said. "Very well."

"What sort of thing?"

"Actually, I'm a musician and a singer and I can sing just about anything that you want to put in front of me," Gene explained, "as long as it doesn't come up into opera or semi-opera or something like that. I love to listen to that type of music, but I can sing just about anything I want to sing."

"Yeah, but could you—"

"I'm an artist," Gene told Simmonds. "That's what I'm paid to do."

"But if, as you say, you don't attract the kids anymore," the interviewer said, "it's mainly people who are still old rock 'n' rollers and older, haven't you thought of changing your style so you come on as a straight country artist?"

"No," Gene said flatly. "I can never do that."

"You couldn't do that? Why not?" Simmonds asked.

"Jerry don't do it as well."

"Well, he plays a lot of country music records now, I mean—"

"Yeah," Gene interrupted. "Well, he plays a lot, but he still does his 'Whole Lotta Shakin' Goin On.' In England he can't get off the stage unless he does it."

"Yes," Simmonds conceded. "Do you think kids, the sort of kids that used to come to your performances in the late fifties, today are missing out on something by not appreciating the old style of rock 'n' roll?"

"Oh, they do appreciate it," Gene assured. "The biggest group in the world used to be called the Beatles and the Rolling Stones. But our biggest group in the United States is called Creedence Clearwater, and he does old, stinking rock 'n' roll and it's funky and it's lowdown and he pulls it right from the bottom of his feet, right from his heart. To see Creedence, you'd probably hate him, to see him. But I love him. That man can sing, and as far as I'm concerned I haven't ever seen an artist I didn't like, really. They can do something well. Some of the things they do I don't like, but some of the things— I cannot judge their music. Now a lot of people and a lot of promoters will pay you to do a show and they want to enter your personal life as well, which to me is not right on. It's not good. They want to enter the artist's private life, which my life is private and I like to keep it that way. But what I do when I get on stage is entirely different, and what my public wants me to do is what I'll do. And I will not have no cigar-smoking middle-man sitting out there judging my public or telling my public what they should do, what they should like. 'Cause if the public don't like me, they won't pay and come to see me. And I think I speak for not only myself, but for every British artist in the country, and they know what I'm talking about."

"But this sort of tough line, this sort of independence you want, must have got you into trouble or lost you work in the past," Simmonds said.

"I don't need your work, really," Gene told him. "I don't have to work, I don't have to. I'm paid by the United States government."

"I'm sorry?" Simmonds asked, not sure he heard the singer correctly. "You're paid by the United States government? How is that?"

"Yes," Gene told him. "I'm in the Navy. I was hurt."

"I see. You get a pension?"

"I told you before, when I was seventeen I was in the Navy. It's not a pension, it's a—"

"A disability payment?"

"Yes," Gene said. "Right."

"Oh, so you don't have to work?"

"No."

"And where do you spend most of your time?"

"I spend most of my time with my wife and four children."

"Very wise, too."

"My son was just accepted in the Naval Academy, which being a disabled officer," Gene said, spewing the same fantasy he'd told Adrian back in Ealing, "I'm allowed to recommend him. And he was accepted, thank God. You know, I'm very proud of that. But I think it's just about high time that some artist got up and stood up and said, Look, these cigar-smoking fat slobs are not allowed to tell the British public what they like and what they dislike. Let them decide."

"Okay," Simmonds said, groping for a different subject. "Turning from the people behind artists to the people in front of them, the audience. People still—I mean, you may say this is nonsense—but people still identify you as somebody who will go up and play in front of rockers and get bigger cheers than anybody else because of your black leather gear and your motorcycle accident. I'm not saying that you're surrounded by Hell's Angels, but people sometimes say they are today's true underground in this country. Is this true, do you think? You're very close to them?"

"Really?" Gene asked. "I am? I don't think it's that way. They consider me as a fighter for them. I will get up and say what they think, what they'd like to say if they were here."

"This is your platform."

"Right," Gene said.

"What would they like you to say?"

"Well, just what I've said, really. And it's not the gear that I dress in. It's the way that I'm not afraid to tell you exactly what I— I'm not afraid of the BBC, I'm not afraid of Radio One. 'Cause I'm in a position to be that way. And they can't get up here and talk for themselves. So I will."

"They're a group of people who are often in trouble, and people often think of them as violent, unthinking people. Now, when you've done your stage act over the years, have you ever had any trouble from an audience?"

"Yes, sir," Gene said. "I have, almost always older people."

"How do you mean by older people?"

"About forties, forty-fives and fifties."

"And what sort of trouble?"

"Jeering," Gene said. "I've never been arrested in my whole life. Never been in any kind of trouble. And you call me a black leather— Have you?"

"You wear black leather on stage—"

"Yeah," Gene interrupted, "but have you ever been arrested?"

"Yes," Simmonds said.

"Well, I haven't, you see."

"Well, that's neither here nor there," Simmonds snipped. "I mean—"

"Well, you're kinda putting me in a category which—"

"No," Simmonds interrupted. "I simply said to you that here is a group of kids who wear black leather and are known as rockers and Hell's Angels—"

"Yeah, but just because they wear black leather and you call them Hell's Angels, you're putting them in a category. You're saying they're bad people."

"No, I'm not," the interviewer disagreed. "I'm saying that people say they're bad. Now, you know them because they are your audience. Have they ever given you trouble?"

"Who is the people that say they're bad?"

"Newspapers, the establishment—"

"Aah, peace!" Gene jumped in. "The establishment. But the establishment will fall. Guaranteed. But they'll fall when these kids grow up and outvote them. Violence is unnecessary. And they will grow up someday, and someday they'll be in a position to change your government."

"You're anti-violence, are you?" Simmonds asked.

"Oh, definitely," Gene replied.

"But you have a violent act," Simmonds countered. "Or it used to be when I used to see it."

"What do you call violent?" Gene asked him.

"Well, you know, sort of— You used to use the microphone like a cattle prod. And stick your leg out and scream at the other people in the band. You know, 'come and get me' sort of thing."

"No," Gene said. "Usually I cue 'em by that way, and I'll speed them up or slow them down as I feel what should be done. I'll feel the people, I'll feel what they want, and I'll speed them up or slow them down. As far as being violent onstage, I use the microphone more or less as a crutch, you see. But you didn't know that, did you?"

"It just looked violent to me."

"I know," Gene said. "Well, what it looked to you and what it seemed to you is exactly what I meant it to be. Thank you. Actually, you paid me a compliment, 'cause you didn't know my leg hurt, did you?" Gene laughed.

"Wish I hadn't said that now," Simmonds demurred. "But anyway, you're obviously a thinking man, Gene. I don't mean that in a condescending way. But so many people who sing either haven't got anything to say—they just can't speak, they just play—or they say 'I just play my music and there's nothing behind it anyway, I'm just me.' Now, do you think there is anything, any sort of message in your music? That might sound silly, but—"

"Yes," Gene said. "God, yes. Oh, Lord. I get on stage sometimes and I'll be singing and I'll start thinking about something else and what the song was written about, and I'll put myself in the place of the song, which is the only way I can sing. If you was to put me in a room by myself, I couldn't sing a note. 'Cause I sing from people, I sing from experience, I sing from things that's happened to me. I sing from the way I walk down the road or what I've seen. There's lots of things I sing about, and these are the songs that made a lot of money for me."

"Would you say you're a 'clean' singer?" Simmonds asked.

"What do you call 'clean'?" Gene asked.

"Well, how do you justify lyrics like— There's a short piece on your last album, I think it was your last album, that starts off, 'I'm wise to the rise in your Levi's.' "

"You can take that any way you please, sir," Gene said. "You can take that dirty or clean. How do you take it?"

"No, you tell me, first of all," Simmonds protested. "You wrote it. It's my question to you."

"Yes, but how do you take it?" Gene persisted.

"No, I'm asking you, first of all, because you wrote it. You justify to me what those words mean, how you came to get them into your song. 'I'm wise to the rise in your Levi's.' "

"I was standing on the corner of Hollywood Boulevard one day," Gene explained, "and I heard a girl say that to a boy. So, therefore, I just said it. You can take anything clean or dirty. You can take sex clean or dirty." Gene laughed. "Can't you? It's just according to how you want it. My wife and kids, to me is clean. We have a beautiful home, and I don't drive a Rolls Royce or I'm not flashy. I'm not a big-headed little smart aleck, which I can be if I want to be. Now, can't I? But I'm not. I feel that God has given me something that a lot of people don't have. He's given me a talent that I can use and I must use it well."

"How can people get the kids back into rock 'n' roll?" Simmonds asked, changing the subject again. "The kids who now say it's old-fashioned, who think of rock 'n' roll as—"

"Well, I don't think kids think of rock 'n' roll as old-fashioned," Gene said. "Otherwise, Creedence Clearwater wouldn't be a hit."

"Yeah, Creedence Clearwater weren't around when you and Roy Orbison and—"

"No," Gene interrupted, "but it's bringing it back."

"Yeah," Simmonds agreed.

"To me, I think Creedence Clearwater, with the help of the Beatles and—"

"Yeah," Simmonds broke in, "but what about the old records? You see, Shelby Singleton is reissuing the old Sun records, the old Carl Perkins and Jerry Lee Lewis—"

"No, it's the same type of music what you're speaking about. Creedence Clearwater, the Beatles and everybody, like 'Good Golly Miss Molly,' that stuff they're coming out with, you know."

"Yeah, but you're not bothered about seeing the original versions of the late fifties being reissued?"

"Lord, no," Gene said. "I appreciate that. Mercy, it helps all of us. It really helps our business, and it helps to establish new artists that's coming up now. That's what I'd like to do. I'd like to help some new artists that's coming up today."

"Any names you'd like to throw out that we wouldn't have heard of possibly here yet?"

"I don't know, because I haven't heard of them. I've only arrived about five days ago, so the climate, you know, is a bit—"

"I was thinking of American bands," Simmonds said. "I thought possibly—"

"Not really," Gene said. "There's a lot of them coming up, but— I'm working with a gentleman with Capitol Records now called Paul Rose, and he's helping me out quite a bit, and we've got a couple of new groups in mind, you know. But I can't say anything about them yet because I haven't seen them that much."

"Do you think any particular sort of musical development in the last ten years has harmed the old rockabilly, rock 'n' roll, as you know it?" Simmonds asked.

"No," Gene said. "I think all music is good. It's just how you want to take it."

"That's a very generous statement: 'All music is good.' "

"Well, opera is fantastic, but I am too stupid in my mind to accept what the artist is trying to put across to me, you see. So that's not his fault, that's mine. So I blame myself. Okay?"

As Gene jetted west across the Atlantic, Margaret Russell Craddock was unburdening herself to the *Sun* at her flat in London. While still married to Gene Vincent, she had given birth to a secret baby, she told the tabloid, four-year-old Jamie, a little brother to Sherri Ann, her daughter with Gene. "Until now, no one has known anything about my little Jamie, or his father," she said. "But I've finally decided to marry again, and I can't let it stay a secret."

Louise Cooper Craddock knew that her son was in England. But she felt compelled to call his house in Simi Valley, anyway. She had a horrible, unshakable feeling that something was wrong with Gene. Something gravely wrong. She'd spent the whole night praying.

To her surprise, Gene answered the phone.

"I just had to come home," he told her. He sounded distraught. "But Mama, she took everything I had, even my record player."

Alarmed, Louise and Kie arranged for a friend to drive them from their trailer park in Saugus to their son's house in Simi Valley. They were shocked at what they found. The house was virtually empty, apparently cleaned out by Marcia. Even the record player her daughters had lovingly given their brother as a gift was gone. Gene's face was gray, nearly lifeless, the color of ashes. He was dying. Kie and Louise pleaded for him to check into the local Veterans Administration Hospital. But he refused. Louise begged him to come home with his mama and daddy, at least. He refused.

Johnny Meeks was playing a gig in Chatsworth, just a few miles over the hill from Gene's house in Simi Valley. He wondered if Gene was going to turn up. His old buddy would often come to his shows when he was in town, mostly to try to get him to go back to England with him on his next tour. No Gene. Must be on the road, Johnny thought.

Kie and Louise returned to the house the next morning. Gene was worse. He'd been drinking steadily through the night and hadn't eaten.

"Mama, did you all pray for me last night?" he asked Louise.

They assisted their failing son out to the car. "Mama, let's hurry and get home," he said again and again. He stumbled and fell. They helped him back up and placed him inside the car. "Mama, if I get through this, I'll be a better man," he told her.

They begged Gene to check into the Inter-Valley Hospital in Saugus as they passed by it on their way to the Craddocks' trailer. Again he refused, murmuring, "I just want to go home, Mama. I just want to go home."

As they entered the trailer, Gene stumbled and lost his footing. He tumbled to the floor. Bent over in a crumpled heap, he vomited, puddling the floor with a growing pool of red. Blood red. Louise took hold of his hand. He looked up at her helplessly. "Mama," he gasped, "you can phone the ambulance now."

*The Triumph Tiger was tough, Gene thought. But now, flying through the hills north of Hollywood, their long, green grasses turned dry and yellow, the live oaks and scrub pines thirsty with the change of season, he felt his once-powerful ride falter. He twisted the accelerator with no luck; no matter how much fuel he gave it, the bike moved forward only hesitantly, as if a curious trepidation had taken hold of it. Maybe he was running out of gas, Gene reasoned, or perhaps it was just engine trouble. He thought he'd kept the motorcycle in pretty good condition over the years. Here, in the crisp light of an autumn day, though, he could see that the once-gleaming chrome was rusted in dark, de-feated patches, the tires were deflated with dry rot, and the engine hacked and sputtered painfully. Gene puzzled how it could've hap-pened. The bike sighed to an exhausted halt at the top of the hill.*

*Now what? Gene wondered. He had no choice. He'd have to wait here for the next car to pass and hitch a ride. He checked the horizon below him. Nothing. A parched wind blew, worrying some dead, dry leaves across the gray asphalt, reminding him of how tired, how utterly spent, he suddenly felt. It was growing dark, the shadows sadly deepening and stretching like mothers mourning sons too soon departed. He waited a few moments, then checked again.*

*His gut lurched.*

*The highway unraveled beneath him was empty, save for a sin-*

gle smoky speck. It was moving fast, speeding so swiftly it seemed to be flying. Gene knew exactly what it was.

The jet black car, the hulking chariot with crimson flames emblazoned down both sides, screamed to an abrupt halt in front of him. The door opened.

Gene could hardly believe his eyes. Black leather pants and a black leather jacket encased the lean, strong, limpless body. A tangle of dark, greasy curls hung over the brow, giving symmetry to the cleft chin and thin lips. And the enormous eyes—they gleamed. Glowed, really. Red as spilt blood.

"I know you. I remember you. What the hell do you want from me?" Gene asked, trying hard not to show his blossoming fear. He knew there was no escaping this time.

"I want you to come with me," the man said slowly, succinctly, fixing his tender prey in his sickening crimson stare. His voice was steely and cold, and it scraped like a serrated blade over Gene's aching eardrums. Gene began to tremble.

"Why?" Gene asked, a bilious terror rising in his throat.

"I will take you where you belong," the man hissed. He leapt forward, grabbing Gene by the neck as the sickly eyes glowed madly in their orbits. He smelled sour, like the putrid regret of a thousand miserable souls.

They began to struggle. The red-eyed man plunged a cold, hard hand deep into Gene's belly. Gene fell to the ground. He labored to his knees like a penitent, unable to catch his breath. The devil man scooped him up under the arms and began dragging him across the pavement to the car. Gene tried to resist, tried to fight. But the man, the beast, was strong. Too strong.

"Leave him," commanded a deep, dusky voice from behind them. The voice was familiar. Gene turned to look as the red-eyed man dropped him to the ground and disappeared.

It was Eddie. He was beautiful, shrouded by tawny shafts of sunlight that had escaped the somber clouds, marking a glowing path to heaven.

*"I will take you where you belong,"* he said, *the boundless compassion in his eyes filling the entire valley, quieting all fears, dispelling all sorrows.*

*Eddie opened his arms to Gene. Gene collapsed wearily onto Eddie's strong chest. A sweet smile of peaceful relief settled on his face as Eddie's warm arms enfolded him.*

# A F T E R W O R D

Gene Vincent died on October 12, 1971, at the Inter-Valley Community Hospital in Saugus, California. The Los Angeles County Coroner's autopsy report listed the cause of death as acute hepatic insufficiency due to, or as a consequence of, cirrhosis of the liver due to, or as a consequence of, chronic alcoholism, with upper gastrointestinal hemorrhage as a contributing condition, but not related to the immediate cause of death. The report also listed, incorrectly, Gene's hair color as black and eye color as blue. The document also indicated that "no amputations, deformities, or appliances [were] noted externally on the body," though friends tell that by the time of his death the exposed bone of Vincent's left leg had turned completely black and withered in width to the diameter of a quarter.

The funeral service, attended by only a handful of Vincent's friends and family—"I don't suppose that six hundred pounds will ever be paid now," third wife Margaret Russell complained to the *Sun* just days after the singer's death—was performed by Tony Alamo of the Tony and Susan Alamo Christian Foundation, a religious sect whose ministry would grow into a multi-million dollar enterprise over the next two decades, according to a Memphis prosecutor, with Alamo living lavishly while many of his followers worked for church businesses for subsistence wages or no pay at all.

The Alamos purchased Gene's burial plot in the Eternal Valley Memorial Park in Newhall, California. There was no headstone until 1976, when Jackie Frisco purchased a permanent granite marker, engraved with an incorrect musical notation of "Be-Bop-A-Lula's" chorus. In September 1994, Tony Alamo, also known as Bernie Lazar Hoffman, was sentenced to a maximum of six years in prison and fined $210,000 for income-tax evasion.

It was a sad, sensational end for a formidable talent whose own life had ultimately become utterly sad and sensational.

Yet despite his tragic demise, Gene Vincent and his contributions to the development and iconography of the rock genre live on. With his defiant black leather, distinctive limp, and revolutionary spirit, Vincent remains an almost mythic figure, a wellspring of musical, sartorial, and attitudinal style long departed yet very much alive in the hearts and music of subsequent generations of rockers.

In the years following his death, countless reissue and tribute albums have appeared, particularly in Europe, some including material only available posthumously. "Be-Bop-A-Lula" has been recorded time and again by a heady phalanx of famous fans, including both John Lennon and Paul McCartney, Carl Perkins, and Jerry Lee Lewis. Johnny Carroll waxed "Black Leather Rebel" in '74 in honor of his late friend. In 1977, Cockney rocker Ian Dury released "Sweet Gene Vincent," his musical tribute to the legend. "There was something mystical about his voice that got to me," Dury explained.

In 1980, Ronny Weiser issued the four songs Vincent had recorded in the Weiser family apartment on *Forever Gene Vincent*, which also featured a rendition of "Say Mama" sung by Vincent's daughter Melody Jean and covers of the singer's material by various other artists. After Vincent's death, Weiser helped kick-start a rockabilly revival in Los Angeles, discovering, recording, and releasing music from groups like the Blasters, and reviving the forgotten careers of original rockabillies like Mac Curtis and Ray Campi. Campi, in fact, led the group of musicians—which also included Jimmie Lee Maslon, Rip Masters, and Jim Durbon—Weiser assembled to record posthumous accompaniment for the Vincent material.

In 1993, esteemed rock guitarist Jeff Beck issued *Crazy Legs*, a note-for-note tribute to Gene and his wildly influential guitarist Cliff Gallup. "He was one of the reasons I actually pursued a musical career," Beck said of the Black Leather Rebel. "I had just walked out of school and I was sitting in the front row [of one of Vincent's earliest UK performances]. Having this guy come across the stage with a black suit on, black leathers, and leaning forward and just screaming—it was too much to handle."

In the 1950s, Vincent took his place alongside fellow musical miscegenators like Elvis Presley, Bill Haley, Chuck Berry, and Little Richard at the forefront of the ground-breaking new sound. For the artists—typically poor, unskilled Southern boys—the music, more often than not, represented a glamorous and liberating way out of decades of generational poverty. For the fans, rock 'n' roll was much more—on many levels an articulation of independence, a denunciation of hypocritical authority, and an early, unprecedented embracing of multi-culturalism.

But if Elvis—with his seductive good looks and suggestive gyrations—was disturbing to the arbiters of middle-class taste, the rebellious, microphone-crushing Vincent—with his mangled left leg, earthy lyrics, nearly obscene moans and pants, and uncontrollable band of whooping, hollering hoodlums, the Blue Caps—was downright shocking. And revolutionary.

Vincent's life and music—as well as the example set by the Blue Caps, rock's very first punk band—established a precedent and a standard for decades of artists, from the Beatles to the Sex Pistols and beyond, who have, knowingly or not, borrowed liberally from Vincent's radical oeuvre. Shades of Vincent can be found in just about every category and subcategory of the pop-music pantheon, from the obvious heavy-metal and punk—where the black leather, menacing stage presence, and instrument-thrashing, microphone-bashing, and hotel-room trashing are *de rigeur*—to new wave psychobilly, swing revivalism, and beyond.

Guitarist Brian Setzer, who mines multi-platinum from dormant musical forms—rockabilly with his eighties band the Stray Cats and swing with his seventeen-piece Brian Setzer Orchestra—counts Vincent as one of his most indelible influences. He can still recall the first time he ever heard a Vincent tune. "I was at Max's Kansas City [in New York City in the seventies], and 'Be-Bop-A-Lula' came on the jukebox. I just flew across the room. It was just so tough and so clean. Hipper than country and cooler than rock 'n' roll."

In 1992, Adam Ant, new wave's British Prince Charming, teamed up with Doors drummer John Densmore to produce *Be-Bop-A-Lula*, a musical stage play about the friendship between Vincent and Eddie Cochran, which ran in Los Angeles. "I just thought those two, between them were these fabulous stylists who had brought the look—not fashion, a style; there's a difference—into rock 'n' roll and had never been given any credit," Ant said of his dramatic tribute. "I thought these guys deserved a place in the theater, as a testament to them and paying a bit of dues to them. Because where would we be? There would be no John Lennon without Gene Vincent, and there would be no Jim Morrison without Gene Vincent."

When once asked what was the smartest thing he'd ever heard anybody in rock 'n' roll ever say, Paul Simon responded with a smile and a chuckle, "Be-bop-a-lula, she's my baby." "Be-Bop-A-Lula" was pivotal in the creation of pop crooner Chris Isaak's rockabilly-inflected sound, too; it actually brought the singer and his first guitarist together. "I had a three-piece band and [guitarist] Jimmy Wilsey knew all the riffs to 'Be-Bop-A-Lula,' " Isaak recalled. "I remember him backstage showing me the riffs, and I went, 'Wow! That sounds just like the Gene Vincent record—so come on!' He hopped out on the stage and just played. I remember I was playing a Silvertone and he borrowed my Gretsch, played that, people seemed to like it, and I went, 'Stay.' "

His earliest experiences listening to Gene Vincent and the Blue Caps' music in the late fifties also helped give shape to his career, former Creedence Clearwater Revival frontman John Fogerty recalled. "You could take the vocal away and the music was just as good. I would listen to it and would imagine it without the singing. I'd say, 'Man, listen how cool the music is, what the guitars are doing and stuff.' So I learned a lot from that as a guy who was going to grow up and become a band leader."

In 1998, Vincent's accomplishments were officially recognized, validated, and sanctified when he was inducted into the Rock and Roll Hall Of Fame. Fogerty presented the award, opening his remarks with an a capella verse of "Be-Bop-A-Lula." "It doesn't get much better than that," he said. "I do believe that this record is probably one of the greatest records ever made. That voice, man, Gene Vincent.

"The sound of Cliff Gallup's guitar, the drummer screaming in the background—it's what we call attitude. And I sure learned that from 'Be-Bop-A-Lula.' Gene Vincent gave to me an image that was perfect for rock 'n' roll, not that I have always lived up to it. Gene's image was loud, self-assured, and greasy. And what better way to talk about rock 'n' roll."

Melody Jean Vincent Craddock, Gene's daughter with his second wife, Darlene, accepted the award, dressed in all-black leather like her famous dad, and a rendition of "Lula" followed from a combo featuring Jeff Beck and teenaged bluesman Jonny Lang, who handled earnestly strained vocal duties. " 'Be-Bop-A-Lula' was Elvis's greatest record," Fogerty quipped later.

Demand for Vincent's music has waxed and waned over the years, but it has never sputtered out. His songs are continually repackaged and re-released, recycled in films and advertisements, and reverently learned and performed by new generations of fledgling musicians. And now the original Vincent fans—those for whom the transcendent memories of The Screaming End still burn large and bright—tote their children and grandchildren to concerts by the Blue Caps, who continue to tour Europe regularly.

"It's kind of spooky, if you think about it," clapper boy Tommy "Bubba" Facenda said of Vincent's fandom in Europe. "It's like a cult following. They raise their children to love Gene Vincent and Eddie Cochran. We play for kids who are younger than teenagers. How do they know Gene Vincent?"

The race may be over, but the voice is living still.

# NOTES

3    Navy medals and history. Britt Hagarty, *The Day the World Turned Blue: A Biography of Gene Vincent* (Vancouver: Talonbooks, 1983).

6    Hospital and accident. Gene Vincent's Official Website, www.rockabillyhall.com/index20.html, Hagarty.

6    Addresses in Norfolk. Norfolk City Directories, 1934–63

7    Sisters, favorite songs. Hagarty.

7    "You have the strangest palate." *Hillbilly and Cowboy Hit Parade*, Winter 1956, no. 2, vol. 7.

7–8  Gene at movies, with Roy and Hazel Cooper, 'Joe Brown Talent Show.' Interview, Leona Cooper Lilley, 1998; Interview, Hazel Cooper, 1998.

8    She remembered how. Hagarty.

8    Munden Point. Norfolk City Directories.

8    He especially liked hearing. Unidentified British press clip, 1960, from Derek Henderson, Home Page and Archive, www.psc.ao.uk/~dhenders/.

9    Cooperative Mills. Norfolk City Directories.

9    Broad Creek Village. Interview, Lilley.

9    But just like John Wayne. Hagarty.

9–10 Gene joins the Navy. Hagarty.

10   Gene sees Elvis. Hagarty.

10   Those songs sounded. Rob Finnis and Bob Dunham, *Gene Vincent and the Blue Caps* (London: Rob Finnis and Bob Dunham, 1974).

10     The one he'd bought for twenty-two American dollars. *The Ledger-Dispatch*, May 29, 1956.

10–11   "To keep the neighbors neighborly." *Teenage Rock & Roll Review*, December 1956.

11     It wasn't at all. Interview, Aileene Cooper, 1999.

11     "No. That's for someone else." *Rock 'n' Roll Jamboree*, Fall 1956.

11–13   Davis meets Gene. Interview, Bill Davis, 1998.

13     One of the giants of the music industry. Chapple and Garofalo, *Rock 'n' Roll Is Here to Pay* (Chicago: Nelson-Hall, 1977).

14     Gene on "Country Showtime." Interview, Davis.

14     Even got a sweet deal. Hagarty.

14–15   Carl Perkins thought the boy had something, too. Carl Perkins and David McGee, *Go, Cat, Go!: The Life and Times of Carl Perkins* (New York: Hyperion, 1996).

15–16   Recording demo. Interview, Davis; Interview, Dickie Harrell, 1993–2000; Interview, Joe Hoppel, 1993, 1998, 1999; Letter, Jack Neal, 1998; Finnis and Dunham.

17     Nelson. Interview, Ken Nelson, 1998; Finnis and Dunham.

17     With the emergence of Presley. Simon Frith, "The Industrialization of Popular Music" in James Lull, ed., *Popular Music and Communication* (Newbury Park, CA: Sage Publications, 1987).

18     "Look, you guys are out of your minds." Finnis and Dunham.

18     "Can you get these people down to Nashville?" Finnis and Dunham.

18     Owen Bradley, Buddy Holly. Interview, Owen Bradley, 1995.

19     Gene gets news of Capitol contract. Finnis and Dunham; Interview, Harrell.

19     "This I believe was the happiest." Finnis and Dunham.

19     Ken Nelson felt a little apprehensive. Interview, Nelson.

19     Looking like a motorcycle gang. Hagarty.

19–23   First recording session. Interview, Harrell; Interview, Nelson; Finnis and Dunham; Hagarty.

20–21   Cliff's Gretsch. *Guitar Player*, December 1993.

24    Gene's got a hit. Interview, Davis; Interview, Nelson; Interview, Harrell; Finnis and Dunham; Hagarty.

25    In April, he signed a two-year contract. *The Virginian-Pilot*, April 3, 1957.

25    Gene learns songs from 78s. Interview, Hoppel.

25    Nelson also requested. Finnis and Dunham.

25    Gene plays "Lula" for barracks B-17. Finnis and Dunham.

26    Gene marries Ruth Ann Hand. Marriage Records, Circuit Court, Chesapeake, Virginia; Hagarty; Piper Vincent, Gene Vincent's Official Website; Interview, Lilley.

27    They started their married life. *The Ledger-Dispatch*, April 30, 1957.

27    Gene stayed with friends or family. Hagarty; Gene Vincent's Official Website.

27    To Ruth Ann, it was abandonment. Divorce Records, Circuit Court, Portsmouth, Virginia.

27–28    Recording at Quonset Hut, June 1956. Interview, Nelson; Interview, Harrell; Finnis and Dunham; Thierry Liesenfeld, *Gene Vincent: The Story Behind His Songs* (Zimmerbach: Thierry Liesenfeld, 1992).

29    "Dickie, are you ready to go on the road?" Finnis and Dunham.

29    He'd been living a double life. Interview, Harrell.

29    Outdoor fair dates. Finnis and Dunham.

29    Elvis on TV. David Halberstam, *The Fifties* (New York: Villard Books, 1993).

30    Gene and Caps rehearse for tour. Interview, Hoppel.

30    WCMS preparations for Caps tour. Interview, Hoppel; Interview, Harrel; Interview, Davis; Finnis and Dunham.

30    "I'll never forget what WCMS did for me." Interview, Hoppel.

30–31    Gene and the Blue Caps first tour. Interview, Harrell.

31    Gene meets Elvis. Peter Guralnick, *Last Train to Memphis: The Rise of Elvis Presley* (Boston: Little, Brown, and Company, 1994); Letter, Peter Guralnick, 1998.

31    Later that day, in the company of his mother. *The Virginian-Pilot*, April 3, 1957.

32 Perry Como Show. Interview, Harrell; Letter, Neal; Finnis and Dunham; Hagarty.

32 "Lula" chart action. Joel Whitburn, *The Billboard Book Of Top 40 Hits* (New York: Billboard Books, 1992).

32–33 Alan Freed. Chapple and Garofalo; Halberstam.

34 Blue Caps loosen up. Interview, Harrell; Letter, Neal.

34 New York and Pennsylvania. Chapple and Garofalo.

34–35 Shamokin, Pennsylvania gig. Interview, Harrell; Finnis and Dunham.

36 Black coffee and an eternal chain of Camel cigarettes. Interview, Harrell; Interview, Tommy Facenda, 1993–1999.

36 Eagle Mountain. Interview, Harrell; Unidentified press clip, September 22, 1956, in *Gene Vincent: The Screaming End*, Alan Clark, ed., (West Covina, CA: National Rock 'n' Roll Archives, 1988).

36 *Bluejean Bop* peaks at sixteen. Joel Whitburn, *Top Pop Albums 1955–1985* (Menomonee Falls, WI: Record Research, 1985).

37 Paul joins the Blue Caps. Finnis and Dunham; Bill Mack and Bob Erskine, Gene Vincent's Official Website; Peek on "Echoes," BBC Radio, May 1987.

38 *Blackboard Jungle, Rock Around the Clock*. Chapple and Garofalo; Guralnick.

38 Capitol Records. Chapple and Garofalo.

38–39 Tashlin. David Shipman, *The Story of Cinema* (New York: St. Martin's Press, 1982).

39 "The quiet, plain type of girl." *Dig*, January 1957.

39–40 Filming *The Girl Can't Help It*. Interview, Harrell; Peek on "Echoes," BBC Radio, May 1987.

40 Caps at Capitol Tower. Finnis and Dunham.

40–41 Recording in Nashville, October 1956. Finnis and Dunham.

41–42 Criterion, Toronto, Canada. Hagarty; John Reynolds, Gene Vincent's Official Website.

42 Sands, Jack Entratter. Nick Tosches, *Dino: Living High in the Dirty Business of Dreams* (New York: Dell Publishers, 1992).

43–46    Gene and the Blue Caps in Vegas. Interview, Harrell; Interview, Davis; Hagarty.

45    Their applause. Facenda on "Race with the Devil," BBC Radio 2, March, 1998.

49    The doctors, alarmed at how badly. Finnis and Dunham.

49–50    L&B litigation. *The Virginian-Pilot*, February 15, 22, March 1, April 3, 6, 23, 1957; *The Ledger-Dispatch*, February 21, 28, March 25, April 3, 6, 22, 1957.

50–52    Gene forms new band. Interview, Facenda; *Now Dig This*, July 1987; Interview, Johnny Meeks, 1998.

53    House on Leckie St. Interview, Harrell; Hagarty; Piper Vincent, Gene Vincent's Official Website.

53–54    Gene and Dickie drive to Nashville. Interview, Harrell.

54    During one show, when Gene hit the deck. Interview, Al Casey, 1998.

55    One night in Cincinnati. *Rollin' Rock*, No. 16/17.

55    Eddie Cochran. Colin Escott, *Somethin' Else: The Fine Lookin' Hits of Eddie Cochran* (EMI-Capitol/Razor & Tie, 1997).

56    They became fast friends. Interview, Harrell.

56    Bubba, Paul, and Gene. Interview, Facenda.

56–57    Cherry bomb. Interview, Harrell; Interview, Facenda.

57    At the end of April he was ordered to pay. *The Ledger-Dispatch*, April 30, 1957.

57    The L&B flap was settled. *The Ledger-Dispatch*, May 31, 1957.

57    He'd actually become a paid-up member. Bob Erskine and Roger Nunn, Gene Vincent's Official Website.

58    Ed McLemore's Artists Service Bureau. Interview, Nelson; Derek Henderson, *Gene Vincent and His Blue Caps: The Lost Dallas Sessions 1957–58* (Dragon Street, 1998); Finnis and Dunham; Hagarty.

58    McLemore, a classy dresser. *Dallas Observer*, January 6, 2000.

58    Gene always traveled real light. Interview, Harrell.

59–61    Tom Fleeger. Henderson, *Gene Vincent and His Blue Caps*; Dennard interview, Tom Fleeger.

61   Gene and Jerry Lee Lewis. Escott, *Jerry Lee Lewis: The Killer 1963–1968* (Bremen: Bear Family Publications, 1986); Lewis, Myra and Murray Silver, *Great Balls of Fire! The Uncensored Story of Jerry Lee Lewis* (New York: St. Martin's Press, 1982), *Rollin' Rock*, No. 13; Finnis and Dunham.

62–63  Buck Owens records with Gene. Interview, Buck Owens, 1998.

63   For Johnny, the whole thing was a thrill. Interview, Meeks; Finnis and Dunham.

64   With his divorce finalized from Ruth Ann. Divorce records, Circuit Court, Portsmouth, Virginia.

64   Louise and the girls in Dallas. Piper Vincent, Gene Vincent's Official Website.

65   The local musicians. *Rollin' Rock*, No. 14.

65–66  Gene and the Caps on the road. Interview, Harrell.

66   Johnny marveled. Interview, Meeks.

66–67  Paul fakes a suicide, gets snowed on, trashes TV, practical jokes. Interview, Harrell; Bob Erskine and Roger Nunn, Gene Vincent's Official Website.

67–68  Howard Miller Show. Interview, Facenda; Finnis and Dunham; Hagarty.

68   Dickie mishaps. Interview, Harrell.

68–69  Fringe benefits, Bubba gets arrested. Interview, Facenda.

68   Gene and kitten. Letter, Dianne Corey, 1999.

69–71  Australia. Interview, Harrell; Interview, Facenda; Interview, Meeks; Piper Vincent, Gene Vincent's Official Website; Hagarty; Charles White, *The Life And Times of Little Richard* (New York: Harmony Books, 1984).

70   Despite their good-natured professional rivalry. Charles White, *The Life And Times of Little Richard*.

71   He came face to face. Timothy White, *Rock Lives* (New York: Henry Holt & Company, Incorporated, 1990).

72   Ed Sullivan Show. Interview, Harrell; Hagarty; Gene Vincent's Official Website.

72   "Dance to the Bop" charts. Joel Whitburn, *Top Pop Singles 1955–1993* (Menomonee Falls, WI: Record Research, 1994).

73    Fender guitars. Interview, Meeks; Finnis and Dunham; *Guitar Player*, December 1983.

73    Nelson always found. Finnis and Dunham.

74    Johnny picked with a penny. Liesenfeld.

74    They'd come up short of material. *Now Dig This*, July 1987.

74–75    *American Bandstand*. Chapple and Garofalo.

78    He thought of pretty Darlene Hicks. Interview, Pat Mason, 1998; Hagarty.

84    Christmas, 1957. Hagarty; Piper Vincent, Gene Vincent's Official Website.

85    Austin, Texas performance. Interview, Ray Campi, 1998; Ray Campi, World Wide Web Rockabilly Hall of Fame Website, www.rockabillyhall.com.

85    "Louisiana Hayride." Hagarty.

86    Milwaukee riot. Hagarty.

86–87    Gene persuades Bubba to rejoin. Interview, Facenda.

87–93    Juvey Gomez and Globe, Arizona. Interview, Juvey Gomez, 1999; Interview, Facenda; Interview, Meeks; Dennard interview, Juvey Gomez.

89    Eddie joins in. *Now Dig This*, July 1987; Tommy Facenda on "Echoes," BBC Radio, May 1987.

88–90    Recording at Capitol Tower, March 1958. Dennard interview, Gomez.

92    Bubba misses his scene. Interview, Facenda.

93    It was just too inconvenient. Interview, Meeks.

93–94    Gene holds court in his hotel room, Juvey and Ricky. Interview, Meeks; Interview, Facenda; Dennard interview, Gomez.

94    Johnny called it quits. Interview, Meeks.

94    On the first of May. Hagarty.

94–95    Bill Mack returns. Mack and Erskine, Gene Vincent's Official Website.

95    D. J. Fontana joins. Finnis and Dunham; Mack and Erskine, Gene Vincent's Official Website.

95    Mounties in Winnipeg. Ibid.

95–96      Bennies. Mack and Erskine, Gene Vincent's Official Website; Interview, Meeks.

96         Canadian tour. Mack and Erskine, Gene Vincent's Official Website; Finnis and Dunham.

96–97      Fontana quits. Hagarty; *Original Cool*, February/March 2000.

97         Dallas, Gene pulls gun on Bill. Mack and Erskine, Gene Vincent's Official Website.

97         Johnny rejoins. Interview, Meeks.

97–98      He could see the writing. Dennard interview, Gomez.

98–99      Juvenile delinquency films. James Gilbert, *A Cycle of Outrage: America's Reaction to the Juvenile Delinquent in the 1950s* (New York: Oxford University Press, 1986).

99–100     Gene and band arrested for murder. Interview, Meeks; Mack and Erskine, Official Gene Vincent Website; *Minneapolis Star*, August 30, 1958, reprinted on Gene Vincent's Official Website.

100        South Dakota, Wisconsin, Michigan, back to Minneapolis. Mack and Erskine, Gene Vincent's Official Website, September, 1998.

101        Girl in Gene's room, Bill quits. Mack and Erskine, Gene Vincent's Official Website; Hagarty.

103        *Town Hall Party* appearance. Saddler, Ian, *The Town Hall Party TV Shows Starring Eddie Cochran and Gene Vincent* (Rockstar, 1999).

103        Johnny took it hard. Interview, Meeks.

103–104    Jerry Lee Merritt. Interview, Merritt.

104        Gene had recently lost. Hagarty.

104–105    Gene had met Buddy. Jim Dawson and Spencer Leigh, *Memories of Buddy Holly* (Milford, NH: Big Nickel Publications, 1996).

105        Changes in rock 'n' roll. Chapple and Garofalo.

106–108    Gene and Jerry in Japan. Interview, Jerry Merritt, 1998; Interview, Mason; Hagarty.

109–110    Jerry stays with Gene and Darlene. Interview, Merritt.

110        Gene and Johnny Cash. Interview, Merritt; Interview, Johnny Cash via Lou Robin, 1999.

110        *Town Hall Party* appearance. Saddler.

110–111    Garden of Allah. Interview, Johnnie Wayne, 1998.

111        Gene and Ronnie Dawson. Interview, Ronnie Dawson, 1996; Henderson, *Gene Vincent and His Blue Caps.*

111–113    Payola. Chapple and Garofalo.

117–118    Gene arrives in London. Alan Vince, *I Remember Gene Vincent* (Merseyside, U.K.: Vintage Rock 'n' Roll Appreciation Society, 1977).

118        Radio interview. Ray Orchard interview with Gene Vincent, Radio Luxembourg, December, 1959.

118–119    Gene's Granada Theatre, Tooting performance. *Disc,* 1959, Henderson Home Page and Archive.

119        Gene's third *Boy Meets Girls* appearance. Hagarty; *Original Cool,* June/July 1997.

120–121    England's teen revolution. Johnny Stuart, *Rockers!* (London: Plexus Publishing Limited, 1987); Iain Chambers, "British Pop: Some Tracks From the Other Side of the Record" in Lull, ed., *Popular Music and Communication*; Dick Hebdige, *Hiding In the Light* (London: Routledge, 1988); *Original Cool* (June/July 1997).

121        Gene's Paris debut. Hagarty.

121–122    Adrian Owlett sees Gene. Ibid.

123–124    Larry Parnes. *Arena: The Eddie Cochran Story,* BBC TV, 1982; Chet Flippo, *Yesterday: The Unauthorized Biography of Paul McCartney* (New York: Doubleday & Company, Incorporated, 1998).

124–125    Glasgow. Hagarty.

125        Darlene realized she was pregnant. Hagarty.

125–126    The reception was the same everywhere. Joe Brown on "Race with the Devil," BBC Radio 2, March 1998; Brown on "Eddie Cochran's Final Tour," BBC Radio 2, 1996.

126        Eddie was extremely homesick. *Arena,* BBC TV, 1982.

126–127    Sharon Sheeley. *Arena,* BBC TV, 1982; Interview, Sharon Sheeley, 1998.

128        Suicidal sorrows. Ibid.

128        He just didn't like the record. Unidentified British press clip, Henderson Home Page and Archive.

129   Manchester Hippodrome performance. Unidentified British press clip, Henderson Home Page and Archive; *Now Dig This*, October 1996.

130   John Peel. Finnis and Dunham.

130   Silver Beetles. Flippo.

130   Lennon yells at girls. Williams, Kay and Pauline Sutcliffe, *Stuart: The Life and Art of Stuart Sutcliffe* (London: Genesis Publications Limited, 1996).

130–135  Goodwin interview. *New Musical Express*, April 1960.

131   His nagging certainty. Interview, Sheeley; Hagarty; *Arena*, BBC TV, 1982.

131   He always denied. *New Musical Express*, 1960, Henderson Home Page and Archive.

132   He didn't go in for the habit. Unidentified British press clip, Henderson Home Page and Archive.

134   Gene and Jack Good. Unidentified British press clip, Henderson Home Page and Archive.

135   He was looking forward to the small stuff. *Hit Parader*, 1960.

135   Sweet, soothing drink. Interview, Sheeley.

137–138  Post-accident. Interview, Sheeley.

138–139  Gene's return to England, airport. Vince.

138   "Eddie and I started out together." *The Virginian-Pilot* and *The Ledger-Star*, April 21, 1960.

139–140  Lewisham Gaumont performance. *New Musical Express*, May 1960.

140   Liverpool Stadium performance. Flippo.

140–141  Rochester. Vince.

141   "Weeping Willow." Craddock, Kie, and Louise. *Gene Vincent Story, Volumes 7 and 8: The Capitol Golden Years* (EMI, 1975).

141–142  Post war England. Welch interview, Carter, 1998.

142   Gene and his switchblade. Welch interview, Carter; Hagarty.

142–143  Gene throwing a knife in the dressing room. Vince.

143–144  Sharon hobbles onstage. Interview, Sheeley.

143–144  Eddie in Manchester. *Arena*, BBC TV, 1982.

144        Billy Fury came to Sharon's hospital room. Interview, Sheeley.

144        "My daughter has died of pneumonia." *Hit Parader*, 1960, Henderson Home Page and Archive.

144–145    After asking to be released. *New Musical Express*, 1960, Henderson Home Page and Archive.

145        Sharon couldn't believe. Interview, Sheeley.

145        Gene claimed that he was the victim. *Hit Parader*, 1960. Henderson Home Page and Archive; unidentified British press clip, Henderson Home Page and Archive.

145        "He put me through so much pain." Interview, Sheeley.

146        Gene really seemed to like. Liesenfeld.

147–148    Gene returns to England, January 1961. Vince.

147        *State Fair*. Letter, Pat Boone, 1998; Vince; Hagarty.

148–149    Darlene leaves Gene. Hagarty; Interview, Wayne.

149–150    Henri Henriod. Interview, Adrian Owlett, 1998.

150        At their rehearsals. Hagarty.

150        Gene lunches with Adrian. Interview, Owlett; Hagarty.

151        Gene and Sounds Incorporated. Hagarty.

151–152    Gene phones Bubba. Interview, Facenda.

152–153    The King of Ballrooms was not well. Unidentified British press clips, May and June 1961, Henderson Home Page and Archives; *The Ledger-Dispatch*, August 15, 1961; *New Musical Express*, August 1961.

153        "That record should never have been released." *Record Mirror*, December 1961.

155        "Was just wonderful." Interview, Brenda Lee, 1995.

155        Gene and Brenda Lee performances. Unidentified British press clip, 1962, in Eddie Muir, ed., *Wild Cat: A Tribute to Gene Vincent* (East Sussex, U.K.: Eddie Muir, 1977); unidentified British press clip, March 1962, Henderson Home Page and Archive.

155        Gene and Margie. Interview, Owlett; Hagarty; Vince.

156        Gene got along very well. Unidentified British press clip, July 1962, Henderson Home Page and Archive.

156–157    Gene and Margie in Italy. Interview, Owlett; Hagarty.

157–158 Star Club. Hagarty; Barry Miles, *Paul McCartney: Many Years From Now* (New York: Henry Holt & Company Incorporated, 1997) Alan Clayson, *Ringo Starr: Straight Man or Joker?* (London: Sanctuary Publishing Limited, 1996).

158 Gene and Margie move to Kent. Unidentified British press clip, August 1962, Henderson Home Page and Archive.

158–159 Gene in Israel. Hagarty.

159 While he was at home. Unidentified British press clip, Henderson Home Page and Archive.

159 Gene and Adam Faith tour. *Disc*, 1962, Henderson Home Page and Archive.

159–160 Gene and Margie get married. Hagarty.

160 Gene in the hospital. Unidentified British press clip, Henderson Home Page and Archive.

160 Gene's drinking was beginning to soil. Hagarty; Interview, Owlett.

160–161 Gene and Margie in Majorca, Paris. Hagarty.

161 Capitol contract expires, Gene's drinking worsens. Hagarty.

161–162 Ritchie Blackmore. Interview, Ritchie Blackmore, 1998.

162–163 Gene felt as savage. *Daily Express*, September 24, 1963; *Daily Mail*, September 24, 1963; *Daily Mirror*, September 24, 1963.

164 Nazi memorabilia. Interview, Casey; *Fusion*, 1969 in *Kicks*, No. 2.

164 Gene took it especially hard. Interview, Casey; *Original Cool*, April/May 1994.

164–165 *Whole Lotta Shakin' Goin On*, Granada TV. Unidentified British press clip in *Jerry Lee Lewis: The Killer: 1963–1968*.

165 Lausanne riot. Interview, Pierre Pennone, 1999.

166 Gene pulls gun on Shouts. Interview, Vic Clark, 1999.

166–167 Gene in hospital for ear. Interview, Harrell; Interview, Mike Warner, 1998.

166 Gene wanted someone. Interview, Merritt; Interview, Meeks.

167–168 Jackie Frisco. Interview, Owlett.

167–169 Blackpool. Interview, Owlett; Hagarty.

168 Medication and alcohol consumption. Interview, Owlett.

173 Gene visits Bubba. Interview, Facenda.

173 Gene didn't tell Bubba. Interview, Owlett; Hagarty.

174 "We were friends." *The Ledger-Star*, February 1, 1966.

174 Gene just couldn't go through with it. Hagarty.

174–175 Gene at Jerry's. Interview, Merritt; *Blue Suede News*, No. 20.

175–176 Gene had seen his buddies the Beatles. *Yakima Republic*, January 9, 1967.

176–177 Gene and Del Worrell. Interview, Del Worrell, 1998.

177–178 Tour of France and Switzerland. Interview, Pennone; Hagarty.

178–186 Jim Pewter. Interview, Jim Pewter, 1998.

186–188 Ronny Weiser meets Gene. Interview, Ronny Weiser, 1998; *Las Vegas Weekly*, August 19–25, 1998; *Goldmine*, January/February 1977.

188–189 Jim Pewter at Gene's. Interview, Pewter.

189–190 Adrian Owlett had taken the demo tape. Interview, Owlett.

190–191 Gene wants out of Playground contract. Interview, Pewter.

190 Fowley was an acquaintance. Interview, Bones Howe, 1999; *Fusion*, 1969 in *Kicks*, No. 2; unidentified press clip, 1969.

191–194 Kim Fowley session at Elektra. Interview, Owlett; Interview, Kim Fowley, 1999; Interview, Rodney Bingenheimer, 1998, 1999; Interview, Robby Krieger, 2000; Interview, Linda Ronstadt, via Ira Koslow, 1999; Interview, Meeks; *Goldmine*, November 25, 1993; *Mojo*, March, 1996.

195 Tom Ayres takes over management. Interview, Tom Ayres, 1998; Interview, Fowley; Interview, Pewter.

195–196 Rock 'n' Roll Revival, Toronto. Interview, Ayres; Interview Fowley; Interview, Bingenheimer.

196–197 The stars loved Gene. Interview, Ayres.

196 Bob Dylan. Bob Spitz, *Dylan: A Biography* (New York: McGraw-Hill Publishing Company, 1989).

197–201 Henroid tour. Interview, Owlett; Hagarty; *The Rock 'n' Roll Singer*, BBC TV, 1969; Eric Dunsdon, Gene Vincent's Official Website.

198        Jackie walked out. *Fusion*, 1969 in *Kicks*, No. 2.

201–203    Sir Douglas Quintet session. Interview, Ayres; Interview, Chris
           Darrow, 1999; *Rolling Stone*, May 28, 1970.

203        Jackie was good for Gene. Interview, Ayres.

204        Gene and Jim Morrison. Interview, Ayres; Interview, Bingen-
           heimer.

204–207    French tour with Houseshakers. Interview, Owlett; Hagarty;
           Interview, Graham Fenton, 1999.

204        Henry Henroid had washed his hands. Henry Henroid on "Race
           with the Devil," BBC Radio 2, March, 1998.

207–209    Gene and Commander Cody. Interview, Bill Kirchen, 1995,
           1998; Interview, John Tichy, 1998; Interview, Ayres.

209–211    Gene and Marcia Avron on tour. Interview, Owlett; Hagarty;
           Interview, Fenton.

211–214    Ronny Weiser session. Interview, Weiser.

214–215    Gene and Monument Records. Interview, Davis; Letter, Fred
           Foster, 1998.

215        Gene calls Jerry Merritt. *Blue Suede News*, No. 20.

216        The man was very ill. Interview, Owlett.

216–230    Gene's last interview. *Now Dig This*, October 1997; *Sun*, October
           14 and 15, 1971; Mortuary Death Report, Department of
           Coroner, County of Los Angeles, October 12, 1971; Muir.

230        Margaret Russell talks to *Sun*. *The Sun*, October 11, 1971.

231        Gene's parents find him at home. Hagarty.

231        Johnny Meeks was playing a gig. Interview, Meeks.

231–232    Gene's last day. Hagarty.

235        Gene's death. Certificate of Death, Department of Public Health,
           State of California; Autopsy Report, Department of Coroner,
           County of Los Angeles, October 14, 1971.

235        Funeral. Interview, Meeks; Interview, Ayres.

235        "I don't suppose that six hundred pounds." *The Sun*, October
           14, 1971.

235–236    Burial plot and gravestone. Records, Eternal Valley Memorial
           Park.

236      Alamo. Associated Press story reprinted in *The Cult Observer*, Vol. 12, No. 1, 1995.

236      "There was something mystical." Interview, Ian Dury, by Chris Welch, date unknown.

237      "He was one of the reasons." Interview, Jeff Beck, 1993.

238      "I was at Max's Kansas City." Interview, Brian Setzer, 1993.

238      "I just thought those two." Interview, Adam Ant, 1995.

238      Paul Simon. Timothy White, *RockLives* (New York: Henry Holt & Company, Incorporated, 1990).

238      "I had a three-piece band." Interview, Chris Isaak, 1998.

239      "You could take the vocal away." Interview, John Fogerty, 1998.

240      "It's kind of spooky." Interview, Facenda.

          Discography. *Goldmine*, November 26, 1993; Derek Henderson, *Gene Vincent: A Discography* (Southampton: Spent Brothers Productions, 1998); Liesenfeld.

# SOURCES

## INTERVIEWS AND CORRESPONDENCE

*By the author*

Anonymous family member, 1998

Ant, Adam, 1995

Ayres, Tom, 1998

Beck, Jeff, 1993

Bingenheimer, Rodney, 1998, 1999

Blackmore, Ritchie, 1998

Boone, Pat, 1998

Bradley, Owen, 1995

Bruce, Michael, 1999

Campi, Ray, 1998

Casey, Al, 1998

Cash, Johnny, via Lou Robin, 1999

Clark, Vic, 1999

Cooper, Aileene, 1999

Cooper, Hazel, 1998

Cory, Dianne, 1999

Darrow, Chris, 1999

Davis, Bill, 1998

Dawson, Ronnie, 1996

Facenda, Tommy, 1993–1999

Fenton, Graham, 1999

Fogerty, John, 1998

Foster, Fred, 1998

Fowley, Kim, 1999

Gomez, Juvey, 1999

Guralnick, Peter, 1998

Harrell, Dickie, 1993–2000

Haugh, Sterling, 1998

Hoppel, Joe, 1993, 1998, 1999

Howe, Bones, 1999

Isaak, Chris, 1998

Kirchen, Bill, 1995, 1998

Krieger, Robby, 2000

Lee, Brenda, 1995

Lilley, Leona Cooper, 1998

Mason, Pat, 1998

Meeks, Johnny, 1998

Merritt, Jerry, 1998

Miller, Peter, 1998

Neal, Jack, 1998

Nelson, Ken, 1998

Owens, Buck, 1998

Owlett, Adrian, 1998

Pennone, Pierre, 1999

Pewter, Jim, 1998

Ronstadt, Linda, via Ira Koslow, 1999

Setzer, Brian, 1993

Sheeley, Sharon, 1998

Tichy, John, 1998

Warner, Mike, 1998

Wayne, Johnnie, 1998

Weiser, Ronny, 1998

Worrell, Del, 1998

Zoom, Billy, 1998

*By others*

Carter, Hal, by Chris Welch, 1998
Dury, Ian, by Chris Welch, date unknown
Fleeger, Tom, by David Dennard, 1998
Gomez, Juvey, by David Dennard, 1998

# BOOKS

Barnard, Russell D., ed. *The Comprehensive Country Music Encyclopedia.* New York: Times Books, 1994.

Berman, Jay. *The Fifties Book.* New York: Berkley Medallion Books, 1974.

Brown, Ashley, ed. *The Marshall Cavendish Illustrated History of Popular Music.* Freeport, NY: Marshall Cavendish, 1989.

Chapple, Steve, and Reebee Garofalo, *Rock 'n' Roll Is Here to Pay.* Chicago: Nelson-Hall, 1977.

Clayson, Alan. *Ringo Starr: Straightman or Joker?* London: Sanctuary Publishing Limited, 1996.

Cotten, Lee. *Did Elvis Sing in Your Hometown? Elvis On Tour in the Fifties.* Sacramento: High Sierra Books, 1995.

Cross, Ricky, and Charles Wittkopp. *Elvis in Tidewater.* Norfolk, VA: Donning Company Publishers, 1982.

Dalton, David. *James Dean: The Mutant King.* New York: St. Martin's Press, 1974.

Davis, Daphne. *Stars!* New York: Stewart, Tabori & Chang Publishers, 1983.

DeCurtis, Anthony, and James Henke. *The Rolling Stone Illustrated History of Rock and Roll.* New York: Random House, 1992.

Escott, Colin. *Jerry Lee Lewis: The Killer 1963–1968.* Bremen: Bear Family Publications, 1986.

Finnis, Rob, and Bob Dunham. *Gene Vincent and the Blue Caps.* London: Rob Finnis and Bob Dunham, 1974.

Flippo, Chet. *Yesterday: The Unauthorized Biography of Paul McCartney.* New York: Doubleday & Company, Incorporated, 1988.

Gilbert, James. *A Cycle of Outrage: America's Reaction to the Juvenile Delinquent in the 1950s.* New York: Oxford University Press, 1986.

Giuliano, Geoffrey. *Blackbird: The Life and Times of Paul McCartney*. New York: Da Capo Press, 1997.

Glennon, Lorraine, ed. *Our Times: The Illustrated History of the 20th Century*. Atlanta: Turner Publishing, Incorporated, 1995.

Guralnick, Peter. *Last Train to Memphis: The Rise of Elvis Presley*. Boston: Little, Brown, and Company, 1994.

Hagarty, Britt. *The Day the World Turned Blue: A Biography of Gene Vincent*. Vancouver: Talonbooks, 1983.

Halberstam, David. *The Fifties*. New York: Villard Books, 1993.

Hardy, Phil, and Dave Laing. *Encyclopedia of Rock*. New York: Schirmer Books, 1988.

Hebdige, Dick. *Hiding in the Light*. London: Routledge, 1988.

Helander, Brock. *The Rock Who's Who*. New York: Schirmer Books, 1996.

Larkin, Colin, ed. *The Guinness Encyclopedia of Popular Music*. New York: Guinness Stockton Publishing Press, 1995.

Larkin, Colin, ed. *The Encyclopedia of Popular Music*. London: Muze, 1998.

Lewis, Myra, and Murray Silver. *Great Balls of Fire! The Uncensored Story of Jerry Lee Lewis*. New York: St. Martin's Press, 1982.

Lull, James, ed. *Popular Music and Communication*. Newbury Park, CA: Sage Publications, 1987.

Martin, Annabel, and Lorna Damms, eds. *Encyclopedia of Rock Stars*. New York: DK Publishing Incorporated, 1996.

Miles, Barry. *Paul McCartney: Many Years From Now*. New York: Henry Holt & Company, Incorporated, 1997.

Murrells, Joseph. *Million-Selling Records From the 1900s to the 1980s*. New York: Arco, 1985.

Perkins, Carl, and David McGee. *Go, Cat, Go! The Life and Times of Carl Perkins*. New York: Hyperion, 1996.

Shipman, David. *The Story of Cinema*. New York: St. Martin's Press, 1982.

Spitz, Bob. *Dylan: A Biography*. New York: McGraw-Hill Publishing Company, 1989.

Stambler, Irwin. *The Encyclopedia of Pop, Rock and Soul*. New York: St. Martin's Press, 1989.

Stuart, Johnny. *Rockers!* London: Plexus Publishing Limited, 1987.

Tosches, Nick. *Dino: Living High in the Dirty Business of Dreams.* New York: Dell Publishing, 1992.

Tosches, Nick. *Hellfire.* New York: Grove Press, 1982.

Vince, Alan. *I Remember Gene Vincent.* Merseyside, U.K.: Vintage Rock 'n' Roll Appreciation Society, 1977.

Whitburn, Joel. *The Billboard Book of Top 40 Hits.* New York: Billboard Books, 1992.

Whitburn, Joel. *Top Pop Albums 1955–1985.* Menomonee Falls, WI: Record Research, 1985.

Whitburn, Joel. *Top Pop Singles 1955–1993.* Menomonee Falls, WI: Record Research, 1994.

White, Charles. *The Life and Times of Little Richard.* New York: Harmony Books, 1984.

White, Timothy. *Rock Lives.* New York: Henry Holt & Company, Incorporated, 1990.

Williams, Kay and Pauline Sutcliffe. *Stuart: The Life and Art of Stuart Sutcliffe.* London: Genesis Publications Limited, 1996.

# PICTURE BOOKS, COLLECTIONS, MEMORABILIA, INTERNET

*The Big Show.* 1957 Australian tour program.

Clark, Alan. *Gene Vincent: The Screaming End.* West Covina, CA: National Rock and Roll Archives, 1988.

Dawson, Jim, and Spencer Leigh. *Memories of Buddy Holly.* Milford, NH: Big Nickel Publications, 1996.

*Gene Vincent and the Blue Caps Picture Album.* 1958 tour program.

*Gene Vincent Story, 1956.* Saulon-La-Chapelle: Crazy Times, date unknown.

Gene Vincent's Official Website, www.rockabillyhall.com/index20.html.

Henderson, Derek, Home Page and Archive, www.psc.ac.uk/~dhenders/.

*Larry Parnes Presents Eddie Cochran and Gene Vincent.* 1960 U.K. tour program.

Muir, Eddie, ed. *Wild Cat: A Tribute to Gene Vincent.* East Sussex, U.K.: Eddie Muir, 1977.

World Wide Web Rockabilly Hall of Fame Website, www.rockabillyhall.com.

# RADIO

"Echoes," BBC Radio, May 1987.

"Eddie Cochran's Final Tour," BBC Radio 2, 1996.

"Race with the Devil," BBC Radio 2, March, 1998.

Ray Orchard interview with Gene Vincent, Radio Luxembourg, December, 1959.

# TELEVISION

*Arena: The Eddie Cochran Story*, BBC TV, 1982.

*Ed Sullivan Show*, November 17, 1957.

*The Rock 'n' Roll Singer*, BBC TV, 1969.

# MOVIES

*The Girl Can't Help It*, 1956.

*Hot Rod Gang*, 1958.

*It's Trad Dad*, 1962.

*Live It Up*, 1964.

# DISCOGRAPHIES

Unless otherwise noted, all information regarding dates, locations, and sequences of recording sessions and the origin, composition, release, and publishing of songs was taken from the following:

Henderson, Derek. *Gene Vincent: A Discography*. Southampton: Spent Brothers Productions, 1998.

Liesenfeld, Thierry. *Gene Vincent: The Story Behind His Songs*. Zimmerbach: Thierry Liesenfeld, 1992.

# LINER NOTES

Braley, John. *Gene Vincent: The Last Session*. BBC/Strange Fruit, 1987.

Craddock, Kie and Louise. *Gene Vincent Story, Volumes 7 and 8: The Capitol Golden Years*. EMI, 1975.

Escott, Colin. *Somethin' Else: The Fine Lookin' Hits of Eddie Cochran*. EMI-Capitol/Razor & Tie, 1998.

Henderson, Derek. *Gene Vincent and His Blue Caps: The Lost Dallas Sessions 1957–58*. Dragon Street, 1998.

Hyde, Bob. *The Screaming End: The Best of Gene Vincent & His Blue Caps*. EMI-Capitol/Razor & Tie, 1997.

Kolanjian, Steve. *The Capitol Collector's Series: Gene Vincent*. Capitol, 1990.

Nunn, Roger. *Gene Vincent: The EP Collection*. See For Miles, 1989.

Saddler, Ian. *The Town Hall Party TV Shows Starring Eddie Cochran and Gene Vincent*. Rockstar, 1999.

Travis, Dave. *Best of Gene Vincent*. Capitol/EMI, 1967.

# DISCOGRAPHY

*(does not include material reissued after Vincent's death)*

## U.S. SINGLES

| LABEL | RECORD # | TITLE | YEAR |
|-------|----------|-------|------|
| Capitol | 3450 | Woman Love/Be-Bop-A-Lula | 1956 |
| Capitol | 3530 | Race With the Devil/Gonna Back Up Baby | 1956 |
| Capitol | 3558 | Blue Jean Bop/Who Slapped John | 1956 |
| Capitol | 3617 | Crazy Legs/Important Words | 1957 |
| Capitol | 3678 | B-I-Bickey-Bi Bo-Bo-Go/Five Days, Five Days | 1957 |
| Capitol | 3763 | Lotta Lovin'/Wear My Ring | 1957 |
| Capitol | 3839 | Dance to the Bop/I Got It | 1957 |
| Capitol | 3874 | I Got a Baby/Walkin' Home From School | 1958 |
| Capitol | 3959 | Baby Blue/True to You | 1958 |
| Capitol | 4010 | Rocky Road Blues/Yes I Love You, Baby | 1958 |
| Capitol | 4051 | Git It/Little Lover | 1958 |
| Capitol | 4105 | Say Mama/Be Bop Boogie Boy | 1959 |
| Capitol | 4153 | Over the Rainbow/Who's Pushin' Your Swing? | 1959 |
| Capitol | 4237 | Right Now/The Night Is So Lonely | 1959 |
| Capitol | 4313 | Wildcat/Right Here on Earth | 1960 |
| Capitol | 4442 | Anna Annabelle/Pistol Packin' Mama | 1960 |

| Capitol | 4525 | Mister Loneliness/If You Want My Lovin' | 1961 |
| Capitol | 4665 | Lucky Star/Baby, Don't Believe Him | 1961 |
| Capitol | 6042 | Be-Bop-A-Lula/Lotta Lovin' | 1964 |
| Challenge | 59337 | Bird Doggin'/Ain't That Too Much | 1966 |
| Challenge | 59347 | Lonely Street/I Got My Eyes on You | 1966 |
| Challenge | 59365 | Born To Be a Rolling Stone/Hurtin' For You | 1967 |
| Playground | 100 | Story of the Rockers/Pickin' Poppies | 1968 |
| Elektra | 74067 | Be-Bop-A-Lula/Ruby Baby | 1969 |
| Forever | 6001 | Story of the Rockers/Pickin' Poppies | 1970 |
| Kama Sutra | 514 | Sunshine/Geese | 1971 |
| Kama Sutra | 518 | High on Life/The Day the World Turned Blue | 1971 |

# U . S .  E P s

| LABEL | RECORD # | TITLE | YEAR |
|---|---|---|---|
| Capitol | 1-764 | Bluejean Bop! (Volume 1) | 1956 |
| Capitol | 2-764 | Bluejean Bop! (Volume 2) | 1956 |
| Capitol | 3-764 | Bluejean Bop! (Volume 3) | 1956 |
| Capitol | PRO-438 | Dance to the Bop | 1957 |
| Capitol | 1-811 | Gene Vincent and the Blue Caps (Vol. 1) | 1957 |
| Capitol | 2-811 | Gene Vincent and the Blue Caps (Vol. 2) | 1957 |
| Capitol | 3-811 | Gene Vincent and the Blue Caps (Vol. 3) | 1957 |
| Capitol | 1-970 | Gene Vincent Rocks and the Blue Caps Roll (Vol. 1) | 1958 |
| Capitol | 2-970 | Gene Vincent Rocks and the Blue Caps Roll (Vol. 2) | 1958 |

| Capitol | 3-970 | Gene Vincent Rocks and the Blue Caps Roll (Vol. 3) | 1958 |
| Capitol | PRO-985 | Hot Rod Gang | 1958 |
| Capitol | 1-1059 | A Gene Vincent Record Date (Vol. 1) | 1958 |
| Capitol | 2-1059 | A Gene Vincent Record Date (Vol. 2) | 1958 |
| Capitol | 3-1059 | A Gene Vincent Record Date (Vol. 3) | 1958 |

# U.S. ALBUMS

| LABEL | RECORD # | TITLE | YEAR |
|-------|----------|-------|------|
| Capitol | T-764 | Bluejean Bop | 1957 |
| Capitol | T-811 | Gene Vincent and the Blue Caps | 1957 |
| Capitol | T-970 | Gene Vincent Rocks and the Blue Caps Roll | 1958 |
| Capitol | T-1059 | A Gene Vincent Record Date | 1958 |
| Capitol | T-1207 | Sounds Like Gene Vincent | 1959 |
| Capitol | T-1342 | Crazy Times (mono) | 1960 |
| Capitol | ST-1342 | Crazy Times (stereo) | 1960 |
| Capitol | DKAO-380 | Gene Vincent's Greatest | 1969 |
| Dandelion/Elektra | 9-102 | I'm Back and I'm Proud | 1970 |
| Kama Sutra | 2019 | Gene Vincent | 1970 |
| Kama Sutra | 2027 | The Day the World Turned Blue | 1971 |
| Rollin' Rock | | Forever Gene Vincent | 1980 |

# UK SINGLES

| LABEL | RECORD # | TITLE | YEAR |
|-------|----------|-------|------|
| Capitol/EMI | 14599 | Woman Love/Be-Bop-A-Lula | 1956 |

| Capitol/EMI | 14628 | Race With the Devil/Gonna Back Up Baby | 1956 |
| Capitol/EMI | 14637 | Blue Jean Bop/Who Slapped John | 1956 |
| Capitol/EMI | 14693 | Crazy Legs/Important Words | 1957 |
| Capitol/EMI | 14722 | B-I-Bickey-Bi Bo-Bo-Go/Five Days, Five Days | 1957 |
| Capitol/EMI | 14763 | Lotta Lovin'/Wear My Ring | 1957 |
| Capitol/EMI | 14808 | Dance to the Bop/I Got It | 1957 |
| Capitol/EMI | 14681 | Jumps, Giggles and Shouts/Wedding Bells | 1957 |
| Capitol/EMI | 14830 | I Got a Baby/Walkin' Home From School | 1958 |
| Capitol/EMI | 14868 | Baby Blue/True to You | 1958 |
| Capitol/EMI | 14908 | Rocky Road Blues/Yes I Love You, Baby | 1958 |
| Capitol/EMI | 14935 | Git It/Little Lover | 1958 |
| Capitol/EMI | 14974 | Say Mama/Be Bop Boogie Boy | 1959 |
| Capitol/EMI | 15000 | Over the Rainbow/Who's Pushin' Your Swing? | 1959 |
| Capitol/EMI | 15035 | Summertime/Frankie and Johnny | 1959 |
| Capitol/EMI | 15053 | Right Now/The Night Is So Lonely | 1959 |
| Capitol/EMI | 15099 | Wildcat/Right Here on Earth | 1959 |
| Capitol/EMI | 15115 | My Heart/I Got To Get to You Yet | 1960 |
| Capitol/EMI | 15136 | Pistol Packin' Mama/Weeping Willow | 1960 |
| Capitol/EMI | 15169 | Anna Annabelle/Accentuate the Positive | 1960 |
| Capitol/EMI | 15179 | Jezebel/Maybe | 1961 |
| Capitol/EMI | 15185 | Mister Loneliness/If You Want My Lovin' | 1961 |
| Capitol/EMI | 15202 | She She Little Sheila/Hot Dollar | 1961 |
| Capitol/EMI | 15215 | I'm Going Home/Love of A Man | 1961 |
| Capitol/EMI | 15231 | Brand New Beat/Unchained Melody | 1961 |
| Capitol/EMI | 15243 | Lucky Star/Baby, Don't Believe Him | 1962 |
| Capitol/EMI | 15264 | King of Fools/Be-Bop-A-Lula '62 | 1962 |

| Capitol/EMI | 15290 | Held for Questioning/You're Still In My Heart | 1963 |
| Capitol/EMI | 15307 | Rip It Up/High Blood Pressure (demo) | 1963 |
| Capitol/EMI | 15307 | Crazy Beat/High Blood Pressure | 1963 |
| Columbia | 7174 | Where Have You Been All My Life/Temptation Baby | 1963 |
| Columbia | 7218 | Humpity Dumpity/A Love 'Em And Leave 'Em Kinda Guy | 1964 |
| Columbia | 7293 | La Den Da Den Da Da/Beginning of the End | 1964 |
| Columbia | 7343 | Private Detective/You Are My Sunshine | 1964 |
| London | 10079 | Bird Doggin'/Ain't That Too Much | 1966 |
| London | 10099 | Lonely Street/I've Got My Eyes On You | 1966 |
| Capitol/EMI | 15546 | Be-Bop-A-Lula/Say Mama | 1968 |
| Dandelion | 4596 | Be-Bop-A-Lula/Ruby Baby | 1969 |
| Dandelion | 5974 | White Lightning/Scarlet Ribbons | 1970 |
| Spark | 1091 | Story of the Rockers/Pickin' Poppies | 1973 |
| Beeb | 001 | Roll Over Beethoven/Say Mama/Be-Bop-A-Lula | 1974 |

## U K   E P s

| LABEL | RECORD # | TITLE | YEAR |
| --- | --- | --- | --- |
| Capitol/EMI | PRO-985 | Hot Rod Gang | 1958 |
| Capitol/EMI | 1-1059 | A Gene Vincent Record Date (Vol. 1) | 1959 |
| Capitol/EMI | 1-20173 | If You Want My Lovin' | 1960 |
| Capitol/EMI | 1-20354 | Race With the Devil | 1961 |
| Capitol/EMI | 1-20453 | Crazy Beat No. 1 | 1962 |
| Capitol/EMI | 2-20453 | Crazy Beat No. 2 | 1962 |
| Capitol/EMI | 3-20453 | Crazy Beat No. 3 | 1962 |
| Capitol/EMI | 1-20461 | True to You | 1962 |

# UK ALBUMS

| LABEL | RECORD # | TITLE | YEAR |
|-------|----------|-------|------|
| Capitol/EMI | T-764 | Bluejean Bop | 1956 |
| Capitol/EMI | T-811 | Gene Vincent and the Blue Caps | 1957 |
| Capitol/EMI | T-970 | Gene Vincent Rocks and the Blue Caps Roll | 1958 |
| Capitol/EMI | T-1059 | A Gene Vincent Record Date | 1958 |
| Capitol/EMI | T-1207 | Sounds Like Gene Vincent | 1959 |
| Capitol/EMI | T-1342 | Crazy Times (mono) | 1960 |
| Capitol/EMI | ST-1342 | Crazy Times (stereo) | 1960 |
| Capitol/EMI | 20453 | The Crazy Beat of Gene Vincent | 1963 |
| Columbia | 1646 | Shakin' Up a Storm | 1964 |
| London | 8333 | Gene Vincent | 1967 |
| Capitol | 20957 | Best of Gene Vincent | 1967 |
| Capitol/EMI | 21144 | Best of Gene Vincent Volume Two | 1968 |
| Dandelion | 63754 | I'm Back and I'm Proud | 1970 |
| Kama Sutra | 2361009 | If Only You Could See Me Today | 1971 |
| Kama Sutra | 2316005 | The Day the World Turned Blue | 1971 |

# INDEX